Building Web and Mobile ArcGIS Server Applications with JavaScript

Master the ArcGIS API for JavaScript, and build exciting, custom web and mobile GIS applications with the ArcGIS Server

Eric Pimpler

BIRMINGHAM - MUMBAI

Building Web and Mobile ArcGIS Server Applications with JavaScript

First published: February 2014

Production Reference: 1120214

Published by Packt Publishing Ltd.
Livery Place
35 Livery Street
Birmingham B3 2PB, UK.

ISBN 978-1-84969-796-5

www.packtpub.com

Cover Image by Whitney Pimpler (wpimpler@gmail.com)

Credits

Author
Eric Pimpler

Reviewers
Pouria Amirian
Ken Doman
Joseph Saltenberger

Acquisition Editor
Vinay Argekar

Content Development Editor
Susmita Panda Sabat

Technical Editors
Sharvari H. Baet
Pragnesh Bilimoria
Aparna Chand
Pooja Nair
Nikhil Potdukhe

Copy Editors
Kirti Pai
Stuti Srivastava

Project Coordinator
Joel Goveya

Proofreaders
Simran Bhogal
Ameesha Green

Indexers
Mehreen Deshmukh
Tejal Soni

Graphics
Sheetal Aute
Ronak Dhruv
Disha Haria
Yuvraj Mannari
Abhinash Sahu

Production Coordinator
Melwyn D'sa

Cover Work
Melwyn D'sa

About the Author

Eric Pimpler is the founder and owner of GeoSpatial Training Services (geospatialtraining.com) and has over 20 years of experience in implementing and teaching GIS solutions using Esri, Google Earth/Maps, and open source technology. Currently, he focuses on ArcGIS scripting with Python and the development of custom ArcGIS Server web and mobile applications using JavaScript. He is the author of *Programming ArcGIS 10.1 with Python Cookbook.*

Eric has a bachelor's degree in Geography from Texas A&M University and a master's degree in Applied Geography with a concentration in GIS from Texas State University.

About the Reviewers

Pouria Amirian is a GIS/Computer Science lecturer, researcher, and developer working with the National University of Ireland, Maynooth. In addition to his collaboration with the University of Ireland, he has several scientific and academic collaborations with world class universities in Germany, France, and the UK. He is the author of the best-selling book on ArcGIS development, *Beginning ArcGIS for Desktop Development using .NET*, published by Wiley in 2013. He has extensive experience in the design and development of various kinds of small-scale to enterprise-distributed, service-oriented (geospatial) information systems. Dr. Amirian is currently interested in cutting-edge research and development projects on (geospatial) Big Data and NoSQL databases and has recently been a technical editor of several books on the mentioned topics. He can be contacted at pouriaamirian.arcobjects@gmail.com.

I would like to thank my friend, Dr. Majid Farahani, for his support, understanding, and encouragement during my career. My thanks also goes to the author and the technical review team for making this book a fun project.

Ken Doman has worked with computers for most of his life and still likes to keep himself occupied with them in his free time. He graduated with a bachelor's degree in Biology from Rice University. From there, he moved from one field to another, until he was asked to launch a GIS department for his hometown in Jacksonville, Texas. He started with a shoebox full of notebook paper for an address database. Before long, he published the first online map of his community. He's been hooked on publishing web maps ever since.

Ken currently works as a GIS web developer at Bruce Harris and Associates, a private company that provides GIS services and products for municipalities across the United States. There, he works on an array of technologies, helping county and city governments make their data available on web browsers.

This is the first book Ken has worked on, but he has high hopes that it won't be his last.

I would first like to thank my wife, Luann, for her love and support. Her love for words inspired me to take this responsibility seriously. I'd also like to thank God, without whom nothing is possible. I would also like to thank Bruce Harris and Associates, the City of Plantation, Florida, and the City of Jacksonville, Texas, for giving me the opportunity to learn more about GIS, which helped me grow in my career.

Joseph Saltenberger works as a data analyst at a GIS software company that specializes in spatial decision support systems for fire and EMS departments. He graduated from the Humboldt State University with a B.S. in Natural Resources (GIS and Remote Sensing emphasis), and the San Diego State University with an M.S. in Geography (GIScience emphasis). His academic and professional career has focused on using GIS for data management and analysis, and for developing custom GIS applications.

www.PacktPub.com

Support files, eBooks, discount offers and more

You might want to visit www.PacktPub.com for support files and downloads related to your book.

Did you know that Packt offers eBook versions of every book published, with PDF and ePub files available? You can upgrade to the eBook version at www.PacktPub.com and as a print book customer, you are entitled to a discount on the eBook copy. Get in touch with us at service@packtpub.com for more details.

At www.PacktPub.com, you can also read a collection of free technical articles, sign up for a range of free newsletters and receive exclusive discounts and offers on Packt books and eBooks.

http://PacktLib.PacktPub.com

Do you need instant solutions to your IT questions? PacktLib is Packt's online digital book library. Here, you can access, read and search across Packt's entire library of books.

Why Subscribe?

- Fully searchable across every book published by Packt
- Copy and paste, print and bookmark content
- On demand and accessible via web browser

Free Access for Packt account holders

If you have an account with Packt at www.PacktPub.com, you can use this to access PacktLib today and view nine entirely free books. Simply use your login credentials for immediate access.

Table of Contents

Preface

ArcGIS Server is the predominant platform used to develop GIS applications for the Web. There are a number of programming languages you can use to develop applications with ArcGIS Server, including JavaScript, Flex, and Silverlight. JavaScript has become the preferred language for developing applications on this platform, since it can be used for both web and mobile applications and doesn't require the installation of a plugin for the application to be used in a browser. Flex and Silverlight both fall short as languages for mobile development and both require the use of a plugin for the application to run in a browser.

This book will teach you how to build web-based GIS applications using the ArcGIS API for JavaScript. Using a practical, hands-on style of learning, you will learn how to develop fully functional applications with ArcGIS Server and develop a skill set that is in high demand.

You will learn how to create maps and add geographic layers from a variety of sources, including tiled and dynamic map services. In addition, you'll learn how to add graphics to the map and stream geographic features to the browser using `FeatureLayer`. Most applications also include specific functionalities implemented by ArcGIS Server as tasks. You'll learn how to use the various tasks provided by ArcGIS Server, including queries, identification of features, finding features by attributes, geoprocessing tasks, and more. Finally, you'll learn just how easy it is to develop mobile applications with the ArcGIS API for JavaScript.

What this book covers

Chapter 1, Introduction to HTML, CSS, and JavaScript, covers fundamental HTML, CSS, and JavaScript concepts before getting started with developing GIS applications with the ArcGIS API for JavaScript.

Chapter 2, Creating Maps and Adding Layers, teaches you how to create a map and add layers to the map. You will learn how to create an instance of the Map class, add layers of data to the map, and display this information on a web page. The Map class is the most fundamental class in the API as it provides the canvas for your data layers and any subsequent activities that occur in your application. However, your map is useless until you add layers of data. There are several types of data layers that can be added to a map, including tiled, dynamic, and feature. Readers will learn more about each of these layer types in this chapter.

Chapter 3, Adding Graphics to the Map, teaches the reader how to display temporary points, lines, and polygons in GraphicsLayer on the map. GraphicsLayer is a separate layer that always resides on top of other layers and stores all the graphics associated with the map.

Chapter 4, The Feature Layer, offers additional capabilities, apart from inheriting from GraphicsLayer, such as the ability to perform queries and selections. Feature layers are also used for online editing of features. Feature layers differ from tiled and dynamic map service layers, because feature layers bring geometry information to the client computer to be drawn and stored by the web browser. Feature layers potentially cut down on round trips to the server. A client can request the features it needs, and perform selections and queries on those features without having to request more information from the server.

Chapter 5, Using Widgets and Toolbars, covers out-of-the-box widgets that you can drop into your application for enhanced productivity. The BasemapGallery, Bookmarks, Print, Geocoding, Legend, Measurement, Scalebar, Gauge, and Overview map widgets are included. In addition, the ArcGIS API for JavaScript also includes helper classes for adding various toolbars to your applications, including navigation and drawing toolbars.

Chapter 6, Performing Spatial and Attribute Queries, covers the ArcGIS Server Query Task, which allows you to perform attribute and spatial queries against data layers in a map service that have been exposed. You can also combine these query types to perform a combination attribute and spatial query.

Chapter 7, Identifying and Finding Features, covers two common operations found in any GIS application. These operations require that the user click a feature on the map in the case of identification, or perform a query in the case of finding features. In either case, information about particular features is returned. In this chapter, the reader will learn how to use the IdentifyTask and FindTask objects to obtain information about features.

Chapter 8, Turning Addresses into Points and Points into Addresses, covers the use of the Locator task to perform geocoding and reverse geocoding. Geocoding is the process of assigning a coordinate to an address, while reverse geocoding assigns an address to a coordinate.

Chapter 9, Network Analyst Tasks, allows you to perform analyses on street networks, such as finding the best route from one address to another, finding the closest school, identifying a service area around a location, or responding to a set of orders with a fleet of service vehicles.

Chapter 10, Geoprocessing Tasks, allows you to execute custom models built in ArcGIS Desktop using ModelBuilder. Models are run in an automated fashion from either a desktop environment or via a centralized server accessed through a web application. Any tool found in ArcToolbox, whether that be a tool for your ArcGIS license level or a custom tool that you've built, can be used in a model and chained together with other tools. Once constructed, these models can be run on a centralized server and accessed via web applications. In this chapter, we will examine how you can access these geoprocessing tasks through the ArcGIS API for JavaScript.

Chapter 11, Integration with ArcGIS Online, details how you can use the ArcGIS API for JavaScript to access the data and maps created with ArcGIS.com. The website ArcGIS.com is for working with maps and other types of geographic information. On this site, you will find applications for building and sharing maps. You will also find useful basemaps, data, applications, and tools that you can view and use, plus communities you can join. For application developers, the really exciting news is that you can integrate ArcGIS.com content into your custom developed applications using the ArcGIS API for JavaScript. In this chapter, you will explore how ArcGIS.com maps can be added to your applications.

Chapter 12, Creating Mobile Applications, details how you can build mobile GIS applications using the ArcGIS API for JavaScript. ArcGIS Server support is currently provided for iOS, Android, and BlackBerry operating systems. The API is integrated with dojox/mobile. In this chapter, you'll learn about the compact build of the API that makes web mapping applications possible through web-kit browsers as well as the built-in gesture support.

Appendix, Application Design with ArcGIS Templates and Dojo, covers one of the most difficult tasks for many web developers which is designing and creating the user interface. The ArcGIS API for JavaScript and Dojo greatly simplifies this task. Dojo's layout dijits provide a simple, efficient way to create application layouts, and Esri has provided a number of sample application layouts and templates that you can use to get up and running quickly. In this appendix, the reader will learn techniques to design an application quickly.

What you need for this book

To complete the exercises in this book, you will need access to a web browser—preferably Google Chrome or Firefox. Each chapter contains exercises designed to supplement the material presented. Exercises will be completed using the ArcGIS API for JavaScript Sandbox to write and test your code. The Sandbox can be found at http://developers.arcgis.com/en/javascript/sandbox/sandbox. html. The exercises will access publicly available instances of ArcGIS Server, so it will not be necessary for you to install ArcGIS Server.

Who this book is for

If you are an application developer who wants to develop web and mobile GIS applications using ArcGIS Server and the API for JavaScript, this book is ideal for you. It is primarily oriented towards beginners and intermediate-level GIS developers or application developers who are more traditional and may not have developed GIS applications in the past, but are now tasked with implementing solutions on this platform. No prior experience with ArcGIS Server, JavaScript, HTML, or CSS is expected, but it is certainly helpful.

Conventions

In this book, you will find a number of styles of text that distinguish between different kinds of information. Here are some examples of these styles, and an explanation of their meaning.

Code words in text, database table names, folder names, filenames, file extensions, pathnames, dummy URLs, user input, and Twitter handles are shown as follows: "Add the onorientationchange() event to the <body> tag."

A block of code is set as follows:

```
routeParams = new RouteParameters();
routeParams.stops = new FeatureSet();
routeParams.outSpatialReference = {wkid:4326};
routeParams.stops.features.push(stop1);
routeParams.stops.features.push(stop2);
```

When we wish to draw your attention to a particular part of a code block, the relevant lines or items are set in bold:

```
function computeServiceArea(evt) {
  map.graphics.clear();
  var pointSymbol = new SimpleMarkerSymbol();
```

```
    pointSymbol.setOutline = new SimpleLineSymbol(SimpleLineSymbol.
STYLE_SOLID, new Color([255, 0, 0]), 1);
    pointSymbol.setSize(14);
    pointSymbol.setColor(new Color([0, 255, 0, 0.25]));
}
```

New terms and **important words** are shown in bold. Words that you see on the screen, in menus or dialog boxes for example, appear in the text like this: "Click on the **Run** button."

Warnings or important notes appear in a box like this.

Tips and tricks appear like this.

Reader feedback

Feedback from our readers is always welcome. Let us know what you think about this book—what you liked or may have disliked. Reader feedback is important for us to develop titles that you really get the most out of.

To send us general feedback, simply send an e-mail to feedback@packtpub.com, and mention the book title via the subject of your message.

If there is a topic that you have expertise in and you are interested in either writing or contributing to a book, see our author guide on www.packtpub.com/authors.

Customer support

Now that you are the proud owner of a Packt book, we have a number of things to help you to get the most from your purchase.

Downloading the example code

You can download the example code files for all Packt books you have purchased from your account at http://www.packtpub.com. If you purchased this book elsewhere, you can visit http://www.packtpub.com/support and register to have the files e-mailed directly to you.

Errata

Although we have taken every care to ensure the accuracy of our content, mistakes do happen. If you find a mistake in one of our books—maybe a mistake in the text or the code—we would be grateful if you would report this to us. By doing so, you can save other readers from frustration and help us improve subsequent versions of this book. If you find any errata, please report them by visiting http://www.packtpub.com/submit-errata, selecting your book, clicking on the **errata submission form** link, and entering the details of your errata. Once your errata are verified, your submission will be accepted and the errata will be uploaded on our website, or added to any list of existing errata, under the Errata section of that title. Any existing errata can be viewed by selecting your title from http://www.packtpub.com/support.

Piracy

Piracy of copyright material on the Internet is an ongoing problem across all media. At Packt, we take the protection of our copyright and licenses very seriously. If you come across any illegal copies of our works, in any form, on the Internet, please provide us with the location address or website name immediately so that we can pursue a remedy.

Please contact us at copyright@packtpub.com with a link to the suspected pirated material.

We appreciate your help in protecting our authors, and our ability to bring you valuable content.

Questions

You can contact us at questions@packtpub.com if you are having a problem with any aspect of the book, and we will do our best to address it.

1
Introduction to HTML, CSS, and JavaScript

There are certain fundamental concepts that you need to understand before you can get started with developing GIS applications with the ArcGIS API for JavaScript. For those of you already familiar with HTML, JavaScript, and CSS, you may wish to skip ahead to the next chapter. However, if you're new to any of these concepts, read on. We are going to cover these topics at a very basic level, just enough to get you started. For a more advanced treatment on any of these subjects, there are many learning resources available, including books and online tutorials. You can refer to *Appendix, Application Design with ArcGIS Templates and Dojo*, for a more comprehensive list of these resources.

In this chapter, we will cover the following topics:

- Basic HTML page concepts
- JavaScript fundamentals
- Basic CSS principles

Basic HTML page concepts

Before we dive into the details of creating a map and adding layers of information, you need to understand the context of where the code will be placed when you're developing applications with the ArcGIS API for JavaScript. The code you write will be placed inside an HTML page or a JavaScript file. HTML files typically have an `.html` or `.htm` file extension and JavaScript files have a `.js` extension. Once you have created a basic HTML page, you can go through the steps required to create a basic map with the ArcGIS API for JavaScript.

The core of a web page is an HTML file. Coding this basic file is quite important as it forms the basis for the rest of your application. Mistakes that you make in the basic HTML coding can result in problems down the line when your JavaScript code attempts to access these HTML tags.

The following is a code example for a very simple HTML page. This example is about as simple as an HTML page can get. It contains only the primary HTML tags `<DOCTYPE>`, `<html>`, `<head>`, `<title>`, and `<body>`. Use your favorite text or web editor to enter the following code. I use Notepad++ but there are many other good editors available. Save this example as `helloworld.html`:

```
<!DOCTYPE html PUBLIC "-//W3C//DTD HTML 4.01//EN" "http://www.w3.org/
TR/html4/strict.dtd">

<html>
  <head>
    <meta http-equiv="Content-Type" content="text/html;
charset=utf-8">
    <title>Topographic Map</title>

  </head>
  <body>
      Hello World
  </body>
</html>
```

There are a different types of HTML currently in use. The new HTML5 is getting a lot of press and you'll likely see this implementation being used almost exclusively for the development of new applications; so, we'll focus on HTML5 throughout the book. However, I do want to make you aware that there are other flavors of HTML in use, the most common being HTML 4.01 (seen in the preceding code example) and XHTML 1.0.

Downloading the example code

You can download the example code files for all Packt books you have purchased from your account at http://www.packtpub.com. If you purchased this book elsewhere, you can visit http://www.packtpub.com/support and register to have the files e-mailed directly to you.

The HTML DOCTYPE declaration

The first line of your HTML page will contain the DOCTYPE declaration. This is used to tell the browser how the HTML page should be interpreted. We'll focus on HTML5 in this book, so the following example you see uses the HTML5 DOCTYPE declaration. The two other common DOCTYPE declarations are HTML 4.01 Strict and XHTML 1.0 Strict:

- HTML 5 uses the following code:

  ```
  <!DOCTYPE html>
  ```

- HTML 4.01 Strict uses the following code:

  ```
  <!DOCTYPE html PUBLIC "-//W3C//DTD HTML 4.01//EN" "http://www.
  w3.org/TR/html4/strict.dtd">
  ```

- XHTML 1.0 Strict uses the following code:

  ```
  <!DOCTYPE html PUBLIC "-//W3C//DTD XHTML 1.0 Strict//EN" "http://
  www.w3.org/TR/xhtml1/DTD/xhtml1-strict.dtd">
  ```

Primary tags

At a minimum, all your web pages will need to contain the `<html>`, `<head>`, and `<body>` tags. The `<html>` tag defines the whole HTML document. All other tags must be placed inside this tag. Tags that define how the web page will appear in the browser are placed inside the `<body>` tag. For instance, your mapping applications will contain a `<div>` tag inside the `<body>` tag that is used as a container for displaying the map.

Loading the `helloworld.html` page in a browser will produce the content you see in the following screenshot. Most of the ArcGIS API for JavaScript code that you write will be placed between the `<head></head>` tags and within a `<script>` tag or inside a separate JavaScript file. As you gain experience, you will likely begin placing your JavaScript code inside one or more JavaScript files and then referencing them from the JavaScript section. We'll explore this topic later. For now, just concentrate on placing your code inside the `<head>` tags.

Validating HTML code

As mentioned earlier, it is very important that your HTML tags be coded correctly. This is all well and good you say, but how do I know that my HTML has been coded correctly? Well, there are a number of HTML code validators that you can use to check your HTML. The W3C HTML validator (`http://validator.w3.org/`) shown in the following screenshot can be used to validate HTML code through URI, file upload, or direct input:

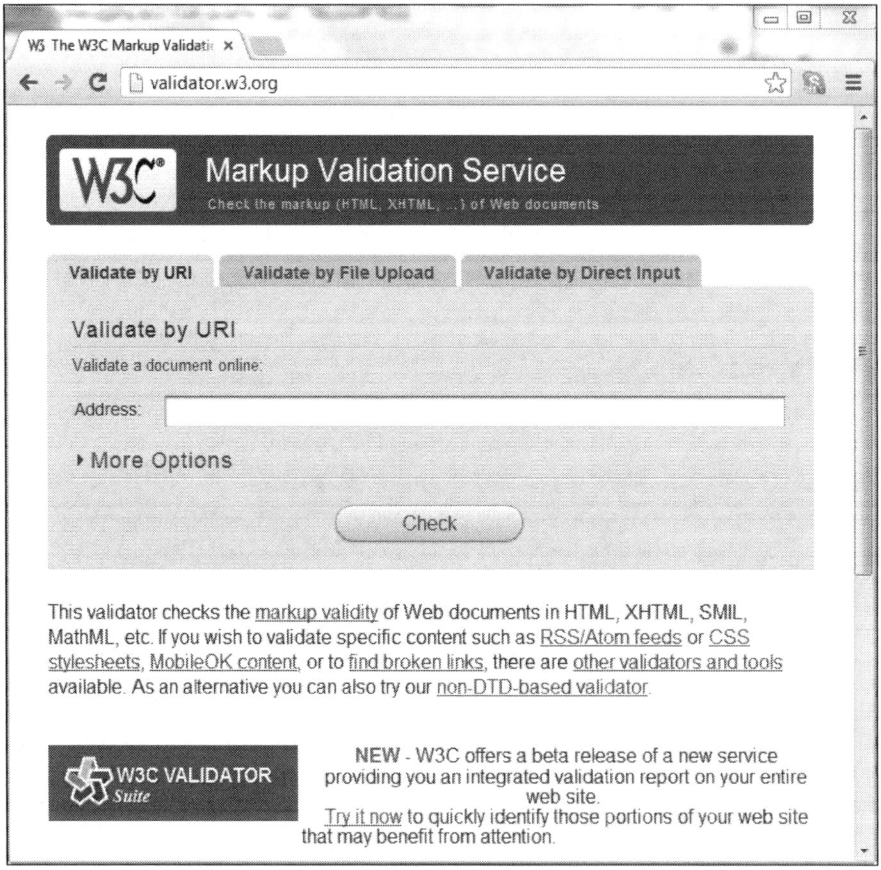

Assuming that your HTML code successfully validates itself, you will get a screen with a message indicating a successful validation as shown in the following screenshot:

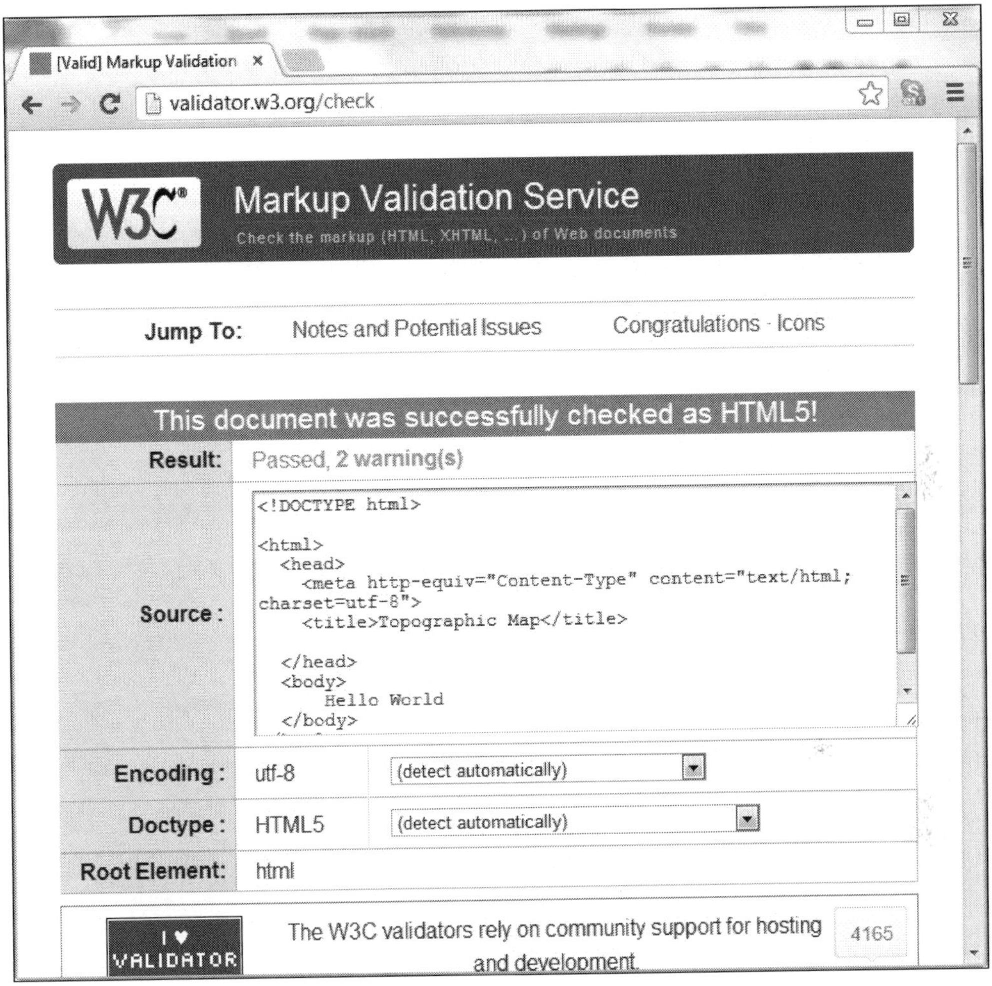

On the other hand, it will identify any problem with an error message displayed in red. Errors are described in detail, which makes it easier to correct problems. Often a single error can lead to many other errors, so it is not uncommon to see a long list of error items. Don't panic if this is the case. Fixing one error often resolves many others.

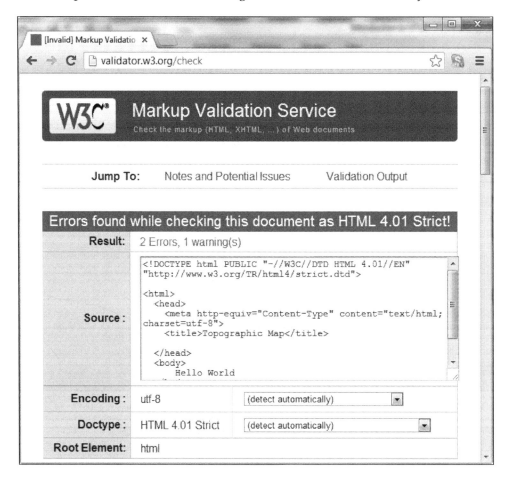

To correct the errors in the preceding document, you would need to surround the text `Hello World` with a paragraph tag similar to `<p>Hello World</p>`.

JavaScript fundamentals

As implied by the name, the ArcGIS API for JavaScript requires that you use the JavaScript language when developing your application. There are some fundamental JavaScript programming concepts that you will need to know before you start building your application.

JavaScript is a lightweight scripting language that is embedded in all modern web browsers. Although JavaScript can certainly exist outside the web browser environment in other applications, it is most commonly known for its integration with web applications.

All modern web browsers, including Internet Explorer, Firefox, and Chrome, have JavaScript embedded. The use of JavaScript in web applications gives us the ability to create dynamic applications that do not require round trips to the server to fetch data, and thus the applications are more responsive and user-friendly. However, JavaScript does have the capability of submitting requests to the server, and is a core technology in the **Asynchronous JavaScript and XML (AJAX)** stack.

 One common misconception regarding JavaScript is that it is a simplified version of Java. The two languages are actually unrelated with the exception of the name.

Commenting in code

It is a best practice to always document your JavaScript code through the use of comments. At a minimum, these should include the author of the code, the date of last revision, and the general purpose of the code. In addition, at various points throughout your code, you should include comment sections that define the purpose of specific sections of the application. The purpose of this documentation is to make it easier for you or any other programmer to quickly get up to speed in the event that the code needs to be updated in some way.

Any comments that you include in your code are not executed. They are simply ignored by the JavaScript interpreter. Commenting in JavaScript can be done in a couple of ways including single line and multiline comments. Single line comments start with // and any additional characters that you add to the line. The following code example shows how single line comments are created:

```
//this is a single line comment.  This line will not be executed
```

Multiline comments in JavaScript start with /* and end with */. Any lines in between are treated as comments and are not executed. The following code example shows an example of multiline comments:

```
/*
Copyright 2012 Google Inc.

Licensed under the Apache License, Version 2.0 (the "License");
you may not use this file except in compliance with the License.
You may obtain a copy of the License at
```

```
http://www.apache.org/licenses/LICENSE-2.0

Unless required by applicable law or agreed to in writing, software
distributed under the License is distributed on an "AS IS" BASIS,
WITHOUT WARRANTIES OR CONDITIONS OF ANY KIND, either express or
implied.
See the License for the specific language governing permissions and
limitations under the License.
*/
```

Variables

The concept of variables is a fundamental concept that you need to understand when working with any programming language. Variables are simply names that we use to associate with some type of data value. At a lower level, these variables are areas of space carved out in a computer's memory that store data.

You can think of a variable as a box that has a name and contains some sort of data. When we initially create the variable, it is empty until data is assigned. Basically, variables give us the ability to store and manipulate data. In the following diagram, we create a variable called ssn. Initially, this variable is empty but is then assigned a value of 450-63-3567. The data value assigned to a variable can be of various types, including numbers, strings, booleans, objects, and arrays.

In JavaScript, variables are declared with the var keyword. In general, the names that you assign to your variables are completely up to you. However, there are certain rules that you need to follow when creating a variable. Variables can contain both text and numbers but should never start with a number. Always start your variable name with a letter or an underscore. In addition, spaces are not allowed within variable names nor are special characters such as percent signs and ampersands. Other than that, you are free to create variable names as you wish but you should try to assign variable names that describe the data that the variable will be assigned to. It is also perfectly legal to declare multiple variables with the same var keyword as seen in the following code example:

```
var i, j, k;
```

You can also combine variable declaration with data assignment, as seen in the following examples:

```
var i = 10;
var j = 20;
var k = 30;
```

You may have also noticed that each JavaScript statement ends with a semicolon. The semicolon indicates the end of a statement in JavaScript and should always be included in JavaScript.

JavaScript and case sensitivity

One very important point that I need to make is that JavaScript is a case-sensitive language and you need to be very careful about this because it can introduce some difficult-to-track-down bugs in your code. All variables, keywords, functions, and identifiers must be typed with a consistent capitalization of the letters. This gets even more confusing when you consider that HTML is not case sensitive. This tends to be a stumbling block for new JavaScript developers. In the following code snippet, I have created three variables, all with the same spelling. But, because they do not follow the same capitalization pattern, you end up with three different variables:

```
Var myName = 'Eric';
var myname = 'John';
var MyName = 'Joe';
```

Variable datatypes

JavaScript supports various types of data that can be assigned to your variables. Unlike other strongly-typed languages such as .NET or C++, JavaScript is a loosely-typed language. What this means is that you don't have to specify the type of data that will occupy your variable. The JavaScript interpreter does this for you on the fly. You can assign strings of text, numbers, boolean true/false values, arrays, or objects to your variables.

Numbers and strings are pretty straightforward for the most part. Strings are simply text enclosed by either a single or double quote. For instance:

```
varbaseMapLayer = "Terrain";
varoperationalLayer = 'Parcels';
```

Numbers are not enclosed inside quote marks and can be integers or floating point numbers:

```
var currentMonth = 12;
var layered = 3;
var speed = 34.35;
```

One thing I would point out to new programmers is that numeric values can be assigned to string variables through the use of single or double quotes that enclose the value. This can be confusing at times for some new programmers. For instance, a value of 3.14 without single or double quotes is a numeric datatype while a value of 3.14 with single or double quotes is assigned a string data type.

Other datatypes include booleans that are simply true or false values and arrays that are a collection of data values. An array basically serves as a container for multiple values. For instance, you could store a list of geographic data layer names within an array and access them individually, as required.

Arrays allow you to store multiple values in a single variable. For example, you might want to store the names of all the layers you want to add to a map. Instead of creating individual variables for each layer, you could use an array to store all of them in a single variable. You can then reference individual values from the array using an index number by looping through them with a *for* loop. The following code example shows one way to create an array in JavaScript:

```
var myLayers=new Array();
myLayers[0]="Parcels";
myLayers[1]="Streets";
myLayers[2]="Streams";
```

You could also simplify the creation of this array variable as seen in the following code example, where the array has been created as a comma-separated list enclosed in brackets:

```
var myLayers = ["Parcels", "Streets", "Streams"];
```

You can access elements in an array through the use of an index as seen in the following code example. Array access is zero based, which means that the first item in the array occupies the 0 position and each successive item in the array is incremented by one:

```
var layerName = myLayers[0];  //returns Parcels
```

Decision-supporting statements

An `if/else` statement in JavaScript and other programming languages is a control statement that allows decision making in your code. This type of statement performs a test at the top of the statement. If the test returns a value of `true`, then the statements associated with the `if` block will run. If the test returns a value of `false`, then the execution skips to the first `else if` block. This pattern will continue until a value of `true` is returned in the test or the execution reaches the `else` statement. The following code example shows how this statement works:

```
var layerName = 'streets';
if (layerName == 'aerial') {
    alert("An aerial map");
}
else if (layerName == "hybrid") {
    alert("A hybrid map");
}
else {
    alert("A street map");
}
```

Looping statements

Looping statements give you the ability to run the same block of code over and over again. There are two fundamental looping mechanisms in JavaScript. The *for* loop executes a code block a specified number of times and the *while* loop executes a code block while a condition is true. Once the condition becomes false, the looping mechanism stops.

The following code sample shows the syntax of a `for` loop. You'll note that it takes a start value, which will be an integer and a condition statement. You can also supply an increment. The code block inside the *for* loop will execute the given condition while the value is less than the end value:

```
for (start value; condition statement; increment)
{
  the code block to be executed
 }
```

In the following example, the start value is set to 0 and is assigned to a variable called i. The condition statement is when i is less than or equal to 10, and the value of i is incremented by 1 for each loop, using the ++ operator. Each time we pass through the loop, the value of i is printed:

```
var i = 0;
for (i = 0; i <= 10; i++) {
    document.write("The number is " + i);
    document.write("<br/>");
}
```

The other basic looping mechanism in JavaScript is the *while* loop. This loop is used when you want to execute a code block while a condition is true. Once the condition is set to false, the execution stops. The *while* loops accept a single argument, which is the condition that will be tested. In the following example, the code block will be executed while i is less than or equal to 10. Initially, i is set to a value of 0. At the end of the code block, you will notice that i is incremented by one (i = i + 1):

```
var i = 0;
while (i <= 10)
{
    document.write("The number is " + i);
    document.write("<br/>");
    i = i + 1;
}
```

Functions

Now let's cover the very important topic of functions. Functions are simply named blocks of code that are executed when called. The vast majority of the code that you write in this book and in your development efforts will occur within the functions.

Best practice calls for you to split your code into functions that perform small, discrete units of operation. These blocks of code are normally defined in the <head> section of a web page inside a <script> tag, but can also be defined in the <body> section. However, in most cases, you will want your functions defined within the <head> section so that you can ensure that they are available once the page is loaded.

To create a function, you need to use the function keyword followed by a function name that you define, and any variables necessary for the execution of the function passed as parameter variables. In the event that you need your function to return a value to the calling code, you will need to use the return keyword in conjunction with the data that you want passed back.

Functions can also accept parameters that are just variables used to pass information into the function. In the following code example, the `prod()` function passes two variables: `a` and `b`. This information, in the form of variables, can then be used inside the function:

```
var x;
function multiplyValues(a,b)
{
    x = a * b;
    return x;
}
```

Objects

Now that we've gone through some basic JavaScript concepts, we'll tackle the most important concept in this section. In order to effectively program mapping applications with the ArcGIS API for JavaScript, you need to have a good fundamental understanding of objects. So, this is a critical concept that you need to grasp to understand how to develop web-mapping applications.

The ArcGIS API for JavaScript makes extensive use of objects. We'll cover the details of this programming library in detail, but for now we'll hit the high-level concepts. Objects are complex structures capable of aggregating multiple data values and actions into a single structure. This differs greatly from our primitive datatypes, such as numbers, strings, and booleans, which can hold only a single value. Objects are much more complex structures.

Objects are composed of both data and actions. Data, in the form of properties, contains information about an object. For example, with a `Map` object found in the ArcGIS API for JavaScript, there are a number of properties, including the map extent, graphics associated with a map, the height and width of the map, layer IDs associated with the map, and others. These properties contain information about the object.

Objects also have actions that we typically call methods, but we can also group constructors and events into this category. Methods are actions that a map can perform, such as adding a layer, setting the map extent, or getting the map scale.

Constructors are special-purpose functions that are used to create new instances of an object. With some objects, it is also possible to pass parameters into the constructor to give more control over the object that is created. The following code example shows how a constructor is used to create a new instance of a Map object. You can tell that this method is a constructor because of the use of the new keyword that I've highlighted. The new keyword, followed by the name of the object and any parameters used to control the new object, defines the constructor for the object. In this case, we've created a new Map object and stored it in a variable called map. Three parameters are passed into the constructor to control various aspects of the Map object including basemap, center of the map, and the zoom scale level:

```
var map = new Map("mapDiv", {
  basemap: "streets",
  center:[-117.148, 32.706], //long, lat
  zoom: 12
});
```

Events are actions that take place on the object and are triggered by the end user or the application. This would include events such as a map click, mouse move, or a layer being added to the map.

Properties and methods are accessed via a dot notation wherein the object instance name is separated from the property or method by a dot. For instance, to access the current map extent you would enter map.extent in your code. A couple of code examples showing how to access properties of an object are as follows:

```
var theExtent = map.extent;
var graphics = map.graphics;
```

The same is the case with methods, except that methods have parentheses at the end of the method name. Data can be passed into a method through the use of parameters. In the first line of the following code, we're passing a variable called pt into the map.centerAt(pt) method:

```
map.centerAt(pt);
map.panRight();
```

Basic CSS principles

Cascading Style Sheets (CSS) is a language used to describe how HTML elements should be displayed on a web page. For instance, CSS is often used to define common styling elements for a page or set of pages, such as the font, background color, font size, link colors, and many other things related to the visual design of a web page. Take a look at the following code snippet:

```
<style>
  html, body {
    height: 100%;
    width: 100%;
    margin: 0;
    padding: 0;
  }

  #map{

    padding:0;
    border:solid 2px #94C7BA;
    margin:5px;
  }
  #header {
    border: solid 2px #94C7BA;
    padding-top:5px;
    padding-left:10px;
    background-color:white;

    color:#594735;

    font-size:14pt;
    text-align:left;
    font-weight:bold;
    height:35px;
    margin:5px;
    overflow:hidden;
  }
  .roundedCorners{
    -webkit-border-radius: 4px;
    -moz-border-radius: 4px;
    border-radius: 4px;
  }
  .shadow{

    -webkit-box-shadow: 0px 4px 8px #adadad;
    -moz-box-shadow: 0px 4px 8px #adadad;
    -o-box-shadow: 0px 4px 8px #adadad;
    box-shadow: 0px 4px 8px #adadad;
  }
</style>
```

CSS syntax

CSS follows certain rules that define what HTML element to select along with defining how that element should be styled. A CSS rule has two main parts: a selector and one or more declarations. The selector is typically the HTML element that you want to style. In the following diagram, the selector is p. A <p> element in HTML represents a paragraph. The second part of a CSS rule comprises of one or more declarations, each of which consists of a property and a value. The property represents the style attribute that you want to change. In our example, we are setting the color property to red. In effect, what we have done with this CSS rule is define that all the text within our paragraph should be in red.

We have used p {color:red}, as shown in the following diagram:

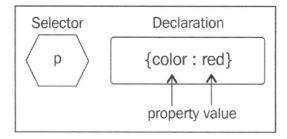

You can include more than one declaration in a CSS rule as you see in the following example. A declaration is always surrounded by curly brackets and each declaration ends with a semicolon. In addition, a colon should be placed between the property and the value. In this particular example, two declarations have been made: one for the color of the paragraph and another for the text alignment of the paragraph. Notice that the declarations are separated by a semicolon:

```
p {color:red;text-align:center}
```

CSS comments are used to explain your code. You should get into the habit of always commenting on your CSS code just as you would in any other programming language. Comments are always ignored by the browser. Comments begin with a slash followed by an asterisk and end with an asterisk followed by a slash. Everything in between is assumed to be a comment and is ignored:

```
/*
h1 {font-size:200%;}
h2 {font-size:140%;}
h3 {font-size:110%;}
*/
```

In addition to specifying selectors for specific HTML elements, you can also use the id selector to define styles for any HTML elements with an id value that matches the id selector. An id selector is defined in CSS through the use of the pound sign (#), followed by an id value.

For instance, in the following code example, you see three id selectors: rightPane, leftPane, and map. In ArcGIS API for JavaScript applications, you almost always have a map. When you define a <div> tag that will serve as the container for the map, you define an id selector and assign it a value that is often the word map. In this case, we are using CSS to define several styles for our map, including a margin of 5 pixels along with a solid styled border of a specific color and a border radius:

```
#rightPane {
    background-color:white;
    color:#3f3f3f;
    border: solid 2px #224a54;
    width: 20%;
}
#leftPane {
    margin: 5px;
    padding: 2px;
    background-color:white;
    color:#3f3f3f;
    border: solid 2px #224a54;
    width: 20%;
```

```
}
#map {
    margin: 5px;
    border: solid 4px #224a54;
    -mox-border-radius: 4px;
}
```

Unlike `id` selectors that are used to assign styles to a single element, the `class` selectors are used to specify styles for a group of elements, all of which have the same HTML class attribute. A class selector is defined with a period, followed by the class name. You may also specify that only specific HTML elements with a particular class should be affected by the style. Examples of both are shown in the following code example:

```
.center {text-align:center;}
p.center {text-align:center;}
```

Your HTML code would then reference the class selector as follows:

```
<p class="center">This is a paragraph</p>
```

There are three ways to insert CSS into your application: inline, internal stylesheets, and external stylesheets.

Inline styling

The first method of defining CSS rules for your HTML elements is through the use of inline styles. This method is not recommended because it mixes style with presentation and is difficult to maintain. It is an option in some cases where you need to define a very limited set of CSS rules. To use inline styles, simply place the `style` attribute inside the relevant HTML tag:

```
<p style="color:sienna;margin-left:20px">This is a paragraph.</p>
```

Internal stylesheets

An internal stylesheet moves all the CSS rules into a specific web page. Only HTML elements within that particular page have access to the rules. All CSS rules are defined inside the `<head>` tag and are enclosed inside a `<style>` tag, as seen in the following code example:

```
<head>
    <style type="text/css">
        hr {color:sienna;}
        p {margin-left:20px;}
        body {background-image:url("images/back40.gif");}
    </style>
</head>
```

External stylesheets

An external stylesheet is simply a text file containing CSS rules and is saved with a `.css` file extension. This file is then linked to all web pages that want to implement the styles defined within the external stylesheet through the use of the HTML `<link>` tag. This is a commonly used method to split the styling from the main web page and gives you the ability to change the look of an entire website through the use of a single external stylesheet.

Now let's put some emphasis on the *cascading* part of cascading stylesheets. As you now know, styles can be defined in external stylesheets, internal stylesheets, or inline. There is a fourth level that we didn't discuss, which is the browser default. You don't have any control over that though. In CSS, an inline style has the highest priority, which means that it will override a style defined in an internal stylesheet, an external stylesheet, or the browser default. If an inline style is not defined, any style rule defined in an internal stylesheet would take precedence over styles defined in an external stylesheet. The caveat here is that if a link to an external stylesheet is placed after the internal stylesheet in HTML `<head>`, the external stylesheet will override the internal sheet!

That's a lot to remember! Just keep in mind that style rules defined further down the hierarchy override style rules defined higher in the hierarchy, as shown in the following diagram:

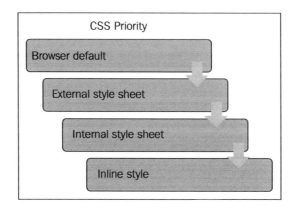

These are the basic concepts that you need to understand with regard to CSS. You can use CSS to define styles for pretty much anything on a web page, including backgrounds, text, fonts, links, lists, images, tables, maps, and any other visible objects.

Separating HTML, CSS, and JavaScript

You may be wondering where all of this code is placed. Should you put all your HTML, CSS, and JavaScript code in the same file or split them into separate files? For very simple applications and examples, it is not uncommon for all the code to be placed into a single file with an extension of `.html` or `.htm`. In this case, the CSS and JavaScript code will reside in the `<head>` section of your HTML page. However, the preferred way of creating an application using this code stack is to separate the presentation from the content and behavior. The user interface items for your application should reside in an HTML page that contains only tags used to define the content of the application, along with references to any CSS (presentation) or JavaScript (behavior) files that are part of the application. The end result is a single HTML page and one or more CSS and JavaScript files. This would result in a folder structure similar to that shown in the following screenshot, where we have a single file called `index.html` and several folders that hold CSS, JavaScript, and other resources, such as images. The `css` and `js` folders will contain one or more files.

CSS files can be linked into an HTML page with the <link> tag. In the following code sample, you will see a code example that shows you how to use the <link> tag to import a CSS file. Links to CSS files should be defined in the <head> tag of your HTML page:

```
<!DOCTYPE html>

<html>
  <head>
    <title>GeoRanch Client Portal</title>
    <meta name="viewport" content="initial-scale=1.0, user-
scalable=no">
    <link rel="stylesheet" href="bootstrap/css/bootstrap.css">
  </head>
  <body>
  </body>
</html>
```

JavaScript files are imported into your HTML page with the <script> tag as seen in the following code example. These <script> tags can be placed in the <head> tag of your web page, as seen in reference to the ArcGIS API for the following JavaScript code, or near the end of the page just before the ending </body> tag, as has been done with the creategeometries.js file. It is often recommended that you import your JavaScript files close to the ending </body> tag because when browsers download JavaScript files, they don't download anything else until the downloading is done. This can make it look like the application is loading slowly.

Adding a <script> tag in the header is recommended for JavaScript libraries, such as Dojo, which need to be parsed before they interact with HTML elements in the body. That's why the ArcGIS API for JavaScript is loaded in the header:

```
<!DOCTYPE html>
<html>
  <head>
    <title>GeoRanch Client Portal</title>
    <meta name="viewport" content="initial-scale=1.0, user-
scalable=no">
```

```
    <script src="http://js.arcgis.com/3.7/"></script>
  </head>
  <body>
    <script src="js/creategeometries.js"></script>
  </body>
</html>
```

Splitting your code into several files allows for a clean separation of your code and it should be much easier to maintain.

Summary

Before we can begin a detailed discussion of the ArcGIS API for JavaScript, you need to have an understanding of some of the fundamental HTML, CSS, and JavaScript concepts. This chapter has provided just that, but you will need to continue learning many additional concepts related to these topics. Right now, you know just enough to be dangerous.

How your application looks is defined through the HTML and CSS code that you develop while the functionality provided by your application is controlled through JavaScript. These are very different skill sets and many people are good at one but not necessarily the other. Most application developers will focus on developing the functionality of the application through JavaScript and will leave HTML and CSS to the designers! Nevertheless, it is important that you have a good understanding of at least the basic concepts of all these topics. In the next chapter, we'll dive into the ArcGIS API for JavaScript and begin learning how to create the Map object and how to add dynamic and tiled map service layers to the map.

2

Creating Maps and Adding Layers

Now that we've got some of the basics of HTML, CSS, and JavaScript out of the way, it's time to actually get to work and learn how to build some great GIS web applications! The material in this chapter will introduce you to some of the fundamental concepts that define how you create a map and add information to it in the form of layers.

In this chapter, we'll cover the following topics:

- The ArcGIS API for JavaScript Sandbox
- Basic steps to create an application with the ArcGIS API for JavaScript
- More about the map
- Working with map service layers
- Tiled map service layers
- Dynamic map service layers
- Map navigation
- Working with the map extent

Introduction

We all have to start somewhere when learning a new programming language or **application programming interface (API)**. The same applies to creating web-mapping applications with the ArcGIS API for JavaScript. Not only do you need to understand some basic JavaScript concepts, but you also need to have a grasp of HTML, CSS, and of course the ArcGIS API for JavaScript, which is actually built on top of the Dojo JavaScript framework. That's a lot to put on your plate all at once, so in this chapter, I'm going to have you create a very basic application, which will serve as a foundation that you can build on in the coming chapters. Mimicry is an excellent way to learn programming skills, so in this chapter, I'm just going to have you type in the code that you see and I'll provide some explanation along the way. I'll save the detailed descriptions of the code for later chapters.

To get your feet wet with the ArcGIS API for JavaScript, you're going to create a simple mapping application in this chapter, which creates a map, adds a couple of data layers, and provides some basic map navigation capabilities.

There are some basic steps that you must follow to create any web-mapping application with the ArcGIS API for JavaScript. You'll see each of these steps for the first time in this chapter, and we'll describe them in greater detail later in the book. These basic steps will be followed each time you create a new application using the API for JavaScript. The first few times that you create an application, these steps will seem a little strange but you'll quickly gain an understanding of what they do and why they are necessary. Pretty soon you can just think of these steps as a template you use with every application.

Let's get started!

The ArcGIS API for JavaScript Sandbox

In this book, you're going to use the ArcGIS API for JavaScript Sandbox to write and test your code. The Sandbox can be found at `http://developers.arcgis.com/en/javascript/sandbox/sandbox.html` and will appear as seen in the following screenshot, when loaded. You'll write your code in the left pane and click the **Run** button to see the results in the right pane, as shown in the following screenshot:

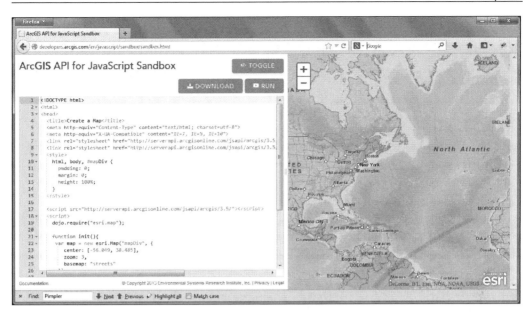

Basic steps for creating an application with the ArcGIS API for JavaScript

There are several steps that you'll need to follow to create any GIS web application with the ArcGIS API for JavaScript. These steps will always need to be performed if you intend to have a map as part of your application. And I can't imagine that you wouldn't want to do that, given that you're reading this book! In a nutshell, there are several steps you need to follow:

1. Creating the HTML code for the page.
2. Referencing the ArcGIS API for JavaScript and stylesheets.
3. Loading modules.
4. Making sure the DOM is available.
5. Creating the map.
6. Defining the page content.
7. Styling the page.

This was just a brief description of what needs to be done. We'll examine each of these steps in greater detail in the coming pages.

Creating HTML code for a web page

In the previous chapter, you learned the basic concepts of HTML, CSS, and JavaScript. Now, you're going to start putting those skills to work. You first need to create a simple HTML document that will ultimately serve as the container for your map. Since we're using the ArcGIS API for JavaScript Sandbox, this step has already been done for you. However, I do want you to spend some time examining the code so that you have a good grasp of the concepts. In the left pane of the Sandbox, the code you see highlighted in the following code example references the basic HTML code for the web page. There's obviously some other HTML and JavaScript code in there as well, but the following code forms the basic components of the web page. This code includes several basic tags, including `<html>`, `<head>`, `<title>`, `<body>`, and a few others:

```
<!DOCTYPE html>
<html>
<head>
  <title>Create a Map</title>
  <meta http-equiv="Content-Type" content="text/html; charset=utf-8">
  <meta name="viewport" content="initial-scale=1, maximum-
scale=1,user-scalable=no">
  <link rel="stylesheet" href="http://js.arcgis.com/3.7/js/dojo/dijit/
themes/claro/claro.css">
  <link rel="stylesheet" href="http://js.arcgis.com/3.7/js/esri/css/
esri.css">
  <style>
    html, body, #mapDiv {
      padding: 0;
      margin: 0;
      height: 100%;
    }
  </style>

  <script src="http://js.arcgis.com/3.7/"></script>
  <script>
    dojo.require("esri.map");

    function init(){
     var map = new esri.Map("mapDiv", {
        center: [-56.049, 38.485],
        zoom: 3,
        basemap: "streets"
      });
    }
    dojo.ready(init);
```

```
      </script>

    </head>
    <body class="claro">
      <div id="mapDiv"></div>
    </body>
    </html>
```

Referencing the ArcGIS API for JavaScript

To begin working with the ArcGIS API for JavaScript, you need to add references to the stylesheet and API. In the Sandbox, the following lines of code have been added inside the `<head>` tag:

```
    <link rel="stylesheet" href="http://js.arcgis.com/3.7/js/esri/css/
    esri.css">

    <script src="http://js.arcgis.com/3.7/"></script>
```

The `<script>` tag loads the ArcGIS API for JavaScript. At the time of writing this chapter, the current version is 3.7. When new versions of the API are released, you'll want to update this number accordingly. The `<link>` tag loads the `esri.css` stylesheet, which contains styles specific to Esri widgets and components.

Optionally, you can include a reference to one of the stylesheets for a Dojo Dijit theme. The ArcGIS API for JavaScript is built directly on the Dojo JavaScript framework. Dojo comes with four predefined themes that control the look of user interface widgets that are added to your application: Claro, Tundra, Soria, and Nihilo. In the following code example, I'm referencing the Claro theme:

```
    <link rel="stylesheet" href="http://js.arcgis.com/3.7/js/dojo/dijit/
    themes/claro/claro.css">
```

The other available stylesheets can be referenced as seen in the following code example. You don't have to reference any of the style sheets, but if you intend to add Dojo user interface components (Dijits), then you'll want to load one of the stylesheets to control the styling of the components:

```
    <link rel="stylesheet" href="http://js.arcgis.com/3.7/js/dojo/dijit/
    themes/tundra/tundra.css">
    <link rel="stylesheet" href="http://js.arcgis.com/3.7/js/dojo/dijit/
    themes/nihilo/nihilo.css">
    <link rel="stylesheet" href="http://js.arcgis.com/3.7/js/dojo/dijit/
    themes/soria/soria.css">
```

The website www.dojotoolkit.org provides a theme tester that you can use to get a feel for how each of the themes affect the display of the user interface components. The theme tester is located at http://archive.dojotoolkit.org/nightly/ dojotoolkit/dijit/themes/themeTester.html. The following screenshot shows the Dijit Theme Tester interface:

Loading modules

Before you can create a Map object, you must first reference the resource that provides the map. This is accomplished through the use of a require() function.

Legacy or AMD Dojo?

Whether to use the older legacy style of Dojo or the new AMD is currently a source of frustration for many developers. **Asynchronous Model Definition (AMD)** was introduced in Version 1.7 of Dojo. The Version 3.4 release of the ArcGIS Server API for JavaScript was the first version to have all modules rewritten using the new AMD style. For the time being, both the legacy and AMD style will work just fine, but it is advised that any new applications be written using the new AMD style. We'll follow that convention in this book but keep in mind that applications written prior to the release of Version 3.4 of the API and some Esri samples still reflect the older style of coding.

The `require()` function is used to import resources into your web page. Various resources are provided by the ArcGIS API for JavaScript, including the `esri/map` resource, which must be provided before you can create a map or work with geometry, graphics, and symbols. Once a reference to the resource has been provided, you can use the `Map` constructor to create the `Map`. The following points show how to run the code in Sandbox:

- Before you begin adding code to the Sandbox, remove the following highlighted code, if necessary. The code I'm having you remove is from a legacy style of coding the ArcGIS API for JavaScript. We're going to use the new AMD style. In future versions of the Sandbox, it may not be necessary to remove these lines of code. I expect that Esri will eventually migrate this basic code block to the newer AMD style:

```
<script>
    dojo.require("esri.map");

    function init(){
     var map = new esri.Map("mapDiv", {
        center: [-56.049, 38.485],
        zoom: 3,
        basemap: "streets"
      });
    }
    dojo.ready(init);
</script>
```

- The resources you import need to be contained within a new `<script>` tag. Add the following highlighted lines of code to the Sandbox inside the `<script>` tag. The argument names used inside the `require()` function can be named anything you like. However, both Esri and Dojo provide a list of preferred arguments. I recommend using the Esri list of preferred arguments when naming arguments passed to the `require` callback function. Dojo also does the same with their list of preferred argument aliases. For example, in the following code you add, we provide a reference to the `esri/map` resource and then inside the anonymous function, we provide a preferred argument of `Map`. Each resource that you reference in the `require()` function will have an associated argument, which will provide a hook into the object for that resource:

```
<script>
require(["esri/map", "dojo/domReady!"], function(Map) {

    });

</script>
```

Making sure Document Object Model is available

When a web page loads, all the HTML elements that compose the page are loaded and interpreted. This is known as **Document Object Model (DOM)**. It is imperative that your JavaScript does not attempt to access any of these elements until all the elements have loaded. Obviously, if your JavaScript code attempted to access an element that hasn't been loaded yet, it would cause an error. To control this, Dojo has a `ready()` function that you can include inside the `require()` function, which will execute only after all the HTML elements and any modules have loaded. Alternatively, you can use the `dojo/domReady!` plugin to ensure that all the HTML elements have been loaded. We'll use the second method for this exercise.

In the previous code, we have used the plugin with `dojo/domReady!` having been added to the `require()` function.

 Although it is certainly possible to add JavaScript code directly inside your basic HTML file, it is a better practice to create a separate JavaScript file (`.js`). Most of the code that we write in this book will be done inside an HTML file for simplicity, but as your applications become more complex, you'll want to adhere to the practice of writing your JavaScript code in a separate file.

Creating the map

The creation of a new map is done through `esri/map`, which is a reference to the `Map` class found in the `esri/map` module you imported in a previous step. Inside the `require()` function, you're going to create a new `Map` object using a constructor function. This constructor for the `Map` object accepts two parameters, including a reference to the `<div>` tag where the map will be placed on the web page as well as an options parameter that can be used to define various map setup options. The `options` parameter is defined as a JSON object that contains a set of key/value pairs.

Perhaps the most visible option is `basemap`, which allows you to select a predefined basemap from `ArcGIS.com` and can include `streets`, `satellite`, `hybrid`, `topo`, `gray`, `oceans`, `national-geographic`, or `osm`. The `zoom` option is used to define a starting zoom level for the map and can be an integer value that corresponds to a predefined zoom scale level. The `minZoom` and `maxZoom` options define the smallest and largest-scale zoom levels for the map. The `center` option defines the center point of the map that will initially be displayed and uses a `Point` object containing a latitude/longitude coordinate pair. There are a number of additional options that you pass in as parameters to the constructor for the `Map` object.

First, we'll create a global variable called map as well as the require() function by adding the highlighted line of the following code:

```
<script>
    var map;
    require(["esri/map", "dojo/domReady!"], function(Map) {
    });
</script>
```

Add the following highlighted code block to the require() function. This line of code is the constructor for the new Map object. The first parameter passed into the constructor is a reference to the ID of the <div> tag where the map will be placed. We haven't defined this <div> tag yet, but we'll do so in the next step. The second parameter passed into the Map constructor is a JSON object that defines options including the geographic coordinate that will serve as the center of the map, a zoom level, and the topo basemap:

```
basemap.require(["esri/map", "dojo/domReady!"], function(Map) {
  map = new Map("mapDiv", {
    basemap: "topo",
    center: [-122.45,37.75], // long, lat
    zoom: 13,
    sliderStyle: "small"
  });
});
```

Creating the page content

One of the final steps is to create the HTML <div> tag that will serve as the container for the map. You always want to assign a unique ID to the <div> tag so that your JavaScript code can reference the location. In the Sandbox this <div> tag with a unique identifier of mapDiv has already been created for you. You can see this in the highlighted line of following code. In addition, you will also want to define the class attribute for the <body> tag, which should reference the Dojo stylesheet that you referenced.

In the following code, you can see the <body> tag that is already created in the Sandbox accomplishes the preceding two tasks:

```
<body class="claro">
    <div id="mapDiv"></div>
</body>
```

Styling the page

You can add styling information to the `<head>` tag that will define various styling aspects for the web page. In this case, the styling has already been created for you in the Sandbox, as shown in the following code. In this case, the styling includes setting the map so that it fills the entire browser window:

```
<style>
    html, body, #mapDiv {
        padding:0;
        margin:0;
        height:100%;
    }
</style>
```

The complete code

The code for this simple application should appear as follows:

```
<!DOCTYPE html>
<html>
  <head>
    <meta http-equiv="Content-Type" content="text/html;
      charset=utf-8">
    <meta http-equiv="X-UA-Compatible" content="IE=7, IE=9,
      IE=10">
    <meta name="viewport" content="initial-scale=1, maximum-
      scale=1,user-scalable=no"/>
    <title>Simple Map</title>
    <link rel="stylesheet"
      href="http://js.arcgis.com/3.7/js/esri/css/esri.css">
    <link rel="stylesheet"
      href="http://js.arcgis.com/3.7/js/dojo/dijit/themes/claro/
      claro.css">
    <style>
      html, body, #map {
        height: 100%;
        width: 100%;
        margin: 0;
        padding: 0;
      }
    </style>
    <script src="http://js.arcgis.com/3.7/"></script>
    <script>
```

```
        var map;

        require(["esri/map", "dojo/domReady!"], function(Map) {
          map = new Map("map", {
            basemap: "topo",
            center: [-122.45,37.75], // long, lat
            zoom: 13,
            sliderStyle: "small"
          });
        });
      </script>
    </head>

    <body class="claro">
      <div id="map"></div>
    </body>
</html>
```

Execute the code by clicking on the **Run** button and you should see the following output, if everything has been coded correctly:

More about the map

In the process described earlier, we introduced the process that you'll need to follow for each application that you build with the ArcGIS API for JavaScript. You learned how to create an initialization JavaScript function. The purpose of the initialization script is to create your map, add layers, and perform any other setup routines necessary to get your application started. Creating a map is invariably one of the first things that you'll do and in this section, we'll take a closer look at the various options you have to create an instance of the Map class.

In object-oriented programming, the creation of a class instance is often done through the use of a constructor. A constructor is a function that is used to create or initialize a new object. In this case, the constructor is used to create a new Map object. Constructors frequently take one or more parameters that can be used to set the initial state of an object.

The Map constructor can take two parameters including the container where the map should reside and various options for the map. However, before you can call the constructor for a map, you must first reference the resource that provides the map. This is accomplished by importing the esri/map resource. Once a reference to the resource has been provided, you can use the constructor to create the map. A <div> ID is a required parameter for the constructor and is used to specify the container for the map. In addition, you can also pass multiple options that control various aspects of the map, including the basemap layer, the initial display of the map center, display of navigation controls, graphic display during panning, control of the slider, levels of detail, and many more.

Let's take a closer look at how options are specified in the map constructor. Options, the second parameter in the constructor, are always enclosed with brackets. This defines the contents of a JSON object. Inside the brackets, each option has a specific name and is followed by a colon and then the data value that controls the option. In the event that you need to submit multiple options to the constructor, each option is separated by a comma. The following code example shows how options are submitted to the Map constructor:

```
var map = new Map("mapDiv", {
  center: [-56.049, 38.485],
  zoom: 3,
  basemap: "streets"
});
```

In this case, we are defining options for the map coordinate that will serve as the center of the map, along with a zoom level and a basemap layer of streets. These options are enclosed with curly braces and are separated by commas.

Working with map service layers

A map without data layers is sort of like an artist with a blank canvas. The data layers that you add to your map give it meaning and set the stage for analysis. There are two primary types of map services that provide data layers that can be added to your map: dynamic map service layers and tiled map service layers.

Dynamic map service layers reference map services that create a map image on the fly and then return the image to the application. This type of map service may be composed of one or more layers of information. For example, the demographics map service displayed in the following screenshot is composed of nine different layers, representing demographic information at various levels of geography:

Demographics (MapServer)

View In: ArcMap   ArcGIS Explorer   ArcGIS JavaScript   Google Earth

View Footprint In: Google Earth

Service Description:

Map Name: Layers

Layers:

- Demographics/ESRI_Census_USA (0)
  - Census Block Points (1)
  - Census Block Group (2)
  - Counties (3)
    - Coarse Counties (4)
    - Detailed Counties (5)
  - States (6)
- ESRI_StreetMap_World_2D (7)
  - World Street Map (8)

While they can take somewhat longer to display in a client application as they must be generated *on the fly*, dynamic map service layers are more versatile than tiled map service layers. In dynamic map service layers, you can control the features displayed through layer definitions, set the visibility of various layers within the service, and define temporal information for the layer. For example, in the **Demographics** map service layer detailed in the preceding screenshot, you might choose to display only **Census Block Group** in your application. This is the type of versatility provided by dynamic map service layers that you don't get with tiled map service layers.

Tiled map service layers reference a predefined cache of map tiles instead of dynamically rendered images. The easiest way to understand the concept of tiled map services is to think about a grid that has been draped across the surface of a map. Each cell within the grid has the same size and will be used to cut the map into individual image files called tiles. The individual tiles are stored as image files on a server and are retrieved as needed, depending upon the map extent and scale. This same process is often repeated at various map scales. The end result is a cache of tilesets that have been generated for various map scales. When the map is displayed in the application, it will appear to be seamless even though it is composed of many individual tiles.

These tiled or cached map layers are often used as basemaps that include imagery, street maps, topographic maps, or for data layers that don't change often. Tiled map services tend to display faster as they don't have the overhead of creating images on the fly each time there is a request for a map.

Operational layers are then draped on top of the tiled basemaps and these are often dynamic layers. While they can be somewhat slower in terms of performance, dynamic map service layers have the advantage of being able to define their appearance on the fly.

Using layer classes

Using the layer classes from the API for JavaScript, you can reference map services hosted by ArcGIS Server and other map servers. All layer classes inherit from the Layer base class. The Layer class has no constructor, so you can't specifically create an object from this class. This class simply defines properties, methods, and events that are inherited by all classes that inherit from Layer.

As indicated in the following figure, DynamicMapServiceLayer, TiledMapServiceLayer, and GraphicsLayer all inherit directly from the Layer class. DynamicMapServiceLayer and TiledMapserviceLayer also act as base classes. DynamicMapServiceLayer is the base class for dynamic map services while TiledMapServiceLayer is the base class for tiled map services. *Chapter 3, Adding Graphics to the Map*, is devoted entirely to graphics and the GraphicsLayer, so we'll save our discussion on this type of layer for later on in the book. Layer, DynamicMapServiceLayer, and TiledMapServiceLayer are all base classes, meaning that you can't specifically create an object from these classes in your application.

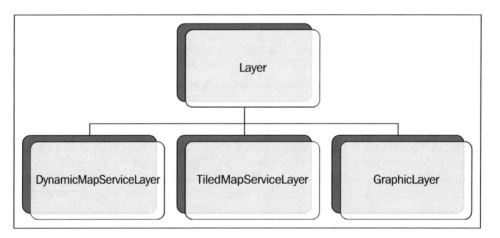

Tiled map service layers

As mentioned earlier, tiled map service layers reference a cache of predefined images that are tiled together to create a seamless map display. These are often used as base maps.

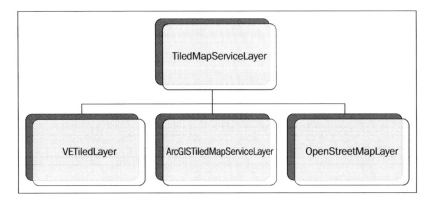

The `ArcGISTiledMapServiceLayer` class is used when referencing a tiled (cached) map service exposed by ArcGIS Server. As this type of object works against a tiled set of maps that have been cached, performance is often improved. The constructor for `ArcGISTiledMapServiceLayer` takes a URL pointer to the map service, along with options that allow you to assign an ID to the map service and control transparency and visibility.

In the following code example, notice that the constructor for `ArcGISTiledMapServiceLayer` takes a parameter that references a map service. After an instance of a layer has been created, it is added to the map using the `Map.addLayer()` method that accepts a variable that contains a reference to the tiled map service layer:

```
var basemap = new ArcGISTiledMapServiceLayer("http://server.
arcgisonline.com/ArcGIS/rest/services/World_Topo_Map/MapServer");
map.addLayer(basemap);
```

`ArcGISTiledMapServiceLayer` is used primarily for the fast display of cached map data. You can also control the levels at which the data will be displayed. For instance, you may want to display data from a generalized `ArcGISTiledMapService`, showing interstates and highways while your users are zoomed out at levels 0-6 and then switch to a more detailed `ArcGISTiledMapService` once the user zooms in further. You can also control the transparency of each layer added to the map.

Dynamic map service layers

As the name suggests, the ArcGISDynamicMapServiceLayer class is used to create dynamic maps served by ArcGIS Server. Just as with ArcGISTiledMapServiceLayer, the constructor for ArcGISDynamicMapServiceLayer takes a URL that points to the map service along with optional parameters that are used to assign an ID to the service, determine the transparency of the map image, and a visibility option that sets the initial visibility of the layer to true or false. The class name ArcGISDynamicMapServiceLayer can be somewhat misleading. Although it appears to reference an individual data layer, this is in fact not the case. It refers to a map service rather than a data layer. Individual layers inside the map service can be turned on/off through the setVisibleLayers() method.

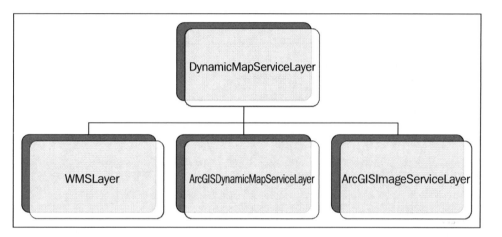

Creating an instance of ArcGISDynamicMapServiceLayer will look very similar to ArcGISTiledMapServiceLayer. The following code example illustrates this. The constructor accepts a URL that points to the map service. The second parameter defines the optional parameters that you can supply to control transparency, visibility, and image parameters:

```
var operationalLayer = new ArcGISDynamicMapServiceLayer("http://
sampleserver1.arcgisonline.com/ArcGIS/rest/services/Demographics/ESRI_
Population_World/MapServer",{"opacity":0.5});
map.addLayer(operationalLayer);
```

Add the preceding two lines of code to the ArcGIS API for JavaScript Sandbox as shown in the following code:

```
<script>
  var map;
  require(["esri/map", "esri/layers/ArcGISDynamicMapServiceLayer",
"dojo/domReady!"], function(Map, ArcGISDynamicMapServiceLayer) {
      map = new Map("mapDiv", {
        basemap: "topo",
        center: [-122.45,37.75], // long, lat
        zoom: 5,
        sliderStyle: "small"
      });
      var operationalLayer = new ArcGISDynamicMapServiceLayer("http://
sampleserver1.arcgisonline.com/ArcGIS/rest/services/Demographics/ESRI_
Population_World/MapServer",{"opacity":0.5});
      map.addLayer(operationalLayer);
    });
  </script>
```

Run the preceding code to see the dynamic layer added to the map, as seen in the following screenshot:

With an instance of `ArcGISDynamicMapServiceLayer`, you can perform a number of operations. Obviously, you can create maps that display the data in the service, but you can also query data from layers in the service, control feature display through layer definitions, control individual layer visibility, set time-related information, export maps as images, control background transparency, and much more.

Adding layers to the map

The `addLayer()` method takes an instance of a layer (`ArcGISDynamicMapServiceLayer` or `ArcGISTiledMapServiceLayer`) as the first parameter, and an optional index that specifies where it should be placed. In the following code example, we have created a new instance of `ArcGISDynamicMapServiceLayer` pointing to a URL for the service. We then call `Map.addLayer()` to pass the new instance of the layer. The layers in the service will now be visible on the map.

```
var operationalLayer = new ArcGISDynamicMapServiceLayer("http://
sampleserver1.arcgisonline.com/ArcGIS/rest/services/Demographics/ESRI_
Population_World/MapServer");
map.addLayer(operationalLayer);
```

The `addLayers()` method takes an array of layer objects and adds them all at once.

In addition to being able to add layers to a map, you can also remove layers from a map using `Map.removeLayer()` or `Map.removeAllLayers()`.

Setting visible layers from a map service

You can control the visibility of individual layers within a dynamic map service layer using the `setVisibleLayers()` method. This applies only to dynamic map service layers, not tiled map service layers. This method takes an array of integers, corresponding to the data layers in the map service.

This array is zero based so the first layer in the map service occupies position 0. In the **Demographics** map service illustrated in the following screenshot, Demographics/ESRI_Census_USA occupies index 0:

Demographics (MapServer)

View In: ArcMap ArcGIS Explorer ArcGIS JavaScript Google Earth

View Footprint In: Google Earth

Service Description:

Map Name: Layers

Layers:

- Demographics/ESRI_Census_USA (0)
  - Census Block Points (1)
  - Census Block Group (2)
  - Counties (3)
    - Coarse Counties (4)
    - Detailed Counties (5)
  - States (6)
- ESRI_StreetMap_World_2D (7)
  - World Street Map (8)

Therefore, in the event that we'd like to display only the **Census Block Points** and **Census Block Group** features from this service, we can use setVisibleLayers() as seen in the following code example:

```
var dynamicMapServiceLayer = new ArcGISDynamicMapServiceLayer("htt
ps://gis.sanantonio.gov/ArcGIS/rest/services/Demographics/MapServer");
dynamicMapServiceLayer.setVisibleLayers([1,2]);
map.addLayer(dynamicMapServiceLayer);
```

Setting a definition expression

In ArcGIS for Desktop, you can use a definition expression to limit the features in a data layer that will be displayed. A definition expression is simply a SQL query set against the columns and rows in a layer. Only the features whose attributes meet the query are displayed. For example, if you only wanted to display cities with a population greater than one million, the expression would be something like POPULATION > 1000000. The ArcGIS API for JavaScript contains a setLayerDefinitions( ) method that accepts an array of definitions that can be applied against ArcGISDynamicMapServiceLayer to control the display of features in the resulting map. The following code example shows how this is done:

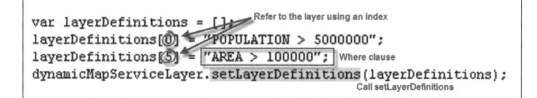

You first create an array that will hold multiple `where` clauses, which will serve as the definition expressions for each layer. In this case, we are defining layer definitions for the first and sixth layer. The array is zero based, so the first array is at index `0`. The `where` clauses are placed into the array and then passed into the `setLayerDefinitions()` method. ArcGIS Server then renders the features that match the `where` clauses for each layer.

Map navigation

Now that you know a little about maps and the layers that reside within those maps, it's time to learn how to control map navigation in your application. In most cases, your users will need to be able to navigate around the map using the panning and zooming features. The ArcGIS API for JavaScript provides a number of user interface widgets and toolbars that you can use in order to allow your user to change the current map extent using the zooming and panning features. Map navigation can also occur through keyboard navigation and mouse navigation. In addition to these user interface components and hardware interfaces, map navigation can also be controlled programmatically.

Map navigation widgets and toolbars

The simplest way to provide map navigation control to your application is through the addition of various widgets and toolbars. When you create a new map and add layers, a zoom slider is included with the map by default. This slider allows the user to zoom in and out of the map. The zoom slider is illustrated in the following screenshot. You don't have to do anything programmatically to have the zoom slider appear on your map; it is present by default. However, you can remove the slider for your application simply by setting the slider option to `false` when creating an instance of the `Map` object, if necessary:

```
{"slider":false,"nav":true,"opacity":0.5,"imageParameters"
:imageParameters}
```

The following screenshot shows the map with the zoom slider:

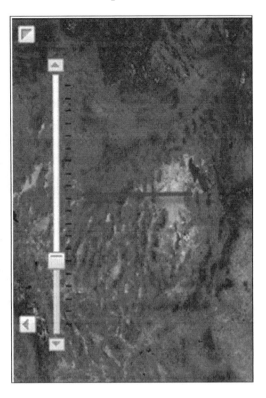

You can also add pan buttons that will pan the map in the direction that the arrow points towards, when clicked. By default, pan buttons will not appear on the map. You must specifically set the nav option to true when creating your Map object:

```
{"nav":true,"opacity":0.5,"imageParameters":imageParameters}
```

The following screenshot shows the pan options:

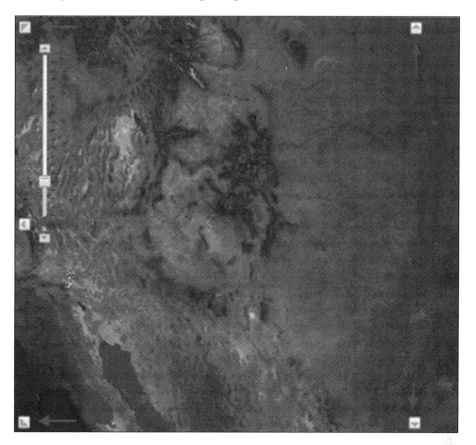

The ArcGIS API for JavaScript also gives you the ability to add several types of toolbars to your application, including a navigation toolbar containing buttons to zoom in and out, panning, full extent, next extent, and previous extent. Toolbar creation is covered in detail in a later chapter, so we'll save that discussion for later.

Map navigation using the mouse and keyboard

Users can also control map navigation using the mouse and/or keyboard devices. By default, users can do the following:

- Drag the mouse to pan
- Use the forward mouse scroll to zoom in
- Use the backward mouse scroll to zoom out
- Press *Shift* and drag the mouse to zoom in
- Press *Shift* + *Ctrl* and drag the mouse to zoom out
- Press *Shift* and click to restore to the center
- Double-click to center and zoom in
- Press *Shift* and double-click to center and zoom in
- Use the arrow keys to pan
- Use the + key to zoom in to a level
- Use the - key to zoom out of a level

The preceding options can be disabled using one of several Map methods. For example, to disable scroll wheel zooming, you would use the Map. disableScrollWheelZoom() method. These navigation features can also be removed after the map has been loaded.

Getting and setting the map extent

One of the first things you'll want to master is getting and setting the map extent. By default, the initial extent of a map within your application is the extent of the map when it was last saved in the map document file (.mxd) used to create the map service. In some cases, this may be exactly what you want, but in the event that you need to set a map extent other than the default, you will have several options.

One of the optional parameters that can be defined in the constructor for the Map object is the center parameter. You can use this optional parameter in conjunction with the zoom object to set the initial map extent. You'll see this illustrated in the following code example, where we define a coordinate pair for the center of the map, along with a zoom level of 3:

```
var map = new Map("mapDiv", {
        center: [-56.049, 38.485],
        zoom: 3,
        basemap: "streets"
    });
```

The initial extent of the map is not a required parameter, and thus if you leave out this information, the map will simply use the default extent. This is shown in the following code example, where only the ID of the container is specified:

```
var map = new Map("map");
```

After a `Map` object has been created, you can also use the `Map.setExtent()` method to change the extent by passing in an `Extent` object as seen in the following code example:

```
var extent = new Extent(-95.271, 38.933, -95.228, 38.976);
map.setExtent(extent);
```

Alternatively, you could set the `Extent` properties individually as seen in the following code example:

```
var extent = new Extent();
extent.xmin = -95.271;
extent.ymin = 38.933;
extent.xmax = -95.228;
extent.ymax = 38.976;
map.setExtent(extent);
```

There may be times when you are using multiple map services in your application. In this case, setting the initial map extent can be done either through the constructor for your map or by using the `Map.fullExtent` method on one of the services. For example, it is common to use a map service that provides base layer capabilities containing aerial imagery along with a map service containing your own local operational data sources. The following code example uses the `fullExtent()` method:

```
map = new Map("mapDiv", {extent:esri.geometry.geographicToWebMercator(
myService2.fullExtent) });
```

The current extent can be obtained either through the `Map.extent` property or the `onExtentChange` event. Note that the `Map.setExtent` property is read only, so don't attempt to set the map extent through this property.

Map events

In the world of programming, events are actions that take place within an application. Normally, these events are triggered by the end user and can include things such as mouse clicks, mouse drags, and keyboard actions, but it can also include the sending and receiving of data, component modification, and others.

The ArcGIS API for JavaScript is an asynchronous API that follows a publish/subscribe pattern wherein an application registers (publishes) events with listeners (subscribers). The following diagram illustrates this process. Listeners are responsible for monitoring the application for these events and then triggering a `handler` function that responds to the event. Multiple events can be registered to the same listener. The `dojo on()` method functions as an event to a handler.

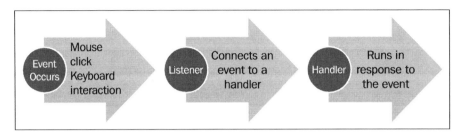

As you may recall, the ArcGIS Server JavaScript API is built on top of Dojo. With Dojo, events are registered to handlers through the `dojo on()` method. This method takes three parameters. Take a look at the code example shown in the following screenshot to get a better understanding of how events are registered:

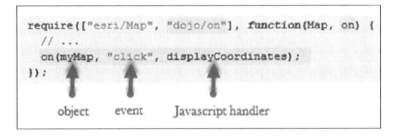

We call the `on()` method with parameters including `map`, `click`, and `displayCoordinates`. The first two parameters indicate the object and the event that we would like to register. In this case, it means we are registering the `click` event found on the `Map` object. This event is fired every time the user clicks the mouse within the confines of the map. The final parameter, `displayCoordinates`, indicates the listener for the event. Therefore, each time the `click` event on the `Map` object is fired, it will trigger the `displayCoordinates` function, which will run and report the current extent of the map. Although the events and the handlers they are registered to will change depending upon your circumstance, the method of registration is the same.

Each time an event occurs, an `Event` object is generated. This `Event` object contains additional event information such as the mouse button that was clicked or perhaps the key on the keyboard that was pressed. This object is automatically passed into the event handler, where it can be examined. In the following code example, you can see that the `Event` object is passed into the handler as a parameter. This is a dynamic object whose properties will change depending upon the type of event that was triggered:

```
function addPoint(evt) {
    alert(evt.mapPoint.x, evt.mapPoint.y);
}
```

There are many different events that are available on a number of different objects in the API. However, it is important to keep in mind that you do not have to register every event with a listener. Only the events that are necessary for your application should be registered. When an event that hasn't been registered with a listener occurs, the event is simply ignored.

The `Map` object contains many different events that you can respond to, including various mouse events, extent change events, basemap change events, keyboard events, layer events, pan and zoom events, and more. Your application can respond to any of these events. In coming chapters, we'll examine events that are available on other objects.

It is a good programming practice to always disconnect your events from their handler when no longer needed. This is normally done when the user navigates away from the page or closes the browser window. The following code example shows how this can be done by simply calling the `remove()` method:

```
var mapClickEvent = on(myMap, "click", displayCoordinates);
mapClickEvent.remove();
```

Summary

We covered a lot of ground in this chapter. All applications created with the ArcGIS API for JavaScript require a certain set of steps. We refer to this as boilerplate code. This includes defining references to the API and stylesheet, loading modules, creating an initialization function, and some other steps. In the `initialization` function, you will most likely create a map, add various layers, and perform other setup operations that need to be performed before the application is used. In this chapter, you learned how to perform these tasks.

In addition, we examined the various types of layers that can be added to a map, including tiled map service layers and dynamic map service layers. Tiled map service layers are precreated and cached on the server and are most often used as basemaps in an application. Dynamic map service layers must be created on the fly each time a request is made and thus may take longer to generate. However, dynamic map service layers can be used to perform many types of operations, including queries, setting definition expressions, and much more.

In addition, you learned how to programmatically control the map extent. Finally, we introduced the topic of events and you learned how to connect an event to an event handler, which is simply a JavaScript function that runs any time a particular event is triggered. In the next chapter, we'll closely examine how you can add graphics to your application.

3
Adding Graphics to the Map

Graphics are points, lines, or polygons that are drawn on top of your map in a layer that is independent of any other data layer associated with a map service. Most people associate a graphic object with the symbol that is displayed on a map to represent the graphic. However, each graphic in ArcGIS Server can be composed of up to four objects, including the geometry of the graphic, the symbology associated with the graphic, attributes that describe the graphic, and an info template that defines the format of the info window that appears when a graphic is clicked on. Although a graphic can be composed of up to four objects, it is not always necessary for this to happen. The objects you choose to associate with your graphic will be dependent on the needs of the application that you are building. For example, in an application that displays GPS coordinates on a map, you may not need to associate attributes or display info window for the graphic. However, in most cases, you will be defining the geometry and symbology for a graphic.

Graphics are temporary objects stored in a separate layer on the map. They are displayed while an application is in use and are removed when the session is complete. The separate layer, called the graphics layer, stores all the graphics associated with your map. In *Chapter 2, Creating Maps and Adding Layers*, we discussed the various types of layers, including dynamic map service layers and tiled map service layers. Just as with the other types of layers, GraphicsLayer also inherits from the Layer class. Therefore, all the properties, methods, and events found in the Layer class will also be present in GraphicsLayer.

Graphics are displayed on top of any other layers that are present in your application. An example of point and polygon graphics is provided in the following screenshot. These graphics can be created by users or drawn by the application in response to the tasks that have been submitted. For example, a business analysis application might provide a tool that allows the user to draw a freehand polygon to represent a potential trade area.

The polygon graphic would be displayed on top of the map, and could then be used as an input to a geoprocessing task that pulls demographic information pertaining to the potential trade area.

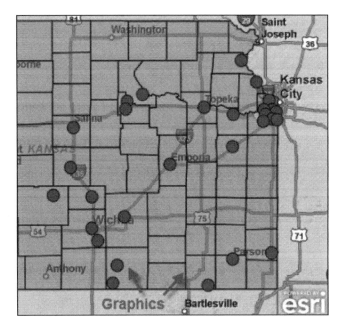

Many ArcGIS Server tasks return their results as graphics. The QueryTask object can perform both attribute and spatial queries. The results of a query are then returned to the application in the form of a FeatureSet object, which is simply an array of features. You can then access each of these features as graphics and plot them on the map using a looping structure. Perhaps you'd like to find and display all land parcels that intersect the 100 year flood plain. A QueryTask object could perform the spatial query and then return the results to your application, where they would then be displayed as polygon graphics on the map.

In this chapter, we will cover the following topics:

- The four parts of a graphic
- Creating geometry for graphics
- Symbolizing graphics
- Assigning attributes to graphics
- Displaying graphic attributes in an info window
- Creating graphics
- Adding graphics to the graphics layer

The four parts of a graphic

A graphic is composed of four items: **Geometry**, **Symbol**, **Attributes**, and **InfoTemplate**, as shown in the following diagram:

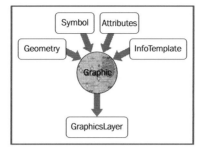

A graphic has a geometric representation that describes where it is located. The geometry, along with a symbol, defines how the graphic is displayed. A graphic can also have attributes that provide descriptive information about the graphic. Attributes are defined as a set of name-value pairs. For example, a graphic depicting a wildfire location could have attributes that describe the name of the fire along with the number of acres burned. The info template defines what attributes should be displayed in the info window that appears when the graphic appears, along with how they should be displayed. After their creation, the graphic objects must be stored inside a `GraphicsLayer` object, before they can be displayed on the map. This `GraphicsLayer` object functions as a container for all the graphics that will be displayed.

All the elements of a graphic are optional. However, the geometry and symbology of a graphic are almost always assigned. Without these two items, there would be nothing to display on the map, and there isn't much point in having a graphic unless you're going to display it.

The following figure shows the typical process of creating a graphic and adding it to the graphics layer. In this case, we are applying the geometry of the graphic as well as a symbol to depict the graphic. However, we haven't specifically assigned attributes or an info template to this graphic.

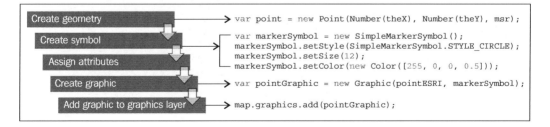

Creating geometry for graphics

Graphics will almost always have a geometry component, which is necessary for their placement on the map. These geometry objects can be points, multipoints, polylines, polygons, or extents and can be created programmatically through a constructor for these objects or can be returned as an output from a task such as a query.

Before creating any of these geometry types, the `esri/geometry` resource needs to be imported. This geometry resource contains classes for `Geometry`, `Point`, `Multipoint`, `Polyline`, `Polygon`, and `Extent`.

`Geometry` is the base class that is inherited by `Point`, `MultiPoint`, `Polyline`, `Polygon`, and `Extent`.

As can be seen from the following code line, the `Point` class defines a location by an X and Y coordinate, and can be defined in either map units or screen units:

```
new Point(-118.15, 33.80);
```

Symbolizing graphics

Each graphic that you create can be symbolized through one of the various symbol classes found in the API. Point graphics are symbolized by the `SimpleMarkerSymbol` class and the available shapes include circle, cross, diamond, square, and X. It is also possible to symbolize your points through the `PictureMarkerSymbol` class, which uses an image to display the graphic. Linear features are symbolized through the `SimpleLineSymbol` class and can include solid lines, dashes, dots, or a combination. Polygons are symbolized through the `SimpleFillSymbol` class and can be solid, transparent, or crosshatch. In the event that you'd prefer to use an image in a repeated pattern for your polygons, the `PictureFillSymbol` class is available. Text can also be added to the graphics layer and is symbolized through the `TextSymbol` class.

Points or multipoints can be symbolized through the `SimpleMarkerSymbol` class, which has various properties that can be set, including style, size, outline, and color. Style is set through the `SimpleMarkerSymbol.setStyle()` method that takes one of the following constants, which corresponds to the type of symbol that is drawn (circle, cross, diamond, and so on):

- `STYLE_CIRCLE`
- `STYLE_CROSS`
- `STYLE_DIAMOND`
- `STYLE_PATH`
- `STYLE_SQUARE`
- `STYLE_X`

Point graphics can also have an outline color, which is created through the `SimpleLineSymbol` class. The size and color of the graphics can also be set. Examine the following code example to get an idea on how this is done:

```
var markerSymbol = new SimpleMarkerSymbol();
markerSymbol.setStyle(SimpleMarkerSymbol.STYLE_CIRCLE);
markerSymbol.setSize(12);
markerSymbol.setColor(new Color([255,0,0,0.5]));
```

Linear features are symbolized with the `SimpleLineSymbol` class and can be a solid line or a combination of dots and dashes. Other properties include color, as defined with `dojo/Color`, and a width property `setWidth` to set the thickness of your line. The following code example explains the process in detail:

```
var polyline = new Polyline(msr);
//a path is an array of points
var path = [new Point(-123.123, 45.45, msr),.....];
polyline.addPath(path);
var lineSymbol = new SimpleLineSymbol().setWidth(5);

//create polyline graphic using polyline and line symbol
var polylineGraphic = new Graphic(polyline, lineSymbol);
map.graphics.add(polylineGraphic);
```

The following screenshot is obtained when the preceding code is run:

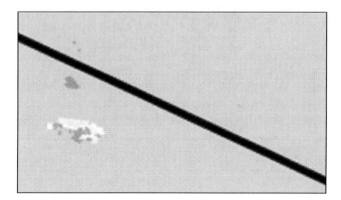

Polygons are symbolized through the `SimpleFillSymbol` class, which allows the drawing of polygons in solid, transparent, or crosshatch patterns. Polygons can also have an outline specified by a `SimpleLineSymbol` object. The following code example explains the process in detail:

```
var polygon = new Polygon(msr);
//a polygon is composed of rings
var ring = [[-122.98, 45.55], [-122.21, 45.21], [-122.13, 45.53],......];
polygon.addRing(ring);
var fillSymbol = new SimpleFillSymbol().setColor(new
Color([255,0,0,0.25]));
//create polygon graphic using polygon and fill symbol
var polygonGraphic = new Graphic(polygon, fillSymbol);
//add graphics to map's graphics layer
map.graphics.add(polygonGraphic);
```

The following screenshot is obtained when the preceding code is run:

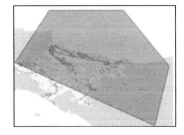

Assigning attributes to graphics

The attributes of a graphic are the name-value pairs that describe that object. In many cases, graphics are generated as the result of a task operation such as `QueryTask`. In such cases, each graphic is composed of both geometry and attributes, and you would then need to symbolize each graphic accordingly. The field attributes associated with the layer become the attributes for the graphic. In some cases, the attributes can be limited through properties such as `outFields`. If your graphics are being created programmatically, you will need to assign the attributes in your code using the `Graphic.setAttributes()` method as seen in the following code example:

```
Graphic.setAttributes( {"XCoord":evt.mapPoint.x, "YCoord".evt.
mapPoint.y,"Plant":"Mesa Mint"});
```

Displaying graphic attributes in an info template

In addition to attributes, a graphic can also have an info template that defines how the attribute data is displayed in a pop-up window. A point attribute variable has been defined in the following code example and contains key-value pairs. In this particular case, we have keys that include the address, city, and state. Each of these names or keys has a value. This variable is the third parameter in the constructor for a new point graphic. An info template defines the format of the pop-up window that appears, and contains a title and an optional content template string:

```
var pointESRI = new Point(Number(theX), Number(theY),msr);
var markerSymbol = new SimpleMarkerSymbol();
markerSymbol.setStyle(SimpleMarkerSymbol.STYLE_SQUARE);
markerSymbol.setSize(12);
markerSymbol.setColor(new Color([255,0,0]));
var pointAttributes = {address:"101 Main Street", city:"Portland",
state:"Oregon"};
var pointInfoTemplate = new InfoTemplate("Geocoding Results");
//create point graphic using point and marker symbol
var pointGraphic = new Graphic(pointESRI, markerSymbol,
pointAttributes).setInfoTemplate(pointInfoTemplate);
//add graphics to maps' graphics layer
map.graphics.add(pointGraphic);
```

The preceding code produces the following screenshot:

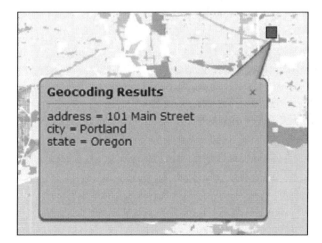

Creating graphics

Once you have defined the geometry, symbology, and attributes for your graphic, a new graphic object can be created with these parameters used as an input to the constructor for the Graphic object. In the following code example, we will create variables for the geometry (pointESRI), symbology (markerSymbol), point attributes (pointAttributes), and info template (pointInfoTemplate), and then apply these variables as an input to the constructor for our new graphic called pointGraphic. Finally, this graphic is added to the graphics layer.

```
var pointESRI = new Point(Number(theX), Number(theY, msr);
var markerSymbol = new SimpleMarkerSymbol();
markerSymbol.setStyle(SimpleMarkerSymbol.STYLE_SQUARE);
markerSymbol.setSize(12);
markerSymbol.setColor(new Color([255,0,0]));

var pointAttributes = {address:"101 Main Street", city:"Portland",
state:"Oregon"};
var pointInfoTemplate = new InfoTemplate("Geocoding Results");
//create the point graphic using point and marker symbol
var pointGraphic = new Graphic(pointESRI, markerSymbol,
pointAttributes).setInfoTemplate(pointTemplate);

//add graphics to maps' graphics layer
map.graphics.add(pointGraphic);
```

Adding graphics to the graphics layer

Before any of your graphics are displayed on the map, you must add them to the graphics layer. Each map has a graphics layer, which contains an array of graphics that is initially empty until you add the graphics. This layer can contain any type of graphic object. This means that you can mix-in points, lines, and polygons at the same time. Graphics are added to the layer through the add() method and can also be removed individually through the remove() method. In the event that you need to remove all the graphics simultaneously, the clear() method can be used. The graphics layer also has a number of events that can be registered, including click, mouse-down, and others.

Multiple graphics layers

Multiple graphics layers are supported by the API, making it much easier to organize different types of graphics. Layers can be easily removed or added, as required. For example, you can put polygon graphics that represent counties in one graphics layer and point graphics that represent traffic incidents in another graphics layer. Then you can easily add or remove either layer as required.

Time to practice with graphics

In this exercise, you will learn how to create and display graphics on a map. We are going to create a thematic map, that shows population density by county for the state of Colorado. You will also be introduced to query tasks. As you will learn in a later chapter, tasks can be executed in ArcGIS Server and include things such as spatial and attribute queries, identification of features, and geocoding. Finally, you will learn how to attach attributes to your graphic features and display them in an info window:

1. Open the JavaScript Sandbox at `http://developers.arcgis.com/en/javascript/sandbox/sandbox.html`.

2. Remove the JavaScript content from the `<script>` tag that I have highlighted in the following code block:

    ```
    <script>
      dojo.require("esri.map");
      function init(){
       var map = new esri.Map("mapDiv", {
          center: [-56.049, 38.485],
          zoom: 3,
          basemap: "streets"
        });
      }
      dojo.ready(init);
    </script>
    ```

3. Create the variables that you'll use in the application.

    ```
    <script>
        var map, defPopSymbol, onePopSymbol, twoPopSymbol,
    threePopSymbol, fourPopSymbol, fivePopSymbol;
    </script>
    ```

4. Add the `require()` function as seen in the following highlighted code:

    ```
    <script>
       var map, defPopSymbol, onePopSymbol, twoPopSymbol,
    threePopSymbol, fourPopSymbol, fivePopSymbol;
    ```

```
    require(["esri/map", "esri/tasks/query", "esri/tasks/QueryTask",
"esri/symbols/SimpleFillSymbol", "esri/InfoTemplate", "dojo/
domReady!"],
        function(Map, Query, QueryTask, SimpleFillSymbol,
InfoTemplate) {

        });
</script>
```

We covered the `esri/map` resource in a past exercise, so no additional explanation should be necessary. The `esri/tasks/query` and `esri/tasks/QueryTask` resources are new and we won't cover them until a later chapter. However, in order to complete this exercise, it is necessary for me to introduce these to you at this point. These resources enable you to perform spatial and attribute queries on a data layer.

5. Inside the `require()` function, you will need to create a `Map` object and add a `basemap: streets` layer by adding the following highlighted code. You will set the initial map extent to display the state of Colorado:

```
<script>
    var map, defPopSymbol, onePopSymbol, twoPopSymbol,
threePopSymbol, fourPopSymbol, fivePopSymbol;
      require(["esri/map", "esri/tasks/query", "esri/tasks/
QueryTask", "esri/symbols/SimpleFillSymbol", "esri/InfoTemplate",
"dojo/_base/Color", "dojo/domReady!"],
        function(Map, Query, QueryTask, SimpleFillSymbol,
InfoTemplate, Color) {
        map = new Map("map", {
            basemap: "streets",
            center: [-105.498,38.981], // long, lat
            zoom: 6,
            sliderStyle: "small"
        });
    });
</script>
```

6. Inside the `require()` function, just below the code block that creates the `Map` object, add the highlighted line of code to create a new polygon symbol that is transparent. This creates a new `SimpleFillSymbol` object and assigns it to the `defPopSymbol` variable. We use RGB values of `255,255,255,`and `0` to ensure that the filled color will be completely transparent. This is accomplished through the value `0`, which ensures that our coloring will be fully transparent. Later, we will add additional symbol objects so that we can display a color-coded map of county population density. For now though, we simply want to create a symbol so that you can understand the basic procedure of creating and displaying graphics on a map. The following code explains the process in detail:

```
map = new Map("mapDiv", {
  basemap: "streets",
  center: [-105.498,38.981], // long, lat
  zoom: 6,
  sliderStyle: "small"
});
defPopSymbol = new SimpleFillSymbol().setColor(new
Color([255,255,255, 0])); //transparent
```

In the next step, you are going to get a preview of how the Query task can be used in an application. We'll cover this task in detail in a later chapter but for now, here is an introduction. The Query task can be used to perform spatial and attribute queries on a data layer in a map service. In this exercise, we are going to use a Query task to perform an attribute query against a county boundary layer provided through an ESRI service.

7. Let's first examine the map service and layer that we will use in our query. Open a web browser and go to http://sampleserver1.arcgisonline. com/ArcGIS/rest/services/Specialty/ESRI_StateCityHighway_USA/ MapServer. This map service provides census information for U.S. states and counties and also includes a highway layer. In this exercise, we are interested in the county layer that has an index number of two. Click on the **counties** option to get detailed information about this layer. There are a lot of fields in this layer, but we are really only interested in the field that will allow us to query by state name and the field that gives us information on the population density. The STATE_NAME field gives us the state name of each county and the POP90_SQMI field gives us the population density of each county.

8. Return to the Sandbox. Below the line of code where we created our symbol, initialize a new QueryTask object by adding the following line of code just below the line that created the defPopSymbol variable. What this line does is create a new QueryTask object that points to the ESRI_StateCityHighway_ USA map service that we just examined in our browser and specifically points to layer index 2, which is our county layer. The following code explains the process in detail:

```
var queryTask = new QueryTask("http://sampleserver1.arcgisonline.
com/ArcGIS/rest/services/Specialty/ESRI_StateCityHighway_USA/
MapServer/2");
```

9. All QueryTask objects need input parameters so that they know what to execute against the layer. This is accomplished through a Query object. Add the following line of code right below the line you just entered:

```
var query = new Query();
```

10. Now we will define some of the properties on our new `Query` object that will enable us to perform an attribute query. Add the following three highlighted lines of code just below the line that created the `query` variable:

```
var query = new Query();
query.where = "STATE_NAME = 'Colorado'";
query.returnGeometry = true;
query.outFields = ["POP90_SQMI"];
```

11. The `where` property is used to create a SQL statement that will be executed against the layer. In this case, we're stating that we'd like to return only those county records that have a state name of `Colorado`. Setting the `returnGeometry` property to `true` indicates that we would like ArcGIS Server to return the geometric definition of all the features that matched our query. This is necessary because we need to plot these features as graphics on top of the map. Finally, the `outFields` property is used to define which fields we would like to be returned along with the geometry. This information will be used later when we create the color-coded map of a county's population density.

12. Finally, we will use the `execute` method on `queryTask` to perform the query against the layer that we have indicated (counties), using the parameters defined on our `query` object. Add the following line of code:

```
queryTask.execute(query, addPolysToMap);
```

In addition to passing the `query` object into ArcGIS Server, we have also indicated that `addPolysToMap` will serve as the callback function. This function will be executed after ArcGIS Server has performed the query and returned the results. It is up to the `addPolysToMap` function to plot the records using the `featureSet` object returned to it.

13. As I mentioned in the previous step, the callback function `addPolysToMap` will be executed when ArcGIS Server returns the `featureSet` object, which contains the records that matched our attribute query. Before creating the callback function, let's first discuss what the code will accomplish. The `addPolysToMap` function will take a single parameter `featureSet`. When a `queryTask` object is executed, ArcGIS Server returns a `featureSet` object to your code. A `featureSet` object contains the graphic objects returned by the query. Inside the `addPolysToMap` function, you will see the line `var features = featureSet.features;`. The `features` property returns an array with all the graphics contained within it. After defining a new feature variable, we create a `for` loop that we will use to loop through each of these graphics and plot the graphics to the map. Create the callback function by adding the following code block:

```
function addPolysToMap(featureSet) {
  var features = featureSet.features;
  var feature;
  for (var i=0, il=features.length; i<il; i++) {
    feature = features[i];
    map.graphics.add(features[i].setSymbol(defPopSymbol));
  }
}
```

As I mentioned earlier, you have to add each graphic that you create to the `GraphicsLayer` object. This is done through the `add()` method as you saw in the preceding code block. You will also notice that we are attaching the symbol we created earlier to each of the graphics (county boundaries).

14. Execute the code by clicking on the **Run** button and you should see the following screenshot as the output if everything has been coded correctly. Notice that each of the counties has been outlined with the symbol that we defined.

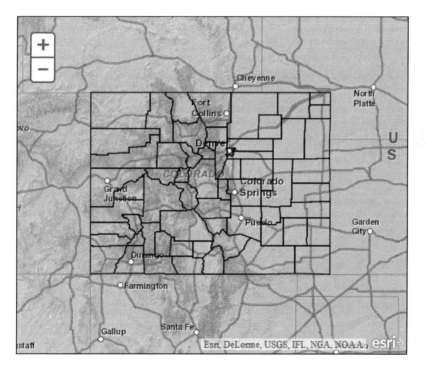

Now we are going to add additional code to the application that will color-code each of the counties based on population. Comment out the `defPopSymbol` variable inside the `require()` function and add five new symbols as follows:

```
//defPopSymbol = new SimpleFillSymbol().setColor(new
Color([255,255,255, 0])); //transparent
onePopSymbol = new SimpleFillSymbol().setColor(new Color([255,255,128,
.85])); //yellow
twoPopSymbol = new SimpleFillSymbol().setColor(new Color([250,209,85,
.85]));
threePopSymbol = new SimpleFillSymbol().setColor(new
Color([242,167,46, .85])); //orange
fourPopSymbol = new SimpleFillSymbol().setColor(new Color([173,83,19,
.85]));
fivePopSymbol = new SimpleFillSymbol().setColor(new Color([107,0,0,
.85])); //dark maroon
```

What we're doing here is basically creating a color ramp of symbols that will be assigned to each county, based on the population density. We are also applying a transparency value of .85 to each symbol so that we will be able to see through each of the counties. This will enable us to see the base map placed below the layer that contains the city names.

Recall that earlier in the exercise, we created `queryTask` and `Query` objects and defined an `outFields` property on `Query` to return the `POP90_SQMI` field. This will now come into play as we will use the values returned in this field to determine the symbol applied to each county based on the population density of that county. Update the `addPolysToMap` function to appear as seen in the following code block, and then we will discuss what we have done:

```
function addPolysToMap(featureSet) {
  var features = featureSet.features;
  var feature;
  for (var i=0, il=features.length; i<il; i++) {
    feature = features[i];
    attributes = feature.attributes;
    pop = attributes.POP90_SQMI;

    if (pop < 10)
    {
                                map.graphics.add(features[i].
setSymbol(onePopSymbol));
    }
    else if (pop >= 10 && pop < 95)
    {                           map.graphics.add(features[i].
setSymbol(twoPopSymbol));
    }
    else if (pop >= 95 && pop < 365)
```

```
    {                    map.graphics.add(features[i].
setSymbol(threePopSymbol));
    }
    else if (pop >= 365 && pop < 1100)
    {                    map.graphics.add(features[i].
setSymbol(fourPopSymbol));
    }
    else
    {                    map.graphics.add(features[i].
setSymbol(fivePopSymbol));
    }
  }
 }
}
```

What we have done with the preceding code block is obtain the population density information from each graphic and save it to a variable called `pop`. An `if/else` code block is then used to assign a symbol to the graphic, based on the population density of that county. For example, a county with a population density (as defined in the `POP90_SQMI` field) of `400` would be assigned the symbol defined by `fourPopSymbol`. Because we are in a `for` loop that examines every county in Colorado, each county graphic will be assigned a symbol.

Execute the code by clicking on the **Run** button and you should see the following screenshot as the output if everything has been coded correctly. Notice that each of the counties has been color-coded with one of the symbols that we defined earlier.

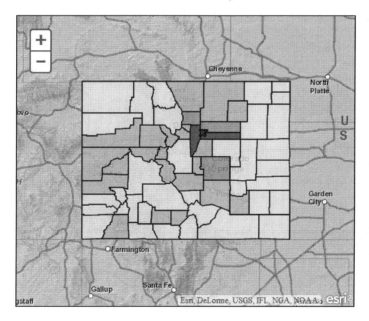

Now you will learn how to attach attributes to a graphic and display them in an info window when the graphic is clicked.

An info window is an HTML pop-up window that gets displayed when you click on a graphic. Normally, it contains the attributes of the clicked graphic but it can also contain custom content that you specify as a developer. The content of these windows is specified through an `InfoTemplate` object that specifies a title for the window and the content to be displayed in the window. The easiest way to create an `InfoTemplate` object is to use a wildcard for the content that will automatically insert all the fields of a dataset into the info window. We are going to add some additional output fields so that more content can be displayed in the info window. Alter the `query.outFields` line to include the fields highlighted in the following code line:

```
query.outFields = ["NAME","POP90_SQMI","HOUSEHOLDS","MALES","FEMALES",
"WHITE","BLACK","HISPANIC"];
```

Then, add the following line of code just below the `queryTask.execute` line:

```
resultTemplate = InfoTemplate("County Attributes", "${*}");
```

The first parameter passed into the constructor (`"County Attributes"`) is the title for the window. The second parameter is a wildcard indicating that all the name-value pairs of the attribute should be printed in the window. Therefore, the new fields that we added to `query.outFields` should all be included in the info window when a graphic is clicked.

Finally, we use the `Graphic.setInfoTemplate()` method to assign the newly created `InfoTemplate` object to a graphic. Alter your `if/else` statement by adding the following highlighted code:

```
if (pop < 10)
{
                         map.graphics.add(features[i].
setSymbol(onePopSymbol).setInfoTemplate(resultTemplate));
}
else if (pop >= 10 && pop < 95)
{
                         map.graphics.add(features[i].
setSymbol(twoPopSymbol).setInfoTemplate(resultTemplate));
}
else if (pop >= 95 && pop < 365)
{
                         map.graphics.add(features[i].
setSymbol(threePopSymbol).setInfoTemplate(resultTemplate));
}
```

```
else if (pop >= 365 && pop < 1100)
{
                         map.graphics.add(features[i].
setSymbol(fourPopSymbol).setInfoTemplate(resultTemplate));
}
else
{
                         map.graphics.add(features[i].
setSymbol(fivePopSymbol).setInfoTemplate(resultTemplate));
}
```

Execute the code by clicking on the **Run** button. Click on any of the counties in the map and you should see an info window similar to the following screenshot:

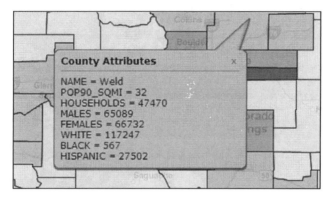

You can view the solution code for this exercise in the graphicexercise.html file of your ArcGISJavaScriptAPI folder to verify that your code has been written correctly.

Summary

In this chapter, you learned that graphics are often used to represent information that is generated as the result of actions performed within a working application. Frequently, these graphics are returned as the result of a task that has been performed, such as an attribute or spatial query. This can include points, lines, polygon, and text. These are temporary objects, only displayed during the current browser session. Each graphic can be composed of geometry, symbology, attributes, and an info template, and is added to the map through the use of a graphics layer, which is always the topmost layer in an application. This ensures that the contents of the layer will always be visible. In the next chapter, we'll introduce you to the feature layer, which can do everything that a graphics layer can do and more!

4
The Feature Layer

The ArcGIS API for JavaScript offers a feature layer for working with client-side graphic features. This FeatureLayer object inherits from the GraphicsLayer object, but also offers additional capabilities, such as the ability to perform queries and selections as well as support definition expressions. It can also be used for web editing. You should already be familiar with the graphics layer from an earlier chapter.

A feature layer differs from tiled and dynamic map service layers in that it transports geometry information for features from ArcGIS Server to the web browser, where it is then drawn on the map. It can also be used to represent data from a nonspatial table, in addition to a feature class that contains geometry.

Streaming data from ArcGIS Server to the browser potentially cuts down on the round trips to the server and can improve the performance of your application. A client can request the features it needs and perform selections and queries on those features, without having to request any more information from the server. The FeatureLayer object is especially appropriate for layers that respond to user interactions such as mouse clicks or hovers. The tradeoff to this is that if you're working with a feature layer that contains a lot of features, it can take a long time to initially transport the features to the client. The feature layer supports several display modes that can help ease this burden of working with a large number of features. We'll examine each of these display modes in this chapter.

A feature layer honors any definition expressions, scale dependencies, and other properties configured on the layer in a map service. Using a feature layer, you can access related tables, perform queries, display time slices, work with feature attachments, and do other useful things.

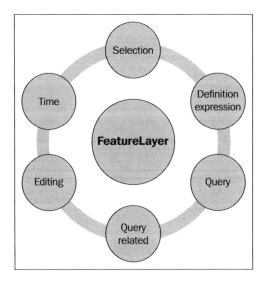

In this chapter, we will cover the following topics:

- Creating a FeatureLayer object
- Defining display modes
- Setting a definition expression
- Feature selection
- Rendering the feature layer
- Time to practice with FeatureLayer

Creating a FeatureLayer object

A feature layer must reference a layer from either a map service or a feature service. Use a map service if you just want to retrieve geometries and attributes from the server and symbolize them yourself. Use a feature service if you want to benefit from symbols in the service's source map document. Also, use a feature service if you plan to edit with the feature layer. Feature layers honor any feature-editing templates configured in the source map document.

In the following code example, you will get details on how to create a `FeatureLayer` object using its constructor. With tiled and dynamic layers, you simply provide a pointer to the rest endpoint but with feature layer, you need to point to a specific layer in the service. In the following code example, we will create a `FeatureLayer` object from the first layer in the service, which is indicated by the number `0`. The constructor for `FeatureLayer` also accepts options such as the display mode, output fields, and info template. Here, the display mode is set to `SNAPSHOT`, which would indicate that we are probably dealing with a fairly small dataset. We'll cover the various types of display modes that can be defined for a feature layer as well as when they should be used, in the next section:

```
var earthquakes = new FeatureLayer("http://servicesbeta.esri.com/
ArcGIS/rest/services/Earthquakes/Since_1970/MapServer/0",{ mode:
FeatureLayer.MODE_SNAPSHOT, outFields: ["Magnitude"]});
```

Optional constructor parameters

In addition to accepting a required layer from the map or feature service for the `FeatureLayer` object as the first parameter, you can also pass a JSON object that defines various options to the constructor. A wide variety of options can be passed into the constructor. I'll discuss the most commonly used options.

The `outFields` property can be used to restrict the fields that are returned with the `FeatureLayer` object. For performance reasons, it's best to only include the fields that you need for the application rather than accepting the default of returning all fields. Only return the fields that you absolutely need for your application. Doing this will ensure that your application performs better. In the following highlighted code, we've defined the `outFields` property to return only the `Date` and `Magnitude` fields:

```
var earthquakes = new FeatureLayer("http://servicesbeta.esri.com/
ArcGIS/rest/services/Earthquakes/Since_1970/MapServer/0",{ mode:
FeatureLayer.MODE_SNAPSHOT, outFields: ["Date", "Magnitude"]});
```

The `refreshInterval` property defines how often (in minutes) to refresh the layer. This property can be used when you have a `FeatureLayer` object containing data that changes often, including new records, or perhaps records that have been updated or deleted. The following highlighted code sets a refresh interval of 5 minutes:

```
var earthquakes = new FeatureLayer("http://servicesbeta.esri.com/
ArcGIS/rest/services/Earthquakes/Since_1970/MapServer/0",{ mode:
FeatureLayer.MODE_SNAPSHOT, outFields: ["Magnitude"], refreshInterval:
5});
```

To define the attributes and styling that should be displayed in an info window when a feature is clicked on, you can set the `infoTemplate` property as explained in the following code example:

```
function initOperationalLayer() {
  var infoTemplate = new InfoTemplate("${state_name}", "Population
(2000):   ${pop2000:NumberFormat}");
  var featureLayer = new FeatureLayer("http://sampleserver6.
arcgisonline.com/arcgis/rest/services/USA/MapServer/2",{
    mode: FeatureLayer.MODE_ONDEMAND,
    outFields: ["*"],
    infoTemplate: infoTemplate
    });

  map.addLayer(featureLayer);
  map.infoWindow.resize(155,75);
}
```

You may want to consider setting the `displayOnPan` property to `false` if you know that Internet Explorer will be the primary browser for your application. By default, this property is set to `true` but setting it to `false` will turn graphics off during pan operations, thus improving the performance of the application on Internet Explorer. The following code block explains this process in detail:

```
var earthquakes = new FeatureLayer("http://servicesbeta.esri.com/
ArcGIS/rest/services/Earthquakes/Since_1970/MapServer/0",{ mode:
FeatureLayer.MODE_SNAPSHOT, outFields: ["Magnitude"], displayOnPan:
false});
```

The display mode, defined with the `mode` parameter, is probably the most important optional parameter. So, we'll cover this in more detail in the next few sections.

Defining display modes

When creating a feature layer, you need to specify a mode for retrieving features. Because the mode determines when and how features are brought from the server to the client, your choice can affect the speed and appearance of your application. You have mode choices as shown in the following diagram:

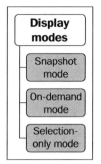

Snapshot mode

The snapshot mode retrieves all the features from the layer and streams them to the client browser, where they are added to the map. So, you need to carefully consider the size of your layer before using this mode. Generally, you will want to use this mode only with small datasets. Large datasets in snapshot mode can significantly degrade the performance of your application. The benefit of snapshot mode is that since all features from the layer are returned to the client, there is no need to return to the server for additional data. This raises the potential for a significant boost in your application's performance.

ArcGIS imposes a limit of 1000 features that may be returned at any one time, though this number is configurable through ArcGIS Server administration. In practical terms, you will want to use this mode only when you're working with small datasets:

```
var earthquakes = new FeatureLayer("http://servicesbeta.esri.com/
ArcGIS/rest/services/Earthquakes/Since_1970/MapServer/0",{ mode:
FeatureLayer.MODE_SNAPSHOT, outFields: ["Magnitude"]});
```

The on-demand mode

The on-demand mode retrieves features only as and when needed. What this amounts to is that all features within the current view extent are returned. Therefore, each time a zoom or pan operation takes place, features are streamed to the client from the server. This tends to work well with large datasets that won't operate efficiently in snapshot mode. It does require a round trip to the server to fetch the features each time the map extent changes but for large datasets, this is preferable. The following code example shows you how to set a FeatureLayer object to the ONDEMAND mode:

```
var earthquakes = new FeatureLayer("http://servicesbeta.esri.com/
ArcGIS/rest/services/Earthquakes/Since_1970/MapServer/0",{ mode:
FeatureLayer.MODE_ONDEMAND, outFields: ["Magnitude"]});
```

The selection-only mode

The selection-only mode does not request features initially. Instead, features are returned only when a selection is made on the client. Selected features are streamed to the client from the server. These selected features are then held on the client. The following code example shows you how to set a FeatureLayer object to SELECTION mode:

```
var earthquakes = new FeatureLayer("http://servicesbeta.esri.com/
ArcGIS/rest/services/Earthquakes/Since_1970/MapServer/0",{ mode:
FeatureLayer.MODE_SELECTION, outFields: ["Magnitude"]});
```

Setting a definition expression

Definition expressions are used to limit the features that are streamed to the client to only those features that match the attribute constraints. FeatureLayer contains a setDefinitionExpression() method that is used to create the definition expression. All features that meet the specified criteria will be returned to be displayed on the map. Expressions are built using traditional SQL expressions as seen in the following code example:

```
FeatureLayer.setDefinitionExpression("PROD_GAS='Yes'");
```

You can retrieve the currently set definition expression by using the FeatureLayer. getDefinitionExpression() method, which returns a string containing the expression.

Feature selection

The feature layer also supports feature selection, which is simply a subset of features in a layer that is used for viewing, editing, analysis, or input to other operations. Features are added to or removed from a selection set using either spatial or attribute criteria and can easily be drawn with a different symbol than those used in the normal display of a layer. The selectFeatures(query) method on FeatureLayer is used to create a selection set and takes a Query object as input. This has been explained in the following code example:

```
var selectQuery = new Query();
selectQuery.geometry = geometry;
featureLayer.selectFeatures(selectQuery,FeatureLayer.SELECTION_NEW);
```

We haven't discussed the `Query` object yet but as you can imagine, it is used to define the input parameters for an attribute or a spatial query. In this particular code example, a spatial query has been defined.

The following screenshot shows a feature that has been selected. A selection symbol has been applied to the selected feature:

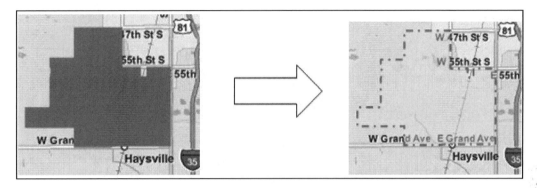

Any definition expression set on a layer either through the application or on the layer inside the map document file will be honored. Setting a symbol that is to be used for the selected features is quite easy and simply involves creating a symbol and then using the `setSelectionSymbol()` method on `FeatureLayer`. Selected features will automatically be assigned this symbol. You can opt to define a new selection set, add features to an existing selection set, or remove features from a selection set through various constants, including `SELECTION_NEW`, `SELECTION_ADD`, and `SELECTION_SUBTRACT`. A new selection set is defined in the following code example:

```
featureLayer.selectFeatures(selectQuery,FeatureLayer.SELECTION_NEW);
```

In addition, you can define the callback and errback functions to process the returned features or handle any errors.

Rendering a feature layer

A renderer can be used to define a set of symbols for a feature layer or a graphics layer. These symbols can have different colors and/or sizes that are based on an attribute. The five types of renderer in the ArcGIS Server API for JavaScript include SimpleRenderer, ClassBreaksRenderer, UniqueValueRenderer, DotDensityRenderer, and TemporalRenderer. We'll examine each of these renderers in this section.

The rendering process will be the same, regardless of the type of renderer you use. You first need to create an instance of the renderer, define the symbology for the renderer, and finally apply the renderer to the feature layer. This rendering process has been illustrated in the following diagram:

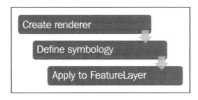

The following code example shows the basic programmatic structure to create and apply a renderer to a FeatureLayer object:

```
var renderer = new ClassBreaksRenderer(symbol, "POPSQMI");
renderer.addBreak(0, 5, new SimpleFillSymbol().setColor(new
Color([255, 0, 0, 0.5])));
renderer.addBreak(5.01, 10, new SimpleFillSymbol().setColor(new
Color([255, 255, 0, 0.5])));
renderer.addBreak(10.01, 25, new SimpleFillSymbol().setColor(new
Color([0, 255, 0, 0.5])));
renderer.addBreak(25.01, Infinity, new SimpleFillSymbol().setColor(new
Color([255, 128, 0, 0.5])));
featureLayer.setRenderer(renderer);
```

The simplest type of renderer is `SimpleRenderer`, which simply applies the same symbol for all graphics.

`UniqueValueRenderer` can be used to symbolize graphics, based on a matching attribute that is typically a field containing string data.

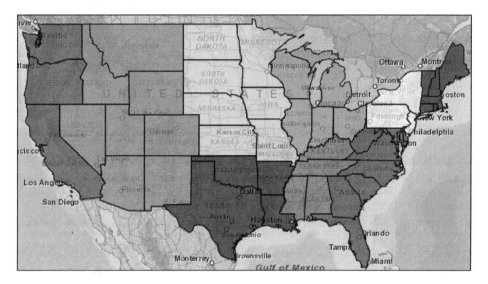

For example, if you have a state feature class, you might want to symbolize each feature based on a region name. Each region would have a different symbol. The following code example shows how you can programmatically create a `UniqueValueRenderer` and add values and symbols to the structure:

```
var renderer = new UniqueValueRenderer(defaultSymbol, "REGIONNAME");
renderer.addValue("West", new SimpleLineSymbol().setColor(new
Color([255, 255, 0, 0.5])));
renderer.addValue("South", new SimpleLineSymbol().setColor(new
Color([128, 0, 128, 0.5])));
renderer.addValue("Mountain", new SimpleLineSymbol().setColor(new
Color([255, 0, 0, 0.5])));
```

A `ClassBreaksRenderer` works with data that is stored as a numeric attribute. Each graphic will be symbolized according to the value of that particular attribute, in accordance with breaks in the data. In the following screenshot, you see an example of a `ClassBreaksRenderer` that has been applied to county-level data for Kansas:

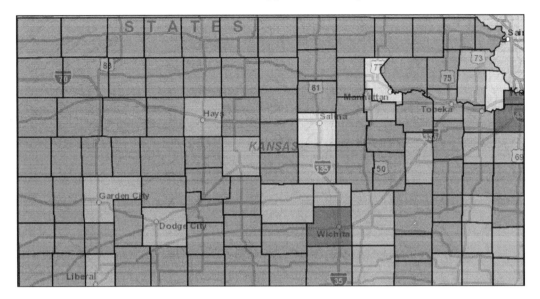

The breaks define the values at which the symbol will change. For example, with a Parcel feature class, you might want to symbolize parcels based on values found in the PROPERTYVALUE field. You'd first want to create a new instance of `ClassBreaksRenderer` and then define the breaks for the data. The `Infinity` and `-Infinity` values can be used as the lower and upper boundaries for your data if needed, as seen in the following code example, where we use the `Infinity` keyword to signify a class break for any values greater than 250,000:

```
var renderer = new ClassBreaksRenderer(symbol, "PROPERTYVALUE");
renderer.addBreak(0, 50000, new SimpleFillSymbol().setColor(new
Color([255, 0, 0, 0.5])));
renderer.addBreak(50001, 100000, new SimpleFillSymbol().setColor(new
Color([255, 255, 0, 0.5])));
renderer.addBreak(100001, 250000, 50000, new SimpleFillSymbol().
setColor(new Color([0, 255, 0, 0.5])));
renderer.addBreak(250001, Infinity, new SimpleFillSymbol().
setColor(new Color([255, 128, 0, 0.5])));
```

A `TemporalRenderer` provides time-based rendering of features. This type of renderer is often used to display historical information or near real-time data. It allows you to define how observations and tracks are rendered.

The following code example explains how to create a `TemporalRenderer` using a `ClassBreaksRenderer` and applying it to a `featureLayer` object. The `ClassBreaksRenderer` is used to define symbols by magnitude; the larger the magnitude, the larger the symbol:

```
// temporal renderer
var observationRenderer = new ClassBreaksRenderer(new
SimpleMarkerSymbol(), "magnitude");

observationRenderer.addBreak(7, 12, new SimpleMarkerSymbol(S
impleMarkerSymbol.STYLE_SQUARE, 24, new SimpleLineSymbol().
setStyle(SimpleLineSymbol.STYLE_SOLID).setColor(new
Color([100,100,100])),new Color([0,0,0,0])));

observationRenderer.addBreak(6, 7, new SimpleMarkerSymbol(S
impleMarkerSymbol.STYLE_SQUARE, 21, new SimpleLineSymbol().
setStyle(SimpleLineSymbol.STYLE_SOLID).setColor(new
Color([100,100,100])),new Color([0,0,0,0])));

observationRenderer.addBreak(5, 6, new SimpleMarkerSymbol(
SimpleMarkerSymbol.STYLE_SQUARE, 18,new SimpleLineSymbol().
setStyle(SimpleLineSymbol.STYLE_SOLID).setColor(new
Color([100,100,100])),new Color([0,0,0,0])));

observationRenderer.addBreak(4, 5, new SimpleMarkerSymbol(
SimpleMarkerSymbol.STYLE_SQUARE, 15,new SimpleLineSymbol().
setStyle(SimpleLineSymbol.STYLE_SOLID).setColor(new
Color([100,100,100])),new Color([0,0,0,0])));

observationRenderer.addBreak(3, 4, new SimpleMarkerSymbol(
SimpleMarkerSymbol.STYLE_SQUARE, 12,new SimpleLineSymbol().
setStyle(SimpleLineSymbol.STYLE_SOLID).setColor(new
Color([100,100,100])),new Color([0,0,0,0])));

observationRenderer.addBreak(2, 3, new SimpleMarkerSymbol(
SimpleMarkerSymbol.STYLE_SQUARE, 9,new SimpleLineSymbol().
setStyle(SimpleLineSymbol.STYLE_SOLID).setColor(new
Color([100,100,100])),new Color([0,0,0,0])));

observationRenderer.addBreak(0, 2, new SimpleMarkerSymbol(
SimpleMarkerSymbol.STYLE_SQUARE, 6,new SimpleLineSymbol().
setStyle(SimpleLineSymbol.STYLE_SOLID).setColor(new
Color([100,100,100])),new Color([0,0,0,0])));

var infos = [
  { minAge: 0, maxAge: 1, color: new Color([255,0,0])},
  { minAge: 1, maxAge: 24, color: new Color([49,154,255])},
  { minAge: 24, maxAge: Infinity, color: new Color([255,255,8])}
];
```

```
var ager = new TimeClassBreaksAger(infos, TimeClassBreaksAger.UNIT_
HOURS);
var renderer = new TemporalRenderer(observationRenderer, null, null,
ager);
featureLayer.setRenderer(renderer);
```

An `ager` symbol has been defined here, which determines how the feature's symbol changes as time progresses.

The final type of renderer that we'll discuss is the `DotDensityRenderer`. The following screenshot depicts a map that has been created using a `DotDensityRenderer`:

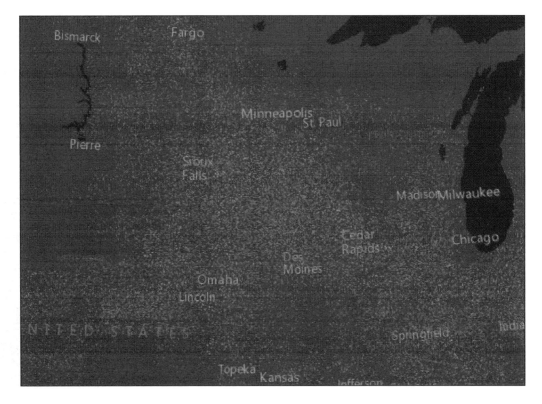

This type of renderer enables you to create dot density visualizations of data that show spatial density of a discrete spatial phenomenon such as population density.

The following code example explains the creation of a DotDensityRenderer based on the pop field and defines a dotValue of 1000 and dotSize equal to 2. This will create one dot per two pixels in size for a population of 1000:

```
var dotDensityRenderer = new DotDensityRenderer({
  fields: [{
      name: "pop",
      color: new Color([52, 114, 53])
  }],
  dotValue: 1000,
  dotSize: 2
});

layer.setRenderer(dotDensityRenderer);
```

Time to practice with FeatureLayer

In this exercise, you will use the FeatureLayer object to set a definition expression on a layer, draw the features that match the definition expression as graphics, and respond to a hover event over the features.

Perform the following steps to complete the exercise:

1. Open the JavaScript Sandbox at http://developers.arcgis.com/en/javascript/sandbox/sandbox.html.

2. Remove the JavaScript content from the <script> tag that I have highlighted in the following code block:

```
<script>
  dojo.require("esri.map");

functioninit(){
var map = new esri.Map("mapDiv", {
        center: [-56.049, 38.485],
        zoom: 3,
        basemap: "streets"
      });
    }
    dojo.ready(init);
</script>
```

3. Create the variables that you'll use in the application inside the
   `<script>` tag:

```
<script>
  var map;
</script>
```

4. Create the `require()` function that defines the resources you'll use in
   this application:

```
<script type="text/javascript" language="Javascript">
  var map;
  require(["esri/map", "esri/layers/FeatureLayer",    "esri/
symbols/SimpleFillSymbol",
"esri/symbols/SimpleLineSymbol", "esri/renderers/SimpleRenderer",
"esri/InfoTemplate", "esri/graphic", "dojo/on",
"dojo/_base/Color", "dojo/domReady!"],
  function(Map,FeatureLayer, SimpleFillSymbol,
      SimpleLineSymbol, SimpleRenderer, InfoTemplate,  Graphic,
on, Color) {

  });

</script>
```

5. In your web browser, navigate to `http://sampleserver1.arcgisonline.`
   `com/ArcGIS/rest/services/Demographics/ESRI_Census_USA/`
   `MapServer/5`.

   We will be using the `states` layer for this exercise. What we want to do is
   apply a definition expression to the `states` layer that will display only those
   states that have a median age greater than `36`. These states will be displayed
   as graphics on the map, and an info window will be displayed containing
   the median age, median age for males, and median age for females for that
   state when the user hovers the mouse over the states that meet the definition
   expression. In addition, the state will be outlined in red. The fields we will
   use from the states layer include STATE_NAME, MED_AGE, MED_AGE_M, and
   MED_AGE_F.

6. Create the `Map` object as seen in the following code example:

```
<script type="text/javascript" language="Javascript">
            var map;
        require(["esri/map", "esri/layers/FeatureLayer",    "esri/
symbols/SimpleFillSymbol",
            "esri/symbols/SimpleLineSymbol", "esri/renderers/
SimpleRenderer", "esri/InfoTemplate", "esri/graphic", "dojo/on",
            "dojo/_base/Color", "dojo/domReady!"],
```

```
        function(Map,FeatureLayer, SimpleFillSymbol,
              SimpleLineSymbol, SimpleRenderer, InfoTemplate,
  Graphic, on, Color) {
          map = new Map("mapDiv", {
            basemap: "streets",
            center: [-96.095,39.726], // long, lat
            zoom: 4,
            sliderStyle: "small"
          });

          });

  </script>
```

7. Add a `map.load` event that triggers the creation of a `map.graphics.`
   `mouse-out` event, which clears any existing graphics and info windows.
   The following code example explains this in detail:

```
map = new Map("map", {
    basemap: "streets",
    center: [-96.095,39.726], // long, lat
    zoom: 4,
    sliderStyle: "small"
});

  map.on("load", function() {
    map.graphics.on("mouse-out", function(evt) {
      map.graphics.clear();
      map.infoWindow.hide();
    });
  });
```

8. Create a new `FeatureLayer` object that points to the `states` layer that you
   had examined earlier. You will also specify that the SNAPSHOT mode be
   used to return the features, define the output fields, and set the definition
   expression. Add the following code to your application for this purpose:

```
map.on("load", function() {
  map.graphics.on("mouse-out", function(evt) {
    map.graphics.clear();
    map.infoWindow.hide();
  });
});

var olderStates = new FeatureLayer("http://sampleserver1.
arcgisonline.com/ArcGIS/rest/services/Demographics/ESRI_Census_
```

```
USA/MapServer/5", {
  mode: FeatureLayer.MODE_SNAPSHOT,
  outFields: ["STATE_NAME", "MED_AGE", "MED_AGE_M", "MED_AGE_F"]
});
olderStates.setDefinitionExpression("MED_AGE > 36");
```

Here, we have used the new keyword to define a new instance of
FeatureLayer that points to the states layer at the rest endpoint noted in
the code. When defining a new instance of FeatureLayer, we have included
a couple of properties including mode and outFields. The mode property
can be set to SNAPSHOT, ONDEMAND, or SELECTION. Since the states layer
contains a relatively small number of features, we can use the SNAPSHOT
mode in this case. This mode retrieves all the features from the layer when
it is added to the map, and therefore does not require any additional trips
to the server to retrieve additional features from the layer. We are also
specifying the outFields property, which is an array of fields that will be
returned. We will be displaying these fields in an info window when the user
hovers over the state. Finally, we set our definition expression on the layer to
display only those features (states) where the median age is greater than 36.

9. In this step, you will create a symbol and apply a renderer to the features
    (states) that are returned from the definition expression. You will also add
    the FeatureLayer to the map. Add the following lines of code just below the
    code that you added in the previous step:

```
var olderStates = new FeatureLayer("http://sampleserver1.
arcgisonline.com/ArcGIS/rest/services/Demographics/ESRI_Census_
USA/MapServer/5", {
  mode: FeatureLayer.MODE_SNAPSHOT,
  outFields: ["STATE_NAME", "MED_AGE", "MED_AGE_M", "MED_AGE_F"]
  });
  olderStates.setDefinitionExpression("MED_AGE > 36");

var symbol = new SimpleFillSymbol(SimpleFillSymbol.STYLE_
SOLID, new SimpleLineSymbol(SimpleLineSymbol.STYLE_SOLID, new
Color([255,255,255,0.35]), 1),new Color([125,125,125,0.35]));
                olderStates.setRenderer(new
SimpleRenderer(symbol));
map.addLayer(olderStates);
```

10. Using the output fields that you defined earlier, create an `InfoTemplate` object. Add the following lines of code to your application just below the lines that you added in the previous step. Note the inclusion of the output fields that are embedded inside brackets and preceded by a dollar sign:

```
var infoTemplate = new InfoTemplate();
infoTemplate.setTitle("${STATE_NAME}");
infoTemplate.setContent("<b>Median Age: </b>${MED_AGE_M}<br/>"
  + "<b>Median Age - Male: </b>${MED_AGE_M}<br/>"
  + "<b>Median Age - Female: </b>${MED_AGE_F}");
map.infoWindow.resize(245,125);
```

11. Then, add the following lines of code to create a graphic that will be displayed when the user hovers the mouse over a state:

```
var highlightSymbol = new SimpleFillSymbol(SimpleFillSymbol.STYLE_
SOLID,
new SimpleLineSymbol(SimpleLineSymbol.STYLE_SOLID,
  new Color([255,0,0]), new Color([125,125,125,0.35]))));
```

12. The final step is to display the highlight symbol and info template that we created in the previous steps. This happens each time the user hovers the mouse over a state. Add the following code block below the last lines of code that you entered previously. Here, we are using `on()` to wire an event (mouse over) to a function, which will respond each time the event occurs. The `mouse-over` event handler in this case will clear any existing graphics from the `GraphicsLayer` object, create the info template that you created in a previous step, create a highlight symbol and add it to the `GraphicsLayer`, and then show the `InfoWindow` object. This has been explained in the following code block:

```
olderStates.on("mouse-over", function(evt) {
  map.graphics.clear();
  evt.graphic.setInfoTemplate(infoTemplate);
  var content = evt.graphic.getContent();
  map.infoWindow.setContent(content);
  var title = evt.graphic.getTitle();
  map.infoWindow.setTitle(title);
  var highlightGraphic = new  Graphic(evt.graphic.
geometry,highlightSymbol);
  map.graphics.add(highlightGraphic);
  map.infoWindow.show(evt.screenPoint,map.getInfoWindowAnchor(evt.
screenPoint));
});
```

You may want to review the solution file (`featurelayer.html`) in your `ArcGISJavaScriptAPI` folder to verify that your code has been written correctly.

Execute the code by clicking on the **Run** button and you should see the following output if everything has been coded correctly. You should see a map similar to the following screenshot. Mouse over one of the highlighted states to see an info window as shown in the following screenshot:

Summary

The JavaScript API for ArcGIS Server offers a `FeatureLayer` object to work with client-side graphic features. This inherits from the graphics layer, but also offers additional capabilities, such as the ability to perform queries and selections and support definition expressions. A feature layer can also be used for web editing. It differs from tiled and dynamic map service layers because feature layers bring geometry information across to the client computer, to be drawn by the web browser. This potentially cuts down on the round trips to the server and can improve the performance of your application on the server side. A client can request the features it needs, and perform selections and queries on those features without having to request more information from the server. The `FeatureLayer` object is especially appropriate for layers that respond to user interactions such as mouse clicks or hovers.

5

Using Widgets and Toolbars

As a GIS web application developer, you want to focus on building a functionality specific to the application you are constructing. Spending valuable time and effort adding basic GIS functions such as zooming and panning to your application detracts from what should be your primary focus. Many applications also need to add an overview map, legend, or scale bar to be added to the user interface. Fortunately, the API provides user interface widgets that you can drop directly into your application and with a little configuration, they are ready to go.

The ArcGIS API for JavaScript also includes helper classes to add the navigation and drawing toolbars to your application. In this chapter, you'll learn how easy it is to add these user interface components to an application.

Let's start by examining a navigation sample that Esri has placed on their resource center website. Open a web browser and go to http://developers.arcgis.com/en/javascript/samples/toolbar_draw/. Take a look at the following screenshot:

At first glance over the preceding screenshot, you'd think that the drawing toolbar is simply a user interface component that you drop into your application, which is not exactly the case. The ArcGIS API for JavaScript provides a toolbar helper class called `esri/toolbars/Draw` to assist in accomplishing this task. In addition, the API also provides a class to handle navigation tasks. What these helper classes do is save you the work of drawing zoom boxes, capturing mouse clicks, and other user-initiated events. As any experienced GIS web developer can tell you, this is no small accomplishment. Adding these basic navigation capabilities into the helper classes provided with the API can easily save hours of development work.

In this chapter, we'll cover the following topics:

- Adding toolbars to an application
- User interface widgets
- Feature editing

Adding toolbars to an application

There are two basic types of toolbars that you can add to your application using the helper classes, `Navigation` and `Draw`, provided by the API. There is also an editing toolbar that can be used to edit features or graphics through a web browser. We'll discuss this toolbar in a later chapter.

Steps for creating a toolbar

The **Navigation** and **Draw** toolbars are not simply user interface components that you can drop into your application. They are helper classes and there are several steps that you need to take to actually create your toolbar with the appropriate buttons. This to-do list for your toolbars may seem a little intimidating, but after you do it once or twice, it becomes pretty simple. The following are the steps to do this, and we'll discuss each item in detail:

1. Define the CSS styles for each button.
2. Create the buttons inside the toolbar.
3. Create an instance of `esri/toolbars/Navigation` or `esri/toolbars/Draw`.
4. Connect button events to handler functions.

Defining CSS styles

The first thing you'll need to do is define the CSS styles for each button that you intend to include on the toolbar. Each button on your toolbar will need an image, text, or both, along with the width and height for the button. Each of these properties are defined within the CSS inside a `<style>` tag as seen in the following code snippet. In the code example shown in the following code snippet, a number of buttons are being defined for the `Navigation` toolbar. Let's examine the **Zoom Out** button and follow it through the entire process to make things a little simpler. I've highlighted the **Zoom Out** button in the following code. As with all the other buttons, we define an image to be used for the button (`nav_zoomout.png`) along with the width and height of the button. In addition, the identifier for this style is defined as `.zoomoutIcon`.

```
<style type="text/css">
  @import
    "http://js.arcgis.com/3.7/js/dojo/dijit/themes/claro/claro.css";
    .zoominIcon{ background-image:url(images/nav_zoomin.png);
      width:16px; height:16px; }
    .zoomoutIcon{ background-image:url(images/nav_zoomout.png);
      width:16px; height:16px; }
    .zoomfullextIcon{ background-
      image:url(images/nav_fullextent.png); width:16px;
        height:16px; }
    .zoomprevIcon{ background-
      image:url(images/nav_previous.png); width:16px;
        height:16px; }
    .zoomnextIcon{ background-image:url(images/nav_next.png);
      width:16px; height:16px; }
    .panIcon{ background-image:url(images/nav_pan.png);
      width:16px; height:16px; }
    .deactivateIcon{ background-
      image:url(images/nav_decline.png); width:16px;
        height:16px; }
</style>
```

Creating buttons

The buttons can to be defined inside a `<div>` container with `data-dojo-type` of the `ContentPane` dijit inside `BorderContainer`, as shown in the following code example. When creating each button, you will need to define the CSS style it should reference and what should happen when the button is clicked. The buttons use the `iconClass` attribute to reference a CSS style. In the case of the **Zoom Out** button in our example, the `iconClass` attribute references `zoomoutIcon`, which is a style we defined earlier. The `zoomoutIcon` style defines an image to use for the button along with a width and height for the button. Take a look at the following code snippet:

```
<div id="mainWindow" data-dojo-type="dijit/layout/BorderContainer"
  data-dojo-props="design:'headline'">
  <div id="header"data-dojo-type="dijit/layout/ContentPane"
    data-dojo-props="region:'top'">
    <button data-dojo-type="dijit/form/Button"
      iconClass="zoominIcon">Zoom In</button>
    <button data-dojo-type="dijit/form/Button"
      iconClass="zoomoutIcon" >Zoom Out</button>
    <button data-dojo-type="dijit/form/Button"
      iconClass="zoomfullextIcon" >Full Extent</button>
    <button data-dojo-type ="dijit/form/Button"
      iconClass="zoomprevIcon" >Prev Extent</button>
    <button data-dojo-type="dijit/form/Button"
      iconClass="zoomnextIcon" >Next Extent</button>
    <button data-dojo-type="dijit/form/Button"
      iconClass="panIcon">Pan</button>
    <button data-dojo-type="dijit/form/Button"
      iconClass="deactivateIcon" >Deactivate</button>
  </div>
</div>
```

The preceding code block defines the buttons on the toolbar. Each button is created using a `Button` user interface control provided by Dijit (a subproject of Dojo). Each control is enclosed within a `<button>` tag inside the `<body>` tag of the web page with all the buttons being enclosed by the surrounding the `<div>` tag that contains the `ContentPane` dijit.

Creating an instance of the Navigation toolbar

Now that the visual interface for the buttons is complete, we need to create an instance of `esri/toolbars/Navigation` and wire up the events and event handlers. Creating an instance of the `Navigation` class is as easy as calling the constructor and passing in a reference to `Map` as you'll see shortly. However, you'll first want to make sure that you add a reference to `esri/toolbars/navigation`. The following code example adds references to the `Navigation` toolbar, creates the toolbar, connects click events to the buttons, and activates the tools. The relevant lines of code have been highlighted and commented so that you understand each section:

```
<script>
  var map, toolbar, symbol, geomTask;

    require([
      "esri/map",
      "esri/toolbars/navigation",
      "dojo/parser", "dijit/registry",

    "dijit/layout/BorderContainer", "dijit/layout/ContentPane",
      "dijit/form/Button", "dojo/domReady!"
      ], function(
      Map, Navigation,
      parser, registry
    ) {
      parser.parse();

    map = new Map("map", {
      basemap: "streets",
      center: [-15.469, 36.428],
      zoom: 3
      });

    map.on("load", createToolbar);

    // loop through all dijits, connect onClick event
      // listeners for buttons to activate navigation tools
      registry.forEach(function(d) {
        // d is a reference to a dijit
        // could be a layout container or a button
        if ( d.declaredClass === "dijit.form.Button" ) {
      d.on("click", activateTool);
      }
      });

    //activate tools
      function activateTool() {
      var tool = this.label.toUpperCase().replace(/ /g, "_");
      toolbar.activate(Navigation[tool]);
      }
```

```
        //create the Navigation toolbar
        function createToolbar(themap) {
        toolbar = new Navigation(map);


        });
    </script>
```

Hopefully, the previous `Navigation` toolbar example has illustrated the steps to add a navigation toolbar to your web mapping application through the JavaScript API. You no longer have to be concerned with adding in JavaScript code to draw and handle the extent rectangle or capture mouse coordinates for a pan operation. In addition, the user interface components of the toolbar can be created easily through various user interface controls supplied by the Dijit library. The `Draw` class makes it equally easy to support the drawing of geometries such as points, lines, and polygons within a similar toolbar.

User interface widgets

The API for JavaScript comes with many out of the box widgets that you can drop into your application for enhanced productivity. Included are the `BasemapGallery`, `Bookmarks`, `Print`, `Geocoder`, `Gauge`, `Measurement`, `Popup`, `Legend`, `Scalebar`, `OverviewMap`, `Editor`, `Directions`, `HistogramTimeSlider`, `HomeButton`, `LayerSwipe`, `LocateButton`, `TimeSlider`, and `Analysis` widgets. Widgets differ from the buttons and tools you create as part of the `Navigation` or `Draw` toolbars we discussed earlier. These widgets are out of the box functionalities that you can drop into your application with just a few lines of code as opposed to the toolbars, which were just helper classes that require a fair amount of HTML, CSS, and JavaScript code.

The BasemapGallery widget

The `BasemapGallery` widget displays a collection of basemaps from `ArcGIS.com` and/ or a user-defined set of map or image services. When a basemap is selected from the collection, the current basemap is removed and the newly selected basemap appears. When adding custom maps to the basemap gallery, they will need to have the same spatial reference as the other layers in the gallery. When using layers from `ArcGIS.com`, this would be the Web Mercator reference with wkids 102100, 102113, or 3857 (well known IDs or 'wkids' are unique identifiers for a spatial reference system). It is also recommended that all basemaps be tiled layers for performance reasons.

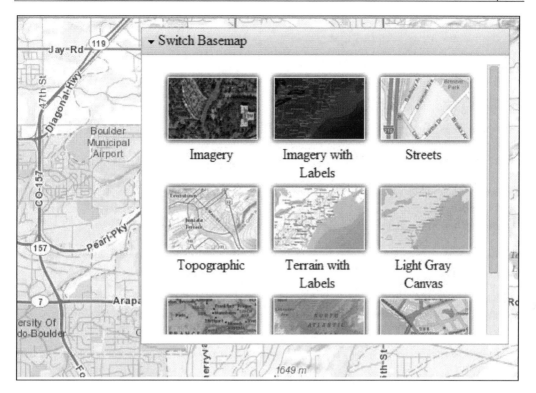

When creating a `BasemapGallery` widget, there are a number of parameters that you can supply in the constructor as shown in the preceding screenshot, which include the ability to show ArcGIS basemaps, define one or more custom basemaps for inclusion in the gallery, supply a Bing maps key and a reference to the map where the gallery will be placed, and so on. After creating the `BasemapGallery` widget, you need to call the `startup()` method to prepare it for user interaction. Take a look at the following code snippet:

```
require(["esri/dijit/Basemap", ...
], function(Basemap, ... ) {
    var basemaps = [];
    var waterBasemap = new Basemap({
      layers: [waterTemplateLayer],
      title: "Water Template",
      thumbnailUrl: "images/waterThumb.png"
    });
    basemaps.push(waterBasemap);
...
});
```

In the preceding code sample, a new `Basemap` object is created with a title, thumbnail image, and an array containing a single layer. This `Basemap` object is then pushed into an array of basemaps that will be added to the widget.

The Bookmarks widget

The `Bookmarks` widget is used to display a set of named geographic extents to the end user. Clicking on a bookmark name from the widget will automatically set the extent of the map to the extent provided for the bookmark. Using the widget, you can add new bookmarks, delete existing bookmarks, and update bookmarks. Bookmarks are defined in JavaScript code as JSON objects with properties that define the name, extent, and bounding coordinates of the bookmark. To add a bookmark to the widget, you call `Bookmark.addBookmark()`. Take a look at the following screenshot:

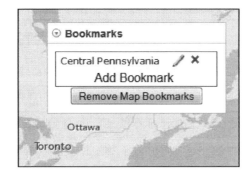

Then take a look at the following code snippet:

```
require([
"esri/map", "esri/dijit/Bookmarks", "dojo/dom", ...
], function(Map, Bookmarks, dom, ... ) {
    var map = new Map( ... );
    var bookmarks = new Bookmarks({
      map: map,
      bookmarks: bookmarks
    }, dom.byId('bookmarks'));
...
});
```

In the previous code example, a new `Bookmarks` object is created. It is attached to the map and a list of bookmarks in the JSON format is added.

The Print widget

The Print widget is a much-welcomed tool, which simplifies printing maps from web applications. It uses a default or user-defined layout for the map. This widget does require the use of an ArcGIS Server 10.1 or higher export web map task. Take a look at the following figure:

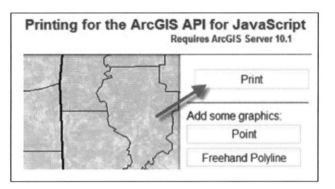

Then take a look at the following code snippet:

```
require([
"esri/map", "esri/dijit/Print", "dojo/dom"...
], function(Map, Print, dom, ... ) {
     var map = new Map( ... );
     var printer = new Print({
       map: map,
       url: "    http://servicesbeta4.esri.com/arcgis/rest/services/
Utilities/ExportWebMap/GPServer/Export%20Web%20Map%20Task"
     }, dom.byId("printButton"));
...
});
```

In the previous code example, a new Print widget is created. The URL property is used to point the widget to a **Print** task and the widget is attached to a HTML element on the page.

The Geocoder widget

The Geocoder widget allows you to easily add geocoding functionality to your application. This widget includes a single textbox that autofilters results as the end user begins typing in an address. Autocompletion is enabled by setting the autoComplete property to true. By default, the Geocoder widget uses the ESRI World Locator service. You can change this by setting the geocoder property. Take a look at the following screenshot:

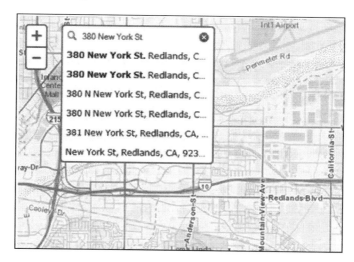

You can also automatically append values to any string that the user enters. For example, in a local application, you might want to always append a specific city and state to any address entered. This is done through the suffix property. To enable the map to display the location of the geocoded address, you can set autoNavigate to true. It is certainly possible for more than one potential location to be returned from Locator. You can set a maximum number of returned locations by setting the maxLocations property. In the practice exercise coming up in the next section, you'll learn how to add the Geocoder widget to your applications.

Time to practice with the Geocoder widget

In this exercise, you'll learn how to add the Geocoder widget to an application.

1. Open the ArcGIS API for JavaScript Sandbox available at http://developers.arcgis.com/en/javascript/sandbox/sandbox.html.

2. Alter the `<style>` tag so that it appears as follows:

```
<style>
html, body, #mapDiv {
height:100%;
```

```css
width:100%;
margin:0;
padding:0;
}
body {
background-color:#FFF;
overflow:hidden;
font-family:"Trebuchet MS";
}
#search {
display: block;
position: absolute;
z-index: 2;
top: 20px;
left: 75px;
}
</style>
```

3. Remove the JavaScript content from the `<script>` tag, highlighted as follows:

```javascript
<script>
dojo.require("esri.map");

function init(){
var map = new esri.Map("mapDiv", {
center: [-56.049, 38.485],
zoom: 3,
basemap: "streets"
});
}
dojo.ready(init);
</script>
```

4. You already have a `<div>` container for the map. In this step, you'll create a second `<div>` tag that will serve as the container for the Geocoding widget. Add the container for the widget as shown in the following highlighted code. Make sure you give the `<div>` tag a particular `id` of search. This corresponds to the CSS styling we defined at the top of the file and highlighted in the following code snippet. It connects the HTML `<div>` tag to the CSS:

```html
<body class="tundra">
  <div id="search"></div>
  <div id="mapDiv"></div>
</body>
```

5. Create variables to hold the map and the `geocoder` object as follows:

```
<script>
var map, geocoder;
</script>
```

6. In the `<script>` tag, add the `require()` function and create a `Map` object as follows:

```
<script>
var map, geocoder;

require([
        "esri/map", "esri/dijit/Geocoder", "dojo/domReady!"
    ], function(Map, Geocoder) {
map = new Map("mapDiv",{
basemap: "streets",
center:[-98.496,29.430], //long, lat
zoom: 13
        });
    });
</script>
```

7. Create the geocoding widget as follows:

```
require([
    "esri/map", "esri/dijit/Geocoder", "dojo/domReady!"
  ], function(Map, Geocoder) {
    map = new Map("map",{
        basemap: "streets",
        center:[-98.496,29.430], //long, lat
        zoom: 13
    });

    var geocoder = new Geocoder({
        map: map,
        autoComplete: true,
        arcgisGeocoder: {
          name: "Esri World Geocoder",
          suffix: " San Antonio, TX"
        }
    },"search");
    geocoder.startup();

});
```

The entire script should appear as follows:

```
<!DOCTYPE html>
<html>
<head>
<meta http-equiv="Content-Type" content="text/html;
  charset=utf-8">
<meta http-equiv="X-UA-Compatible" content="IE=7, IE=9,
  IE=10">
<meta name="viewport" content="initial-scale=1,
  maximum-scale=1,user-scalable=no"/>
<title>Geocoding Widget API for JavaScript | Simple
  Geocoding</title>
<link rel="stylesheet"
  href="http://js.arcgis.com/3.7/js/esri/css/esri.css">
<style>
html, body, #mapDiv {
height:100%;
width:100%;
margin:0;
padding:0;
        }
        #search {
display: block;
position: absolute;
z-index: 2;
top: 20px;
left: 74px;
        }
</style>
<script src="http://js.arcgis.com/3.7/"></script>
<script>
var map, geocoder;

require([
        "esri/map", "esri/dijit/Geocoder", "dojo/
domReady!"
      ], function(Map, Geocoder) {
map = new Map("mapDiv",{
basemap: "streets",
center:[-98.496,29.430], //long, lat
zoom: 13
        });

var geocoder = new Geocoder({
```

```
map: map,
autoComplete: true,
arcgisGeocoder: {
name: "Esri World Geocoder",
suffix: " San Antonio, TX"
            }
        },"search");
geocoder.startup();

        });
</script>
</head>
<body>
<div id="search"></div>
<div id="mapDiv"></div>
</body>
</html>
```

8. Click on the **Run** button to execute the code. You should see something similar to the following screenshot. Notice the Geocoder widget.

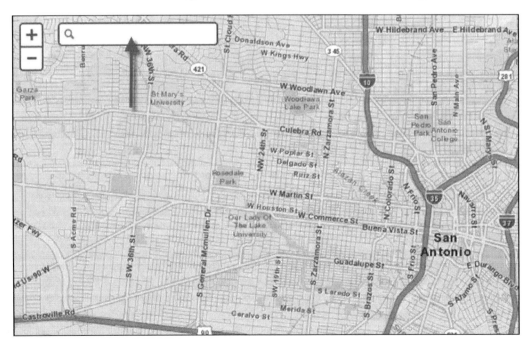

9. Begin typing an address for `San Antonio, TX`. You can use `1202 Sand Wedge` as a sample. Autocompletion should kick in as you begin typing the address. When you see the address, select it from the list. The widget will geocode the address and positions the map so that the address is centered on the map, as shown in the following screenshot:

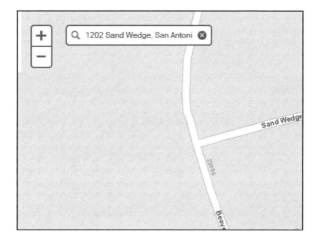

The Gauge widget

The `Gauge` widget displays numeric data from `FeatureLayer` or `GraphicsLayer` in a semicircular gauge interface. You can define the color for the gauge indicator, the field to use for the numeric data that drives the gauge, a label field, a layer to reference, a maximum data value, a title, and a lot more. Take a look at the following screenshot:

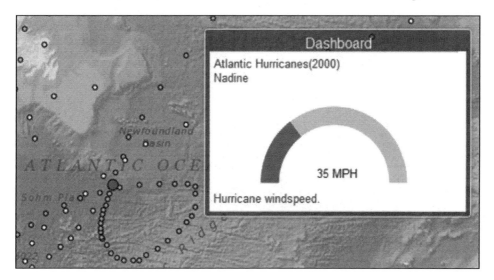

Then take a look at the following code snippet:

```
require([
  "esri/dijit/Gauge", ...
], function(Gauge, ... ) {
var gaugeParams = {
    "caption": "Hurricane windspeed.",
    "color": "#c0c",
    "dataField": "WINDSPEED",
    "dataFormat": "value",
    "dataLabelField": "EVENTID",
    "layer": fl, //fl previously defined as FeatureLayer
    "maxDataValue": 120,
    "noFeatureLabel": "No name",
    "title": "Atlantic Hurricanes(2000)",
    "unitLabel": "MPH"
  };
var gauge = new Gauge(gaugeParams, "gaugeDiv");
  ...
});
```

The previous code example shows the creation of a `Gauge` widget. A number of parameters are being passed into the constructor for the gauge, including a caption, color, data field, layer, max data value, and more.

The Measurement widget

The `Measurement` widget provides three tools that enable the end user to measure the length and area as well as obtain the coordinates of the mouse. Take a look at the following screenshot:

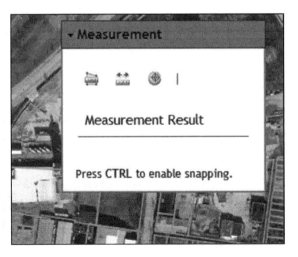

The `Measurement` widget also allows you to change the units of measurement as follows:

```
var measurement = new Measurement({
  map: map
}, dom.byId("measurementDiv"));
measurement.startup();
```

The previous code example shows how to create an instance of the `Measurement` widget and add it to the application.

The Popup widget

The `Popup` widget is functionally similar to the default info window in that it is used to display attribute information about features or graphics. In fact, starting with Version 3.4 of the API, this widget is now the default window for displaying attributes instead of the `infoWindow` parameter. However, it also contains additional functionalities such as the ability to zoom and highlight features, handling of multiple selections, and a button to maximize the window. The interface can also be styled using CSS. Please refer to the following screenshot as an example of the content that can be displayed in the `Popup` widget.

Starting with version 3.4, the `Popup` widget supports rendering text in a **right-to-left** (**RTL**) orientation to support RTL languages such as Hebrew and Arabic. RTL support will automatically apply if the page direction is set to RTL using the `dir` attribute. The default value is **left-to-right** (**LTR**). Take a look at the following code snippet:

```
//define custom popup options
var popupOptions = {
  markerSymbol: new SimpleMarkerSymbol("circle", 32, null, new
  Color([0, 0, 0, 0.25])),
```

```
      marginLeft: "20",
      marginTop: "20"
    };
    //create a popup to replace the map's info window
    var popup = new Popup(popupOptions, dojo.create("div"));

    map = new Map("map", {
      basemap: "topo",
      center: [-122.448, 37.788],
      zoom: 17,
      infoWindow: popup
    });
```

In the previous code example, a JSON `popupOptions` object is created to define the symbol and margin of the pop up. This `popupOptions` object is then passed into the constructor for the `Popup` object. Finally, the `Popup` object is passed into the `infoWindow` parameter, which specifies that the `Popup` object should be used as the info window.

The Legend widget

The `Legend` widget displays a label and symbols for some or all the layers in the map. It does have the ability to respect scale dependencies so that the legend values updates to reflect layer visibility at various scale ranges as you zoom in or out of the application. The `Legend` widget supports `ArcGISDynamicMapServiceLayer`, `ArcGISTiledMapServiceLayer`, and `FeatureLayer`.

When creating a new instance of the Legend widget, you can specify the various parameters that control the contents and display characteristics of the legend. The arrangement parameter can be used to specify the alignment of the legend within its container HTML element and can be defined as alignment left or right. The autoUpdate property can be set to true or false and if true, the legend will automatically update its parameters when the map scale changes or layers are added or removed from the map. The layerInfos parameter is used to specify a subset of layers to use in the legend, and respectCurrentMapScale can be set to true to trigger automatic legend updates based on the scale ranges for each layer. Finally, you need to call the startup() method to display the newly created legend:

```
var layerInfo = dojo.map(results, function(layer,index){
  return {
    layer: layer.layer,
    title: layer.layer.name
  };
});
if(layerInfo.length > 0){
  var legendDijit = new Legend({
    map: map,
    layerInfos: layerInfo
  },"legendDiv");
  legendDijit.startup();
}
```

The previous code example shows how to create a Legend widget and add it to an application.

The OverviewMap widget

The OverviewMap widget is used to display the current extent of the main map within the context of a larger area. This overview map gets updated each time the main map extent changes. The extent of the main map is represented as a rectangle in the overview map. This extent rectangle can also be dragged to change the extent of the main map.

An overview map can be displayed in a corner of the main map and also hidden from display when not in use. It can also be placed inside a <div> element outside the main map window or temporarily maximized for easy access to far away areas of interest. Take a look at the following screenshot:

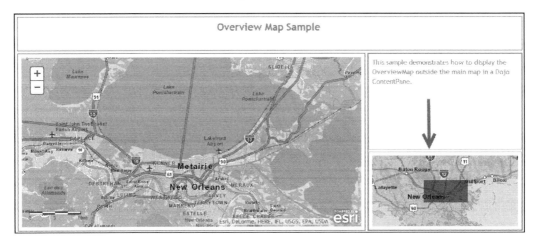

The OverviewMap widget takes a number of optional parameters in the constructor for the object. These parameters allow you to control features such as where the overview map is placed in relation to the main map, the base layer to use for the overview map, the fill color for the extent rectangle, the appearance of a maximize button, and the initial visibility of the overview map. Take a look at the following code snippet:

```
var overviewMapDijit = new OverviewMap({map:map, visible:true});
overviewMapDijit.startup();
```

The previous code example illustrates the creation of an OverviewMap widget.

The Scalebar widget

The Scalebar widget is used to add a scalebar to the map or a specific HTML node. The Scalebar widget displays units in either English or metric values. As of Version 3.4 of the API, it can show both English and metric values at the same time if you set the scalebarUnits property to dual. You can also control scalebar positioning through the attachTo parameter. By default, the scalebar is positioned in the bottom-left-hand corner of the map. Take a look at the following screenshot:

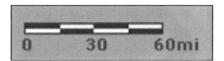

Then take a look at the following code snippet:

```
var scalebar = new esri.dijit.Scalebar({map:map,
    scalebarUnit:'english'});
```

The previous code sample illustrates the creation of a `Scalebar` widget with the units in English.

The Directions widget

The `Directions` widget makes it easy to calculate directions between two or more input locations. The resulting directions, displayed in the following screenshot, are displayed with detailed turn-by-turn instructions and an optional map. If a map is associated with the widget, the direction's route and stops are displayed on the map. The stops displayed on the map are interactive, so you can click on them to display a pop up with stop details or drag the stop to a new location to recalculate the route. Take a look at the following screenshot:

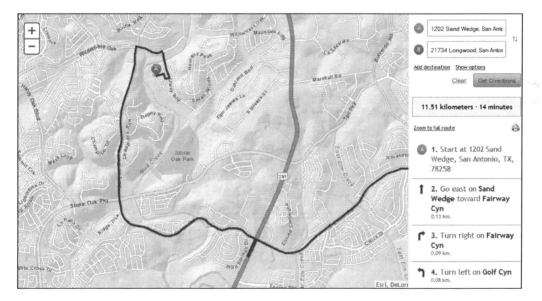

Take a look at the following code snippet:

```
var directions = new Directions({
map: map
},"dir");

directions.startup();
```

The previous code example shows the creation of a `Directions` object.

The HistogramTimeSlider dijit

The `HistogramTimeSlider` dijit provides a histogram chart representation of data for time-enabled layers on a map. Through the UI, users can temporally control the display of data with an extension to the `TimeSlider` widget.

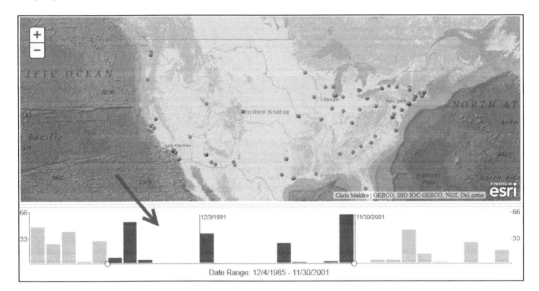

Take a look at the following code snippet:

```
require(["esri/dijit/HistogramTimeSlider", ... ],
function(HistogramTimeSlider, ... ){
  var slider = new HistogramTimeSlider({
    dateFormat: "DateFormat(selector: 'date', fullYear: true)",
    layers : [ layer ],
    mode: "show_all",
    timeInterval: "esriTimeUnitsYears"
  }, dojo.byId("histogram"));
  map.setTimeSlider(slider);
});
```

In the previous code example, a `HistogramTimeSlider` object is created and associated with a map.

The HomeButton widget

The `HomeButton` widget is simply a button that you can add to your application, which returns the map to the initial extent. Take a look at the following screeshot:

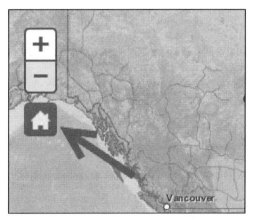

Then take a look at the following code snippet:

```
require([
      "esri/map",
"esri/dijit/HomeButton",
      "dojo/domReady!"
    ], function(
      Map, HomeButton
    ) {

var map = new Map("map", {
center: [-56.049, 38.485],
zoom: 3,
basemap: "streets"
      });

var home = new HomeButton({
map: map
      }, "HomeButton");
home.startup();

    });
```

The previous code example shows the creation of a `HomeButton` widget.

The LocateButton widget

The `LocateButton` widget can be used to find and zoom to the current location of the user. This widget uses the Geolocation API to find the user's current location. Once the location is found, the map zooms to that location. The widget provides options that allow the developer to define the following:

- The HTML5 geolocation position provides options for finding a location such as `maximumAge` and `timeout`. The `timeout` property defines the maximum amount of time that can be used to determine the location of a device, while the `maximumAge` property defines the maximum amount of time before a new location for the device is found.

- The ability to define a custom symbol that will be used to highlight the user's current location on the map.

- The scale to zoom to when a location has been found.

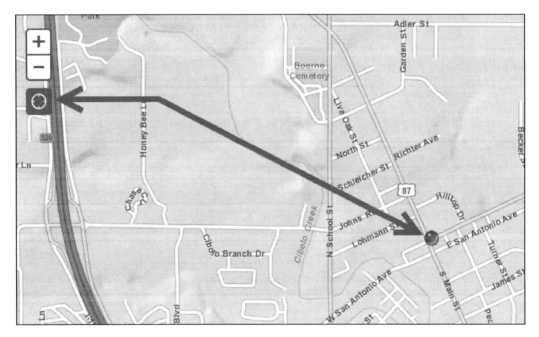

Take a look at the following code snippet:

```
geoLocate = new LocateButton({
map: map,
highlightLocation: false
}, "LocateButton");
geoLocate.startup();
```

The previous code example shows how to create an instance of the `LocateButton` widget and add it to the map.

The TimeSlider widget

The `TimeSlider` widget is used for visualizing time-enabled layers. The `TimeSlider` widget is configured to have two thumbs, so only the data within the time frame of the two thumb locations is displayed. The `setThumbIndexes()` method determines the initial location of each thumb. In this case, a thumb is added at the initial start time and another thumb is positioned one time step higher up. Take a look at the following screenshot:

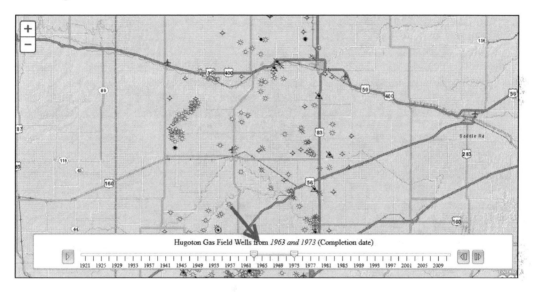

Take a look at the following code snippet:

```
var timeSlider = new TimeSlider({
style: "width: 100%;"
}, dom.byId("timeSliderDiv"));
map.setTimeSlider(timeSlider);

var timeExtent = new TimeExtent();
timeExtent.startTime = new Date("1/1/1921 UTC");
timeExtent.endTime = new Date("12/31/2009 UTC");
timeSlider.setThumbCount(2);
timeSlider.createTimeStopsByTimeInterval(timeExtent, 2,
"esriTimeUnitsYears");
timeSlider.setThumbIndexes([0,1]);
timeSlider.setThumbMovingRate(2000);
timeSlider.startup
```

The previous code example illustrates how you can create an instance of the `TimeSlider` object and set various properties, including the start and end time.

The LayerSwipe widget

The `LayerSwipe` widget provides a simple tool to show a portion of a layer or layers at the top of a map. You can easily compare the content of multiple layers in a map, using this widget to reveal the contents of layer(s) on the map. The widget provides horizontal, vertical, and scope viewing modes.

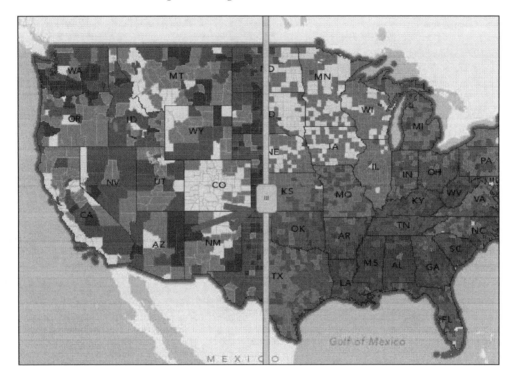

Take a look at the following code snippet:

```
varswipeWidget = new LayerSwipe({
type: "vertical",
map: map,
layers: [swipeLayer]
}, "swipeDiv");
swipeWidget.startup();
```

The previous code example shows how to create an instance of `LayerSwipe` and add it to the map.

Analysis widgets

A number of new analysis widgets have been introduced with the Version 3.7 release of the ArcGIS API for JavaScript. The analysis widgets provide access to the ArcGIS Spatial Analysis Service, which allows you to perform common spatial analyses on your hosted data via the API. The previous screenshot shows part of the `SummarizeNearby` widget, which is one of the 12 Analysis widgets. The analysis widgets include the following 12 widgets:

- `AnalysisBase`
- `AggregatePoints`
- `CreateBuffers`
- `CreateDriveTimeAreas`
- `DissolveBoundaries`
- `EnrichLayer`
- `ExtractData`
- `FindHotSpots`
- `FindNearest`
- `MergeLayers`
- `OverlayLayers`
- `SummarizeNearby`
- `SummarizeWithin`

An `ArcGIS.com` subscription is required for the widgets. Not only will you need to store data using your `ArcGIS.com` account, but will also need to sign in to run an analysis job as a credit-based service. Executing analysis tasks and hosting feature services are not available to personal account users.

Feature editing

Simple feature editing is supported by the ArcGIS API for JavaScript when working against data stored in an enterprise geodatabase format. What this means is that your data needs to be stored in an enterprise geodatabase managed by ArcSDE.

Editing works on the concept of "last in wins." For example, if two people are editing the same feature in a layer and both submit modifications, the last editor to submit changes will overwrite any changes made by the first editor. Obviously, this could pose a problem in some cases, so before implementing editing in your application, you will need to examine how your data could be affected.

Other characteristics of editing include support for domains and subtypes, template style editing, and the ability to edit standalone tables and attachments. To use editing options, you will need to use `FeatureService` and `FeatureLayer`. Editing requests are submitted to the server using a HTTP post request, which in most cases will require the use of a proxy.

Editing support includes feature editing, including the creation and deletion of simple features, along with the ability to modify features through moves, cuts, union, or reshaping. In addition, feature attributes can be edited, documents can be attached to features, and comments can be added to features.

Feature service

Web editing requires a feature service to provide the symbology and feature geometry of your data. The feature service is just a map service with the feature access capability enabled. This capability allows the map service to expose feature geometries and their symbols in a way that is easy for web applications to use and update.

Before you build a web editing application, you need to do some work to create a feature service exposing the layers that you want to be edited. This involves setting up a map document and optionally defining some templates for editing. Templates allow you to preconfigure the symbology and attributes for some commonly used feature types. For example, to prepare editing streams, you might configure templates for "major rivers", "minor rivers", "streams", and "tributaries." Templates are optional, but they make it easy for the end user of the application to create common features.

Once your map is completed, you need to publish it to ArcGIS Server with the Feature Access capability enabled. This creates REST URLs or endpoints to both a map service and a feature service. You will use these URLs to reference the services in your application.

Feature services are accessible in the web APIs through a `FeatureLayer` object, which we examined earlier in a previous chapter. Feature layers can do a variety of things and can reference either map services or feature services. However, when you use `FeatureLayer` for editing purposes, you need to reference a feature service.

With the editing functionality, your web application tells the `FeatureLayer` which attributes have changed and, if applicable, how the geometry has changed. The `FeatureLayer` object also displays the updated features after editing. You can call the `applyEdits()` method on the feature layer to apply the edits, which then commits them to the database.

The editing widgets

The ArcGIS API for JavaScript provides widgets to make it easier for you to add editing function to your Web applications. These widgets include `Editor`, `TemplatePicker`, `AttributeInspector`, and `AttachmentEditor` widgets. The `Editor` widget is the default editing interface and includes everything you need to edit a layer, and also allows you to choose the number and types of tools available. `TemplatePicker` displays a preconfigured template containing symbols for each of the layers in your map document. This template style editing allows your users to simply pick a layer and begin editing. The `AttributeInspector` widget provides an interface for editing the attributes of features and ensures valid data entry. Finally, `AttachmentEditor` associates a downloadable file with a feature. We'll examine each of these widgets in more detail.

The Editor widget

The `Editor` widget, shown in the following screenshot, provides the default editing interface included with API. It combines the functionality of the other widgets to provide everything that you need for editing a layer. You can choose the number and types of tools that are available on the widget.

The `Editor` widget saves your edits immediately after they are made, for example, as soon as you finish drawing a point. If you decide not to use the `Editor` widget, you must determine when and how often you want to apply edits. Take a look at the following screenshot:

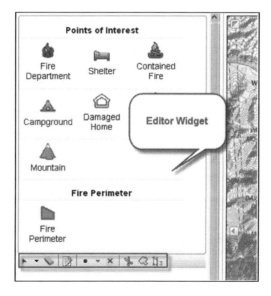

In the following code example, a new `Editor` object is created by passing a `params` object into the constructor. The input `params` object is where the developer defines the functionality that the editing application will include. In this case, only the required options are defined. The required options are the map, the feature layers to edit, and the URL to a geometry service. Take a look at the following code snippet:

```
var settings = {
  map: map,
  geometryService: new GeometryService("http://servicesbeta.esri.com/
arcgis/rest/services/Geometry/GeometryServer"),
  layerInfos:featureLayerInfos
    };

var params = {settings: settings};
var editorWidget = new Editor(params);
  editorWidget.startup();
```

The `Editor` widget provides out of the box editing capabilities using an editable layer in a Feature Service. It combines the out of the box `TemplatePicker`, `AttachmentEditor`, `AttributeInspector`, and `GeometryService` to provide feature and attribute editing. For most editing applications, you should take advantage of the `Editor` widget. This widget allows you to perform all the functions you see listed in the following diagram:

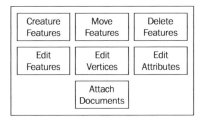

To use the `Editor` widget in your code, you'll need to first load the widget using `dojo.require`. Required parameters for creating a new instance of `Editor` include a reference to the `Map` object and a geometry service.

The TemplatePicker widget

The `TemplatePicker` widget displays a preconfigured set of features to the user, with each feature symbolizing a layer in the service. Editing is initiated very simply by selecting a symbol from the template and then clicking on the map to add features. The symbols displayed in the template come from the editing templates you defined in the feature service's source map or the symbols defined in the application. `TemplatePicker` can also be used as a simple legend. Take a look at the following screenshot:

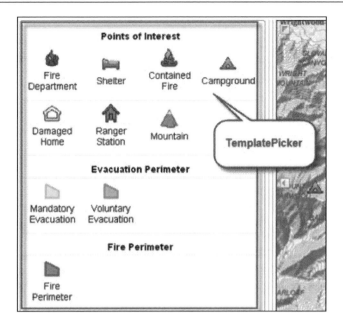

Take a look at the following code snippet:

```
function initEditing(results) {
    var templateLayers = dojo.map(results,function(result){
      return result.layer;
    });
    var templatePicker = new TemplatePicker({
      featureLayers: templateLayers,
      grouping: false,
      rows: 'auto',
      columns: 3
    },'editorDiv');
    templatePicker.startup();
    var layerInfos = dojo.map(results, function(result) {
      return {'featureLayer':result.layer};
    });
    var settings = {
        map: map,
        templatePicker: templatePicker,
        layerInfos:layerInfos
      };
      var params = {settings: settings};
      var editorWidget = new Editor(params);
      editorWidget.startup();
}
```

In the previous code example, a new `TemplatePicker` object is created and attached
to the `Editor` widget.

The AttributeInspector widget

The `AttributeInspector` widget, as shown in the following screenshot, provides an interface for editing feature attributes over the web. It also ensures that the data they enter is valid by matching the input to the expected data type. Domains are also supported. For example, if a coded value domain is applied to a field, the permitted values appear in a drop-down list, restricting the possibility of other values being entered. If a field requires a date value, a calendar appears, helping the user to supply a valid date. Take a look at the following screenshot:

The `AttributeInspector` widget exposes all the available attributes on the layer for editing. If you want to restrict the available attributes, you must code your own interface for entering and validating values. Take a look at the following code snippet:

```
var layerInfos = [{
  'featureLayer': petroFieldsFL,
  'showAttachments': false,
  'isEditable': true,
  'fieldInfos': [
  {'fieldName': 'activeprod', 'isEditable':true, 'tooltip': 'Current
Status', 'label':'Status:'},
  {'fieldName': 'field_name', 'isEditable':true, 'tooltip': 'The name
of this oil field', 'label':'Field Name:'},
  {'fieldName': 'approxacre', 'isEditable':false,'label':'Acreage:'},
  {'fieldName': 'avgdepth', 'isEditable':false,
  'label':'Average Depth:'},
  {'fieldName': 'cumm_oil', 'isEditable':false,
  'label':'Cummulative Oil:'},
  {'fieldName': 'cumm_gas', 'isEditable':false,
  'label':'Cummulative Gas:'}
  ]
```

```
            }];

    var attInspector = new AttributeInspector({
      layerInfos:layerInfos
    }, domConstruct.create("div"));

    //add a save button next to the delete button
    var saveButton = new Button({ label: "Save", "class":
    "saveButton"});
   domConstruct.place(saveButton.domNode,
    attInspector.deleteBtn.domNode, "after");

  saveButton.on("click", function(){
    updateFeature.getLayer().applyEdits(null, [updateFeature], null);
  });

  attInspector.on("attribute-change", function(evt) {
    //store the updates to apply when the save button is clicked
    updateFeature.attributes[evt.fieldName] = evt.fieldValue;
  });

  attInspector.on("next", function(evt) {
    updateFeature = evt.feature;
    console.log("Next " + updateFeature.attributes.objectid);
  });

  attInspector.on("delete", function(evt){
                  evt.feature.getLayer().applyEdits(null,null,[feature]);
    map.infoWindow.hide();
  });

    map.infoWindow.setContent(attInspector.domNode);
    map.infoWindow.resize(350, 240);
```

In the previous code example, an `AttributeInspector` widget is created and added to the application. In addition, several event handlers including the attributes `change`, `next`, and `delete` are set up to handle various attribute changes.

The AttachmentEditor widget

In some situations, you may want to associate a downloadable file with a feature. For example, you might want users to be able to click on a feature representing a water meter and see a link to an image of the meter. In the ArcGIS Web APIs, such an associated downloadable file is known as a feature attachment.

The `AttachmentEditor` widget, as seen in the following screenshot, is a widget that helps users upload and view feature attachments. The `AttachmentEditor` widget includes a list of current attachments (with a **Remove** button), as well as a **Browse** button that can be used to upload more attachments. The `AttachmentEditor` widget works well inside an info window, but can be placed elsewhere on the page.

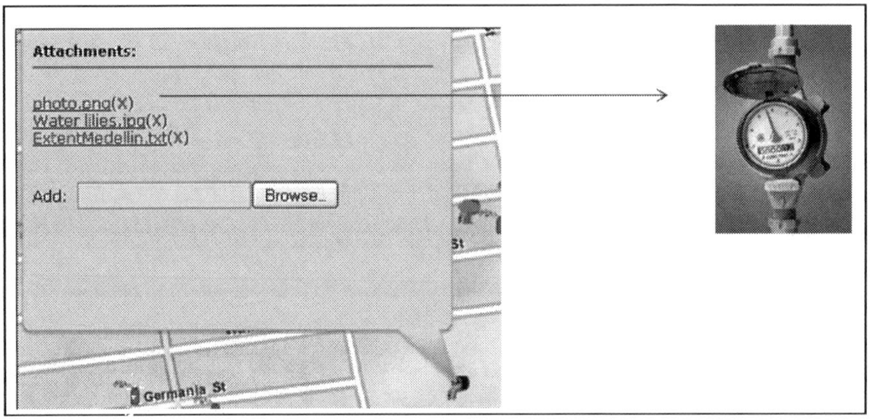

In order to use feature attachments, attachments must be enabled on the source feature class. You can enable attachments for a feature class in ArcCatalog or the **Catalog** window in ArcMap. If the `Editor` widget detects that attachments are enabled, it will include `AttachmentEditor`. Take a look at the following code snippet:

```
var map;

    require([
      "esri/map",
      "esri/layers/FeatureLayer",
      "esri/dijit/editing/AttachmentEditor",
      "esri/config",

      "dojo/parser", "dojo/dom",

      "dijit/layout/BorderContainer", "dijit/layout/ContentPane",
"dojo/domReady!"
      ], function(
        Map, FeatureLayer, AttachmentEditor, esriConfig,
        parser, dom
      ) {
      parser.parse();
      // a proxy page is required to upload attachments
      // refer to "Using the Proxy Page" for more information:
    https://developers.arcgis.com/en/javascript/jshelp/ags_proxy.html
        esriConfig.defaults.io.proxyUrl = "/proxy";
```

```
       map = new Map("map", {
       basemap: "streets",
       center: [-122.427, 37.769],
       zoom: 17
       });
       map.on("load", mapLoaded);

       function mapLoaded() {
           var featureLayer = new FeatureLayer("http://sampleserver3.
arcgisonline.com/ArcGIS/rest/services/SanFrancisco/311Incidents/
FeatureServer/0",{
           mode: FeatureLayer.MODE_ONDEMAND
           });

       map.infoWindow.setContent("<div id='content'
style='width:100%'></div>");
           map.infoWindow.resize(350,200);
   var attachmentEditor = new AttachmentEditor({}, dom.byId("content"));
       attachmentEditor.startup();

           featureLayer.on("click", function(evt) {
           var objectId = evt.graphic.attributes[featureLayer.
objectIdField];
           map.infoWindow.setTitle(objectId);
           attachmentEditor.showAttachments(evt.graphic,featureLayer);
           map.infoWindow.show(evt.screenPoint, map.
getInfoWindowAnchor(evt.screenPoint));
           });
       map.addLayer(featureLayer);
       }
       });
```

The previous code shows how to create an `AttachmentEditor` object and add it to the application.

The Edit toolbar

There may be times when you don't want to use the default `Editor` widget shown in the following screenshot:

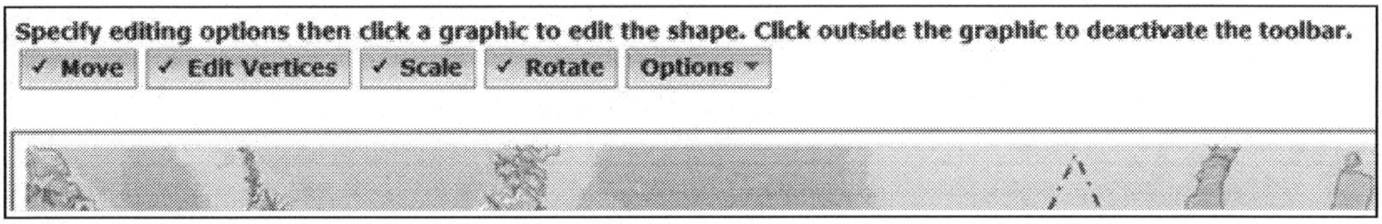

These situations would include times where you want to code your own editing logic, particularly with regards to the client side display of features and graphics. You can use the **Edit** toolbar in these cases. The **Edit** toolbar is simply a JavaScript helper class that is part of the API. It helps with placing and moving vertices and graphics. This toolbar is similar to the **Navigation** and **Draw** toolbars that we examined earlier in the book.

Summary

Widgets and toolbars provide an easy way to add prebuilt functionalities to your application without having to write a lot of code. The wide array of available widgets has increased throughout the various releases of the API, and it is expected that many new widgets will be available in future releases. Toolbars, though similar to widgets, are helper classes that provide the functionality for adding navigation, drawing functionality, and editing tools to your application. However, it is up to the developer to define the appearance of the toolbars and buttons. In the next chapter, you will learn how to create spatial and attribute queries using the `Query` and `QueryTask` classes.

6

Performing Spatial and Attribute Queries

Using ArcGIS Server Query tasks, you can perform attribute and spatial queries against data layers in a map service that has been exposed. You can also combine these query types to perform combined attribute and spatial queries. For example, you might need to find all land parcels with an appraised value greater than $100,000 and that intersect the 100-year floodplain. This would be an example of a combined query that includes both spatial and attribute components. In this chapter, you will learn how to perform attribute and spatial queries using the `Query`, `QueryTask`, and `FeatureSet` objects in the ArcGIS API for JavaScript.

We will cover the following topics in this chapter:

- Introducing tasks in ArcGIS Server
- An overview of attribute and spatial queries
- The Query object
- Executing the query with QueryTask
- Time to practice with spatial queries

Introducing tasks in ArcGIS Server

In the next few chapters of the book, we will discuss the many types of tasks that can be performed with the ArcGIS API for JavaScript. Tasks give you the ability to perform spatial and attribute queries, find features based on text searches, geocode addresses, identify features, and perform various geometry operations including buffering and distance measurements. All tasks are accessed through the `esri/tasks` resource.

All tasks in the ArcGIS API for JavaScript follow the same pattern. This pattern is easily recognizable once you've worked with one or more tasks for any length of time. An input object is used to supply input parameters to the task. Using these input parameters, the task performs its specific function and then an output object is returned containing the results of the task. The following diagram illustrates how each task accepts an input parameter object and returns an output object that can be used in your application.

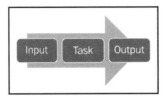

An overview of attribute and spatial queries

As you'll see with other tasks, queries are performed using a sequence of objects that typically include the input to the task, execution of the task, and a result set returned from the task. The input parameters for an attribute or spatial query are stored in a Query object which contains various parameters that can be set for the query. The QueryTask object executes the task using the input provided in the Query object, and a result set is returned in the form of a FeatureSet object, which contains an array of Graphic features that you can then plot on the map.

The Query object, used as input to a QueryTask, is defined by properties that include geometry, where, and text. The geometry property is used to input a geometry that will be used in a spatial query and will be a point, line, or polygon geometry. The where property is used to define an attribute query, while the text property is used to perform a where clause containing a like operator. The Query object can also contain a number of optional properties including the ability to define the fields that will be returned as a result of the query, the output spatial reference for the returned geometry, and the actual geometry of the features that meet the query conditions.

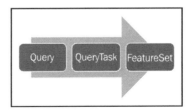

The preceding diagram defines the object sequence you will use when creating attribute and spatial queries.

The Query object

In order for the `QueryTask` object to execute a query against a layer in a map service, it needs input parameters that are defined with a `Query` object. Input parameters define whether the query will be spatial, attribute, or a combination of the two. Attribute queries can be defined by either the `where` or `text` properties. These properties are used to define a SQL attribute query. We'll look at the difference between `Query.where` and `Query.text` in a later section.

Spatial queries require that you set the `Query.geometry` property to define the input geometric shape to be used in a spatial query.

A new instance of the `Query` object can be created through the use of a constructor as seen in the following code example:

```
var query = new Query();
```

Defining the query properties

As I mentioned in the introduction to this section, you can set various parameters on the `Query` object. It is required that you either define the properties for an attribute query (`Query.where` or `Query.text`) or the `Query.geometry` property for a spatial query. You can also use a combination of attribute and spatial query properties.

Attribute queries

The `Query` object provides two properties that can be used in an attribute query: `Query.where` and `Query.text`. In the following code example, I'm setting the `Query.where` property so that only records where the STATE_NAME field equal to 'Texas' are returned. This is just a standard SQL query. Notice that I've enclosed the word Texas with quotes. When performing an attribute query against a text column, you need to enclose the text being evaluated with either single or double quotes. This isn't needed if you are performing an attribute query against a column containing other data types such as numbers or Booleans:

```
query.where = "STATE_NAME = 'Texas'";
```

You can also use the `Query.text` property to perform an attribute query. This is a shorthand way for creating a `where` clause using `like`. The field used in the query is the display field for the layer defined in the map document. You can determine the display field for a layer in the services directory. This is illustrated in the following screenshot where `ZONING_NAME` is the display field. It is this display field that is queried using the `Query.text` property.

```
ArcGIS Services Directory

Home > Louisville > LOJIC_LandRecords_Louisville (MapServer) > Zoning

Layer: Zoning (ID: 2)

Display Field: ZONING_NAME

Type: Feature Layer

Geometry Type: esriGeometryPolygon

Description:

Definition Expression:

Copyright Text:

Min. Scale: 0

Max. Scale: 0

Default Visibility: True

Extent:
        XMin: -85.9471222861492
        YMin: 37.9969113880299
        XMax: -85.4048460192834
        YMax: 38.3802309070567
        Spatial Reference: 4326
```

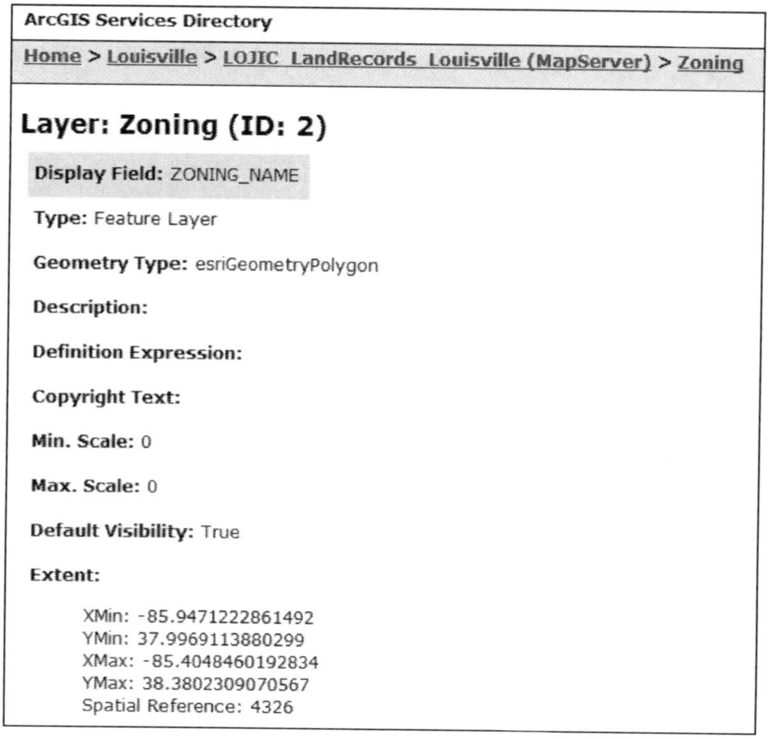

```
//Query.text uses the Display Name for the layer
query.text= stateName;
```

In the following code example, we use `query.text` to perform an attribute query that returns all fields where the state name is entered by the user in a form field on the web page:

```
query = new Query();
query.returnGeometry = false;
query.outFields = ['*'];
query.text = dom.byId("stateName").value;
queryTask.execute(query, showResults);
```

Spatial queries

To perform a spatial query against a layer, you'll need to pass in a valid geometry object to be used in the spatial filter along with a spatial relationship. Valid geometries include instances of `Extent`, `Point`, `Polyline`, and `Polygon`. The spatial relationship is set through the `Query.spatialRelationship` property and is applied during the query. The spatial relationship is defined through the use of one of the following constant values: `SPATIAL_REL_INTERESECTS`, `SPATIAL_REL_CONTAINS`, `SPATIAL_REL_CROSSES`, `SPATIAL_REL_ENVELOPE_INTERSECTS`, `SPATIAL_REL_OVERLAPS`, `SPATIAL_REL_TOUCHES`, `SPATIAL_REL_WITHIN`, and `SPATIAL_REL_RELATION`. The table in the following screenshot describes each of the spatial relationship values:

SPATIAL_REL_CONTAINS	• Part or all of a feature from feature class 1 is contained within a feature from feature class 2.
SPATIAL_REL_CROSSES	• The feature from feature class 1 crosses a feature from feature class 2.
SPATIAL_REL_ENVELOPEINTERSECTS	• The envelope of feature class 1 intersects with the envelope of feature class 2.
SPATIAL_REL_INDEXINTERSECTS	• The envelope of the query feature class intersects the index entry for the target feature class.
SPATIAL_REL_INTERSECTS	• Part of a feature from feature class 1 is contained in a feature from feature class 2.
SPATIAL_REL_OVERLAPS	• Features from feature class 1 overlap feature in feature class 2.
SPATIAL_REL_RELATION	• Allows specification of any relationship defined using Shape Comparison Language.
SPATIAL_REL_TOUCHES	• The feature from feature class 1 touches the border of a feature from feature class 2.
SPATIAL_REL_WITHIN	• The feature from feature class 1 is completely enclosed by the feature from feature class 2

The following code example sets a `Point` object as the geometry passed into the spatial filter in addition to setting the spatial relationship:

```
query.geometry = evt.mapPoint;
query.spatialRelationship = SPATIAL_REL_INTERSECTS;
```

Limiting the fields returned

For performance reasons, you should limit the fields that are returned in the `FeatureSet` object to only those fields that are needed in your application. Every column of information attached to the `FeatureSet` object is additional data that must be passed from the server to the browser, which can cause your application to perform slower than it should. To limit the returned fields, you assign an array containing a list of fields that should be returned to the `Query.outFields` property as seen in the following code example. To return all fields you can use `outFields = ['*']`.

In addition, you can control the return of the geometry for each feature through the `Query.returnGeometry` property. By default, the geometry will be returned; however, in some cases, your application may not need the geometry. For example, if you need to populate a table with the attribute information from a layer, you don't necessarily need the geometry. In this case, you can set `Query.returnGeometry = false`:

```
query.outFields =
  ["NAME", "POP2000", "POP2007", "POP00_SQMI", "POP07_SQMI"];
query.returnGeometry = false;
```

Executing the query with QueryTask

Once you've defined the input properties in a `Query` object, you can use `QueryTask` to execute the query. Before the query can be executed, you must first create an instance of the `QueryTask` object. A `QueryTask` object is created by passing a URL to the layer against which the query will be executed inside the constructor for the object. The following code example shows how a `QueryTask` object is created. Notice that it includes an index number at the end of the URL that references a specific layer in the map service to be queried:

```
myQueryTask = new QueryTask("http://sampleserver1.arcgisonline.com/
ArcGIS/rest/services/Demographics/ESRI_CENSUS_USA/MapServer/5");
```

After creation, the `QueryTask` object can be used to execute a query against the layer with an input `Query` object using the `QueryTask.execute()` method. `QueryTask.execute()` accepts three parameters including an input `Query` object along with success and error callback functions. The syntax for `QueryTask.execute()` is provided in the following code. The input `Query` object is passed as the first parameter:

```
QueryTask.execute(parameters,callback?,errback?)
```

Assuming that the query executes without any error, the success callback function will be called and a `FeatureSet` object is passed into the function. If an error occurs during the execution of the query, then an error callback function is executed. Both the success and error callback functions are optional; however, you should always define functions to handle both cases.

At this point, you may be wondering about these `callback` and `errback` functions. Most tasks in ArcGIS Server return an instance of `dojo/Deferred`. A `Deferred` object is a class that is used as the foundation for managing asynchronous threads in `Dojo`. Tasks in ArcGIS Server can be either synchronous or asynchronous.

Asynchronous and synchronous define how the client (the application using the task) interacts with the server and gets the result from the task. When a service is set to synchronous, the client waits for the task to complete. Typically, a synchronous task executes quickly (several seconds or lesser). An asynchronous task typically takes longer to execute, and the client doesn't wait for the task to complete. The end user is free to continue using the application while the task executes. When a task completes on the server, it calls the callback function and passes the results into this function where they can then be used in some way. They are often displayed on the map.

Let's take a look at a more complete code example. In the following code example, notice that we first create a new variable called myQueryTask, which points to layer 6 (the index numbers are 0 based) in the ESRI_CENSUS_USA map service. We then create the Query object containing the input properties of the query and finally, we use the execute() method on QueryTask to perform the query. The execute() method returns a FeatureSet object that contains the results of the query and these features are processed through a callback function called showResults, which is specified in the execute() method. If an error occurs during the execution of the task, the errorCallback() function will be called:

```
myQueryTask = new QueryTask("http://sampleserver1.arcgisonline.com/
ArcGIS/rest/services/Demographics/ESRI_CENSUS_USA/MapServer/5");
//build query filter
myQuery = new Query();
myQuery.returnGeometry = false;
myQuery.outFields = ["STATE_NAME", "POP2007", "MALES", "FEMALES"];
myQuery.text = 'Oregon';
//execute query
myQueryTask.execute(myQuery, showResults, errorCallback);
function showResults(fs) {
    //do something with the results
    //they are returned as a featureset object
}

function errorCallback() {
  alert("An error occurred during task execution");
}
```

Getting query results

As I mentioned earlier, the results of a query are stored in a `FeatureSet` object that includes an array of graphics, which you can then plot on your map if you wish.

Each feature (graphic) in the array can contain geometry, attributes, symbology, and an InfoTemplate as described in *Chapter 3, Adding Graphics to the Map*. Typically, these features are plotted on the map as graphics. The following code example shows a callback function that is executed when a query has completed execution. A `FeatureSet` object is passed into the callback function and the graphics are drawn on the map:

```
function addPolysToMap(featureSet) {
  var features = featureSet.features;
  var feature;
  for (i=0, il=features.length; i<il; i++) {
    feature = features[i];
    attributes = feature.attributes;
    pop = attributes.POP90_SQMI;
    map.graphics.add(features[i].setSymbol(sym));
  }
}
```

Time to practice with spatial queries

In this exercise, you will learn how to perform spatial queries using the `Query`, `QueryTask`, and `FeatureSet` objects in the ArcGIS API for JavaScript. Using a Zoning layer from the City of Portland, you will query parcel records and display the results on a map.

Perform the following steps to complete the exercise:

1. Open the JavaScript Sandbox at `http://developers.arcgis.com/en/ javascript/sandbox/sandbox.html`.

2. Remove the JavaScript content from the `<script>` tag that I have highlighted in the following code snippet:

```
<script>
dojo.require("esri.map");

function init(){
var map = new esri.Map("mapDiv", {
center: [-56.049, 38.485],
zoom: 3,
```

```
basemap: "streets"
    });
  }
dojo.ready(init);
</script>
```

3. Create the variables that you'll use in the application.

```
<script>
var map, query, queryTask;
var symbol, infoTemplate;
</script>
```

4. Add the `require()` function as seen in the following highlighted code:

```
<script>
  var map, query, queryTask;
  var symbol, infoTemplate;

  require([
      "esri/map", "esri/tasks/query", "esri/tasks/QueryTask",
        "esri/tasks/FeatureSet",
        "esri/symbols/SimpleFillSymbol",
      "esri/symbols/SimpleLineSymbol", "esri/InfoTemplate",
        "dojo/_base/Color", "dojo/on", "dojo/domReady!"
    ], function(Map, Query, QueryTask, FeatureSet,
      SimpleFillSymbol, SimpleLineSymbol, InfoTemplate, Color,
      on) {



  });

</script>
```

5. Inside the `require()` function, create the `Map` object that you'll use in the application. The map will be centered on the Louisville, KY, area:

```
require([
    "esri/map", "esri/tasks/query", "esri/tasks/QueryTask",
      "esri/tasks/FeatureSet",
      "esri/symbols/SimpleFillSymbol",
    "esri/symbols/SimpleLineSymbol", "esri/InfoTemplate",
      "dojo/_base/Color", "dojo/on", "dojo/domReady!"
  ], function(Map, Query, QueryTask, FeatureSet,
    SimpleFillSymbol, SimpleLineSymbol, InfoTemplate,
    Color, on) {
```

```
        map = new Map("mapDiv",{
            basemap: "streets",
            center:[-85.748, 38.249], //long, lat
            zoom: 13
        });

    })
```

6. Create the symbol that will be used to display the results of the query:

```
require([
    "esri/map", "esri/tasks/query", "esri/tasks/QueryTask",
      "esri/tasks/FeatureSet",
      "esri/symbols/SimpleFillSymbol",
    "esri/symbols/SimpleLineSymbol", "esri/InfoTemplate",
      "dojo/_base/Color", "dojo/on", "dojo/domReady!"
], function(Map, Query, QueryTask, FeatureSet,
    SimpleFillSymbol, SimpleLineSymbol, InfoTemplate,
  Color, on) {
    map = new Map("map",{
      basemap: "streets",
      center:[-85.748, 38.249], //long, lat
      zoom: 13
    });

    symbol = new SimpleFillSymbol(SimpleFillSymbol.STYLE_SOLID,
    new SimpleLineSymbol(SimpleLineSymbol.STYLE_SOLID, new
      Color([111, 0, 255]), 2), new Color([255,255,0,0.25]));
    infoTemplate = new InfoTemplate("${OBJECTID}", "${*}");

});
```

7. Now, inside the `require()` function, we are going to initialize the `queryTask` variable and then register the `QueryTask.complete` event. Add the following highlighted lines of code:

```
require([
    "esri/map", "esri/tasks/query", "esri/tasks/QueryTask",
      "esri/tasks/FeatureSet",
      "esri/symbols/SimpleFillSymbol",
    "esri/symbols/SimpleLineSymbol", "esri/InfoTemplate",
      "dojo/_base/Color", "dojo/on", "dojo/domReady!"
], function(Map, Query, QueryTask, FeatureSet,
    SimpleFillSymbol, SimpleLineSymbol, InfoTemplate,
  Color, on) {
```

```
map = new Map("mapDiv",{
    basemap: "streets",
    center:[-85.748, 38.249], //long, lat
    zoom: 13
});

symbol = new SimpleFillSymbol(SimpleFillSymbol.STYLE_SOLID,
new SimpleLineSymbol(SimpleLineSymbol.STYLE_SOLID, new
    Color([111, 0, 255]), 2), new
    Color([255,255,0,0.25]));
infoTemplate = new InfoTemplate("${OBJECTID}", "${*}");

queryTask = new QueryTask("http://sampleserver1.arcgisonline.
com/ArcGIS/rest/services/Louisville/LOJIC_LandRecords_Louisville/
MapServer/2");
queryTask.on("complete", addToMap);

});
```

The constructor for QueryTask must be a valid URL pointer to a data layer
exposed through a map service. In this case, we are creating a reference to
the Zoning layer in the LOJIC_LandRecords_Louisville map service. What
this indicates is that we are going to perform a query against this layer. If you
will remember from a previous chapter, dojo.on() is used to register events.
In this case, we are registering the complete event for our new QueryTask
object. This event fires when the query has been completed, and in this case
will call the addToMap() function specified as a parameter to on().

8. Now we'll define the input parameters for the task by creating a Query
    object. In the first line, we create a new Query instance, and then we set the
    Query.returnGeometry and Query.outFields properties. Setting Query.
    returnGeometry equal to true indicates that ArcGIS Server should return
    the geometric definition of the features that matched the query, while in
    Query.outFields we've specified a wildcard indicating that all fields
    associated with the Zoning layer should be returned for the features returned
    as a result of the query. Add the following highlighted lines of code just
    below the code you entered in the previous step:

```
require([
"esri/map", "esri/tasks/query", "esri/tasks/QueryTask",
  "esri/tasks/FeatureSet", "esri/symbols/SimpleFillSymbol",
"esri/symbols/SimpleLineSymbol", "esri/InfoTemplate",
  "dojo/_base/Color", "dojo/on", "dojo/domReady!"
], function(Map, Query, QueryTask, FeatureSet,
  SimpleFillSymbol, SimpleLineSymbol, InfoTemplate, Color,
  on) {
```

```
map = new Map("mapDiv",{
    basemap: "streets",
    center:[-85.748, 38.249], //long, lat
    zoom: 13
});

symbol = new
  SimpleFillSymbol(SimpleFillSymbol.STYLE_SOLID,
new SimpleLineSymbol(SimpleLineSymbol.STYLE_SOLID, new
  Color([111, 0, 255]), 2), new Color([255,255,0,0.25]));
infoTemplate = new InfoTemplate("${OBJECTID}", "${*}");


    queryTask = new QueryTask("http://sampleserver1.arcgisonline.
com/ArcGIS/rest/services/Louisville/LOJIC_LandRecords_Louisville/
MapServer/2");
    queryTask.on("complete", addToMap);

    query = new Query();
    query.returnGeometry = true;
    query.outFields = ["*"];

});
```

9. Add a line of code that registers the Map.click event to a doQuery function. The doQuery function will be passed the point on the map that was clicked by the user. This map point will be used as the geometry in the spatial query. In the next step, we will create the doQuery function that will accept the point clicked on the map:

```
require([
        "esri/map", "esri/tasks/query", "esri/tasks/QueryTask",
"esri/tasks/FeatureSet", "esri/symbols/SimpleFillSymbol",
        "esri/symbols/SimpleLineSymbol", "esri/InfoTemplate",
"dojo/_base/Color", "dojo/on", "dojo/domReady!"
        ], function(Map, Query, QueryTask, FeatureSet,
SimpleFillSymbol, SimpleLineSymbol, InfoTemplate, Color, on) {

map = new Map("mapDiv",{
  basemap: "streets",
  center:[-85.748, 38.249], //long, lat
  zoom: 13
});
```

```
symbol = new SimpleFillSymbol(SimpleFillSymbol.STYLE_SOLID,
    new SimpleLineSymbol(SimpleLineSymbol.STYLE_SOLID, new
    Color([111, 0, 255]), 2), new Color([255,255,0,0.25]));
infoTemplate = new InfoTemplate("${OBJECTID}", "${*}");


map.on("click", doQuery);

queryTask = new QueryTask("http://sampleserver1.arcgisonline.com/
ArcGIS/rest/services/Louisville/LOJIC_LandRecords_Louisville/
MapServer/2");
queryTask.on("complete", addToMap);

query = new Query();
query.returnGeometry = true;
query.outFields = ["*"];


});
```

10. Now we'll create the doQuery function that executes the QueryTask using
    the Query properties we set in the require( ) function along with the map
    point clicked by the user, which is used in the Query.geometry function.
    The doQuery function accepts a point that was clicked on the map, which can
    be retrieved using the mapPoint property. The mapPoint property returns
    a Point object, which is then used to set the Query.geometry property
    that will be used to find the zoning parcel the user has clicked on the map.
    Finally, the QueryTask.execute() method is executed. After the task has
    executed, a FeatureSet object containing the records that match the query
    will be returned. The question now is where are the results returned? Add the
    following code block just below the closing brace for the require() function:

```
function doQuery(evt) {
    //clear currently displayed results
    map.graphics.clear();

    query.geometry = evt.mapPoint;
    query.outSpatialReference = map.spatialReference;
    queryTask.execute(query);
}
```

11. Remember that we registered the `QueryTask.complete` event to run the `addToMap()` function. We haven't created this function yet. Add the following code to create the `addToMap()` function. This function will accept a `FeatureSet` object returned as a result of the query and plot the features on the map. Also notice that an info template is defined for the feature. This will create an `InfoWindow` object to display the attributes of the returned feature:

```
function addToMap(results) {
  var featureArray = results.featureSet.features;
  var feature = featureArray[0];
  map.graphics.add(feature.setSymbol(symbol).
  setInfoTemplate(infoTemplate));
}
```

You can view the solution code for this exercise in the `spatialquery.html` file.

12. Click on the **Run** button to execute the code. You should see the map in the following screenshot. If not, you may need to recheck your code for accuracy.

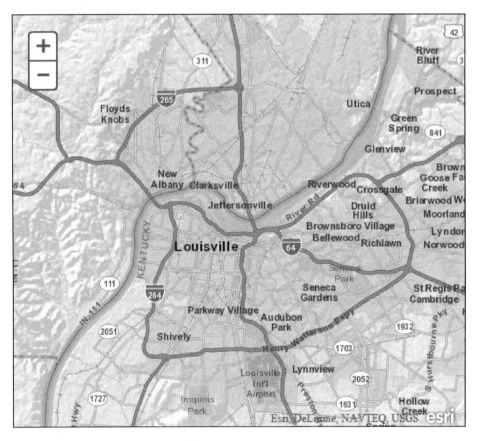

Click anywhere on the map to run the query. You should see the highlighted zoning polygon there, similar to what you can see in the following screenshot:

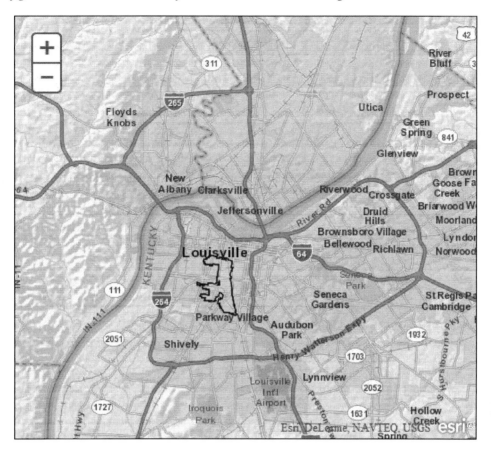

Now, click on the highlighted zoning polygon to display an Info Window that details the attributes associated with the polygon.

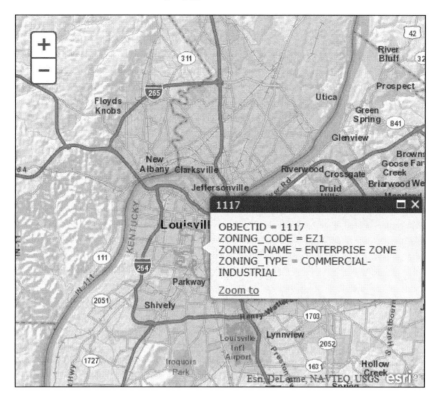

In the task just completed, you learned how to use the `Query` and `QueryTask` objects to create a spatial query that locates the zoning polygon that intersects the point the user has clicked on the map.

Summary

In this chapter, we introduced the concept of tasks in ArcGIS Server. ArcGIS Server provides a number of tasks for commonly used operations in a web mapping application. Attribute and spatial queries are common operations in web mapping applications. To support these queries, the ArcGIS API for JavaScript provides a `QueryTask` object that can be used to execute these queries on the server. When created, the `QueryTask` object accepts a URL that points to a layer that will be queried in a map server. Various input parameters to the `QueryTask` are provided through the `Query` object. Input parameters can include a `where` property to perform attribute queries, a `geometry` property to perform spatial queries, an `outFields` property to define the set of fields that should be returned, and several other supporting properties. After the query has completed on the server, a `FeatureSet` object is returned to a callback function defined in the application. The callback function can then display the `FeatureSet` (which is just an array of `Graphic` objects) on the map. In the next chapter, you will learn how to use two additional tasks: `IdentifyTask` and `FindTask`. Both can be used to return the attributes of features.

7
Identifying and Finding Features

In this chapter, we're going to cover two ArcGIS Server tasks related to returning feature attributes: `IdentifyTask` and `FindTask`. Identifying features is another common operation found in GIS applications. This task returns the attributes of features that have been clicked on a map. The attribute information is often presented in a pop-up window. This functionality is accomplished through the ArcGIS API for JavaScript with the `IdentifyTask` class. As with the other task processes that we have seen, the `IdentifyTask` object uses an input parameter object, which in this case is called `IdentifyParameters`. The `IdentifyParameters` object contains various parameters that control the results of the identify operation. These parameters give you the ability to perform an identification on individual layers, the topmost layer in a service, all visible layers in a service, or all layers in a service along with a search tolerance. An instance of `IdentifyResult` is used to hold the results of the task.

The tasks that you can execute with the ArcGIS API for JavaScript replicate some of the most commonly used functions in ArcGIS Desktop. `FindTask` is one such tool. Just as in the desktop version of ArcGIS, this task can be used to find features in a layer that match a string value. Before executing a Find operation with a `FindTask` object, you will need to set various parameters of the operation in an instance of `FindParameters`. `FindParameters` gives you the ability to set various options, including the search text, fields to search, and others. Using a `FindParameters` object, `FindTask` then executes its tasks against one or more layers and fields then returns a `FindResult` object that contains `layerID`, `layerName`, and feature that matched the search string.

In this chapter, we will deal with the following topics:

- Using IdentifyTask to get feature attributes
- Using FindTask to get feature attributes

Using IdentifyTask to get feature attributes

Attributes from the fields in a layer can be returned to your application using IdentifyTask. In this section, you will learn how to use the various objects associated with IdentifyTask to return this information.

Introducing IdentifyTask

As with the other tasks in ArcGIS Server, the IdentifyTask functionality is separated into three distinct classes in the API including IdentifyParameters, IdentifyTask, and IdentifyResult. These three classes are illustrated in the following figure:

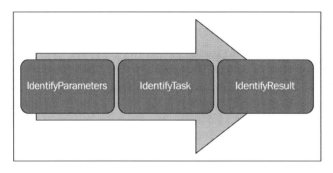

The IdentifyParameters object

The input parameter object for IdentifyTask is IdentifyParameters. A number of properties can be set for your identification operation using the IdentifyParameters class. Parameters include the geometry used to select features (IdentifyParameters.geometry), the layer IDs on which to perform the identification (IdentifyParameters.layerIds), and the tolerance (IdentifyParameters.tolerance) from the specified geometry within which the identification should be performed.

You'll need to import the identify resource shown as follows before you can use the identify functionality provided by ArcGIS Server:

```
require(["esri/tasks/IdentifyTask", ... ], function(IdentifyTask,
    ... ){ ... });
```

Before setting the various parameters on the `IdentifyParameters` object, you need to first create an instance of this object. This can be done with code shown as follows. The code for this constructor doesn't accept any parameters:

```
var identifyParams = new IdentifyParameters();
```

Now that you've created a new instance of `IdentifyParameters`, you can set various properties shown as follows:

```
identifyParams.geometry = evt.MapPoint;
identifyParams.layerIds[0,1,2];
identifyParams.returnGeometry = true;
identifyParams.tolerance = 3;
```

In most cases, an identification operation is performed using a point that the user has clicked on the map. You can obtain this using the point returned from the map-click event as seen in the preceding code example. The layers that should be searched can be defined using an array of layer IDs, which are passed into the `IdentifyParameters.layerIds` property. The array should contain numeric values that reference the layers to be searched. You can obtain the layer index numbers by consulting the services directory. The tolerance property is especially important. It sets the distance in pixels around the geometry. Remember that most of the time the geometry will be a point so you can think of this as a circle that is placed around the point at whatever tolerance value you have set. The value will be in screen pixels. When the `IdentifyTask` attribute is executed, any features from the layers to be identified (that are within or intersect the circle) will be returned.

It's likely that you'll need to experiment with this tolerance value to obtain a value that is best for your application. If the value is set too low, you run the risk of the identify operation not identifying any features and conversely, if the value is set too high, you may get too many features returned. It can be difficult to find the right balance, and the tolerance value that works for one application may not work for another.

The IdentifyTask attribute

`IdentifyTask` performs the identify operation on one or more layers using the parameters specified in `IdentifyParameters`. As with the other tasks that we've examined, `IdentifyTask` needs a pointer to a URL that identifies the map service to be used in the identify operation.

A new instance of `IdentifyTask` can be created with the following code example. The constructor for this task simply accepts a URL that points to the map service containing the layer against which an identify operation can be executed.

```
var identify =
  new IdentifyTask
  ("http://sampleserver1.arcgisonline.com
  /ArcGIS/rest/services/Specialty/ESRI_StatesCitiesRivers_USA/
  MapServer");
```

Once you've created a new instance of the `IdentifyTask` object, you can initiate the execution of this task through the `IdentifyTask.execute()` method, which accepts an `IdentifyParameters` object along with optional success callback and error callback functions. In the following code example, the `IdentifyTask.execute()` method is called. An instance of `IdentifyParameters` is passed as a parameter into the method, along with a reference to an `addToMap()` method, which will process the results that are returned to the method.

```
identifyParams = new IdentifyParameters();
identifyParams.tolerance = 3;
identifyParams.returnGeometry = true;
identifyParams.layerIds = [0,2];
identifyParams.geometry = evt.mapPoint;

identifyTask.execute(identifyParams, function(idResults) {
addToMap(idResults, evt); });

function addToMap(idResults, evt) {
    //add the results to the map
}
```

The results of an identify operation performed with `IdentifyTask` are stored in an instance of `IdentifyResult`. We'll examine this result object in the next section.

IdentifyResult

The result returned by the `IdentifyTask` operation is an array of `IdentifyResult` objects. Each `IdentifyResult` object contains the feature returned from the identify operation, along with the layer ID and layer name where the feature was found. The following code illustrates how an array of `IdentifyResult` objects is processed by a callback function:

```
function addToMap(idResults, evt) {
  bldgResults = {displayFieldName:null,features:[]};
  parcelResults = {displayFieldName:null,features:[]};
  for (vari=0, i<idResults.length; i++) {
```

```
      var idResult = idResults[i];
      if (idResult.layerId === 0) {
        if (!bldgResults.displayFieldName)
          {bldgResults.displayFieldName = idResult.displayFieldName};
          bldgResults.features.push(idResult.feature);
      }
      else if (idResult.layerId === 2) {
          if (!parcelResults.displayFieldName)
            {parcelResults.displayFieldName = idResult.displayFieldName};
            parcelResults.features.push(idResult.feature);
        }
    }
dijit.byId("bldgTab").setContent(layerTabContent(bldgResults,"bldgRes
ults"));
dijit.byId("parcelTab").setContent(layerTabContent(parcelResults,"par
celResults"));
map.infoWindow.show(evt.screenPoint,
map.getInfoWindowAnchor(evt.screenPoint));
}
```

Time to practice – implementing the identify functionality

In this exercise, you will learn how to implement the identify functionality in an application. You are going to create a simple application that will display attribute information from buildings and land parcels in an info window when the user clicks the map. We have prewritten some of the code for you so that you can focus on the functionality directly related to the identification of features. Before we begin, I'll have you copy and paste the prewritten code into the sandbox.

Perform the following steps to complete the exercise:

1. Open the JavaScript Sandbox at http://developers.arcgis.com/en/ javascript/sandbox/sandbox.html.

2. Remove the JavaScript content from the <script> tag that I have highlighted in the following code snippet:

```
<script>
dojo.require("esri.map");

function init(){
var map = new esri.Map("mapDiv", {
center: [-56.049, 38.485],
zoom: 3,
```

```
basemap: "streets"
    });
  }
dojo.ready(init);
</script>
```

3. Create the variables that you'll use in the application:

```
<script>
var map;
var identifyTask, identifyParams;
</script>
```

4. Create the `require()` function that defines the resources you'll use in this application:

```
<script>
  var map;
var identifyTask, identifyParams;
require([
        "esri/map",  "esri/dijit/Popup",
  "esri/layers/ArcGISDynamicMapServiceLayer",
  "esri/tasks/IdentifyTask",
    "esri/tasks/IdentifyResult",
      "esri/tasks/IdentifyParameters",
      "esri/dijit/InfoWindow",
      "esri/symbols/SimpleFillSymbol",
    "esri/symbols/SimpleLineSymbol",
      "esri/InfoTemplate", "dojo/_base/Color" ,
  "dojo/on",
      "dojo/domReady!"
      ], function(Map, Popup, ArcGISDynamicMapServiceLayer,
  IdentifyTask, IdentifyResult, IdentifyParameters,
  InfoWindow,
  SimpleFillSymbol, SimpleLineSymbol, InfoTemplate,
  Color, on) {

    });
</script>
```

5. Create a new instance of the `Map` object:

```
<script>
  var map;
var identifyTask, identifyParams;
require([
    "esri/map",  "esri/dijit/Popup",
      "esri/layers/ArcGISDynamicMapServiceLayer",
      "esri/tasks/IdentifyTask",
```

```
        "esri/tasks/IdentifyResult",
          "esri/tasks/IdentifyParameters",
          "esri/dijit/InfoWindow",
          "esri/symbols/SimpleFillSymbol",
        "esri/symbols/SimpleLineSymbol", "esri/InfoTemplate"
          , "dojo/_base/Color" ,"dojo/on",
          "dojo/domReady!"
          ], function(Map, Popup, ArcGISDynamicMapServiceLayer,
            IdentifyTask, IdentifyResult, IdentifyParameters,
            InfoWindow,
      SimpleFillSymbol, SimpleLineSymbol, InfoTemplate, Color,
        on) {
        //setup the popup window
    var popup = new Popup({
    fillSymbol: new SimpleFillSymbol(SimpleFillSymbol.STYLE_SOLID,
        new SimpleLineSymbol(SimpleLineSymbol.STYLE_SOLID,
        new Color([255,0,0]), 2), new Color([255,255,0,0.25]))
          }, dojo.create("div"));

map = new Map("map", {
  basemap: "streets",
  center: [-83.275, 42.573],
  zoom: 18,
  infoWindow: popup
});

        });
</script>
```

6. Create a new dynamic map service layer and add it to the map:

```
map = new Map("map", {
  basemap: "streets",
  center: [-83.275, 42.573],
  zoom: 18,
  infoWindow: popup
});

var landBaseLayer = new ArcGISDynamicMapServiceLayer
  ("http://sampleserver3.arcgisonline.com/
  ArcGIS/rest/services/BloomfieldHillsMichigan/
  Parcels/MapServer",{opacity:.55});
map.addLayer(landBaseLayer);
```

7. Add a `Map.click` event that will trigger the execution of a function, which will respond when the map is clicked on:

```
map = new Map("map", {
    basemap: "streets",
    center: [-83.275, 42.573],
    zoom: 18,
    infoWindow: popup
});


varlandBaseLayer = new ArcGISDynamicMapServiceLayer
    ("http://sampleserver3.arcgisonline.com/ArcGIS/
    rest/services/BloomfieldHillsMichigan/Parcels/
    MapServer",{opacity:.55});
map.addLayer(landBaseLayer);


map.on("click", executeIdentifyTask);
```

8. Create an `IdentifyTask` object:

```
identifyTask = new
    IdentifyTask("http://sampleserver3.arcgisonline.com/
    ArcGIS/rest/services/BloomfieldHillsMichigan/
    Parcels/MapServer");
```

9. Create an `IdentifyParameters` object and set various properties:

```
identifyTask = new
    IdentifyTask("http://sampleserver3.arcgisonline.com/
    ArcGIS/rest/services/BloomfieldHillsMichigan/Parcels/
    MapServer");


identifyParams = new IdentifyParameters();
identifyParams.tolerance = 3;
identifyParams.returnGeometry = true;
identifyParams.layerIds = [0,2];
identifyParams.layerOption = IdentifyParameters.LAYER_OPTION_ALL;
identifyParams.width  = map.width;
identifyParams.height = map.height;
```

10. Create the `executeIdentifyTask()` function, which is the function that responds to the `Map.click` event. In a previous step, you had set up the event handler for the `Map.click` event. The `executeIdentifyTask()` function was specified as the JavaScript function that will handle this event when it occurs. In this step, you'll create this function by adding the code shown as follows. The `executeIdentifyTask()` function accepts one parameter, which is an instance of the `Event` object. Each event generates an `Event` object, which has various properties. In the case of a `Map.click` event,

this Event object has a property that contains the point that was clicked. This can be retrieved with the Event.mapPoint property and is used when setting the IdentifyParameters.geometry property. The IdentifyTask. execute() method also returns a Deferred object. You then add a callback function to this Deferred object, which parses the results. Add the following code to create the executeIdentifyTask() function. This function should be created outside the require() function:

```
function executeIdentifyTask(evt) {
        identifyParams.geometry = evt.mapPoint;
        identifyParams.mapExtent = map.extent;

        var deferred = identifyTask.execute(identifyParams);

        deferred.addCallback(function(response) {
          // response is an array of identify result objects
          // Let's return an array of features.
          return dojo.map(response, function(result) {
            var feature = result.feature;
            feature.attributes.layerName = result.layerName;
            if(result.layerName === 'Tax Parcels'){
              console.log(feature.attributes.PARCELID);
              var template = new esri.InfoTemplate("", "${Postal
                Address} <br/> Owner of record: ${First Owner
                Name}");
              feature.setInfoTemplate(template);
            }
            else if (result.layerName === 'Building Footprints'){
              var template = new esri.InfoTemplate("", "Parcel ID:
                ${PARCELID}");
              feature.setInfoTemplate(template);
            }
            return feature;
          });
        });


// InfoWindow expects an array of features from each deferred
// object that you pass. If the response from the task execution
// above is not an array of features, then you need to add a
  callback
// like the one above to post-process the response and return an
        // array of features.
        map.infoWindow.setFeatures([ deferred ]);
        map.infoWindow.show(evt.mapPoint);
    }
```

11. You may want to review the solution file (`identify.html`) in your `ArcGISJavaScriptAPI` folder to verify that your code has been written correctly.

12. Execute the code by clicking on the **Run** button and you should see the following output if everything has been coded correctly:

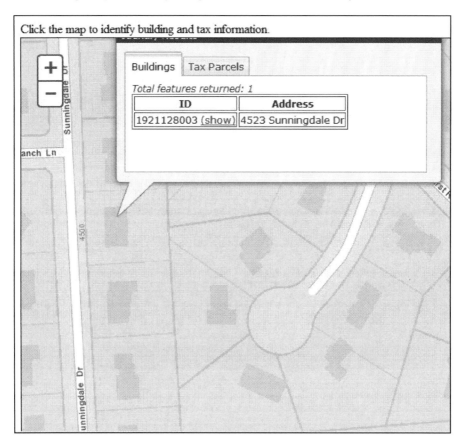

Using FindTask to get the feature attributes

You can use `FindTask` to search a map service exposed by the ArcGIS Server REST API, based on a string value. The search can be conducted on a single field of a single layer, on many fields of a layer, or on many fields of many layers. As with the other tasks that we've examined, the Find operation is composed of three complementary objects including `FindParameters`, `FindTask`, and `FindResult`. The `FindParameters` object serves as the input parameter object, which is used by

FindTask to accomplish its work, and FindResult contains the results returned by the task. Take a look at the following figure:

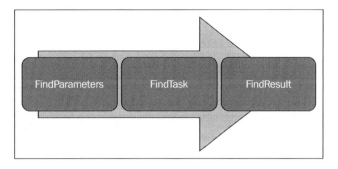

FindParameters

The FindParameters object is used to specify the search criteria for a Find operation and includes a searchText property that includes the text that will be searched for along with properties that specify the fields and layers that will be searched. In addition to this, setting the returnGeometry property to true indicates that you want to return the geometry of the features that matched the Find operation, and can be used to highlight the results.

The following code example shows how to create a new instance of FindParameters and assign various attributes. Before using any of the objects associated with a Find operation, you'll need to import the esri/tasks/find resource. The searchText property defines the string value that will be used in the search across fields, defined in the searchFields property. The layers that will be searched are defined through an array of index numbers assigned to the layerIds property. The index numbers correspond to the layers in the map service. The geometry property defines whether the geometric definition of a feature should be returned in the results. There may be times when you don't need the feature geometry, such as when the attributes simply need to be populated inside a table. In such a case, you would set the geometry property to false.

```
var findParams = new FindParameters();
findParams.searchText = dom.byId("ownerName").value;
findParams.searchFields = ["LEGALDESC","ADDRESS"]; //
    fields to search
findParams.returnGeometry = true;
findParams.layerIds = [0]; //layers to use in the find
findParams.outSpatialReference = map.spatialReference;
```

You can use the `contains` property to determine whether to look for an exact match of the search text or not. If it is set to `true`, it searches for a value that contains the `searchText` property. This is a case-insensitive search. If it is set to `false`, it searches for an exact match of the `searchText` string. The exact match is case-sensitive.

FindTask

`FindTask`, illustrated in the preceding figure, executes a Find operation against the layers and fields specified in `FindParameters` and returns a `FindResult` object, which contains the records that were found. Take a look at the following code snippet:

```
findTask = new FindTask("http://sampleserver1.arcgisonline.com/ArcGIS/
rest/services/TaxParcel/TaxParcelQuery/MapServer/");
findTask.execute(findParams,showResults);

function showResults(results) {
    //This function processes the results
}
```

Just as with `QueryTask`, you must specify a URL pointer to the map service that will be used in the Find operation, but you do not need to include an integer value specifying the exact data layer to be used. This is not necessary because the layers and fields to be used in the Find operation are defined in the `FindParameters` object. Once created, you can then call the `FindTask.execute()` method to initiate the Find operation. The `FindParameters` object is passed into this method as the first parameter, and you can also define optional `success` and `error` callback functions. This is shown in the preceding code example. The `success` callback function passes an instance of `FindResults`, which contains the results of the Find operation.

FindResult

`FindResult` contains the results of a `FindTask` operation and also contains features that can be represented as graphics, layer IDs and names where the feature was found, and the field name that contains the search string. Take a look at the following code snippet:

```
function showResults(results) {
//This function works with an array of FindResult that the task
  returns
  map.graphics.clear();
  var symbol = new SimpleFillSymbol(SimpleFillSymbol.STYLE_SOLID,
  new SimpleLineSymbol(SimpleLineSymbol.STYLE_SOLID,
  new Color([98,194,204]), 2), new Color([98,194,204,0.5]));
  //create array of attributes
```

```
var items = array.map(results,function(result){
  var graphic = result.feature;
  graphic.setSymbol(symbol);
  map.graphics.add(graphic);
  return result.feature.attributes;
});
//Create data object to be used in store
var data = {
  identifier: "PARCELID", //This field needs to have unique values
  label: "PARCELID", //Name field for display. Not pertinent to
    agrid but may be used elsewhere.
  items: items
};
//Create data store and bind to grid.
store = new ItemFileReadStore({ data:data });
var grid = dijit.byId('grid');
grid.setStore(store);
//Zoom back to the initial map extent
map.centerAndZoom(center, zoom);
}
```

Summary

The return of attributes associated with features is one of the most common operations in GIS. ArcGIS Server has two tasks that can return attributes: IdentifyTask and FindTask. The IdentifyTask attribute is used to return the attributes of a feature that has been clicked on the map. FindTask also returns attributes of a feature but uses a simple attribute query to return the attributes. In this chapter, you learned how to use both tasks using the ArcGIS API for JavaScript. In the next chapter, you will learn how to perform geocoding and reverse geocoding using a Locator task.

8
Turning Addresses into Points and Points into Addresses

Plotting addresses or points of interest on a map is one of the most commonly used functions in web mapping applications. To plot an address as a point on a map, you'll first need to get the latitude and longitude coordinates. Geocoding is the process of converting physical addresses into geographic coordinates. In order for your addresses to be added to the map, they must go through a geocoding process that assigns coordinates to the address. Geocoding is accomplished in ArcGIS Server through the use of a Locator service and is executed through the ArcGIS Server JavaScript API with the `Locator` class, which accesses these services to provide address-matching capabilities as well as reverse geocoding. As with the other tasks provided by ArcGIS Server, geocoding requires various input parameters, including an `Address` object to match addresses or a `Point` object in the case of reverse geocoding. This information is then submitted to the geocoding service and an `AddressCandidate` object containing the address matches is returned and can then be plotted on the map.

In this chapter, we will cover the following topics:

- Introducing geocoding
- Geocoding with a Locator service in the ArcGIS API for JavaScript
- The geocoding process
- The reverse geocoding process
- Time to practice with the Locator service

Introducing geocoding

We'll first take a look at a geocoding example to give you a better feel of the process. If you have an address located at 150 Main St, you must first geocode the address before it can be plotted as a point on a map. If 150 Main St lies on a street segment with an address range of 100 to 200 Main St, the geocoding process would interpolate the location of 150 Main St. to be exactly halfway along this street segment. The geocoding software would then assign 150 Main St. to the geographic location that corresponds to the halfway point between 100 and 200 Main St. Now that you have the coordinates for the address, you can plot it on the map. This process is described in the following diagram:

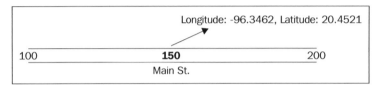

The most common geocoding level is the street segment geocode, which assigns latitude/longitude coordinates based on known geocodes at the intersection of the block or street segment containing an address. This method of geocoding uses an interpolation process as described earlier. This method is the most accurate in urban areas with regularly spaced addresses. However, it does have problems accurately geocoding irregularly spaced addresses and addresses located in a cul de sac. The coordinates of rural areas are also notoriously less complete and this results in lower geocoding rates in those areas.

Geocoding with a Locator service in the ArcGIS API for JavaScript

An ArcGIS Server Locator service can perform geocoding and reverse geocoding. Using the ArcGIS Server API for JavaScript, you can submit an address to the Locator service and retrieve geographic coordinates for the address, which can then be plotted on the map. The following figure illustrates this process. An address, defined by a JSON object in JavaScript, is an input to a Locator object, which geocodes the address and returns the results in an AddressCandidate object, which can then be displayed as a point on your map. This pattern is the same as the other tasks we saw in previous chapters, where an input object (the Address object) provides input parameters to the task (Locator), which submits the job to ArcGIS Server. A result object (AddressCandidate) is then returned to a callback function, which processes the returned data.

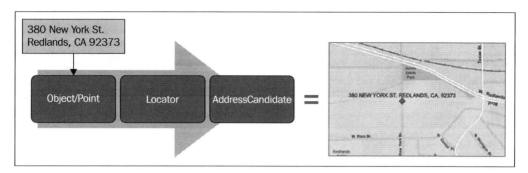

Input parameter objects

The input parameter object for the `Locator` task will take the form of either a JSON address object for geocoding or a `Point` object for reverse geocoding. From a programmatic standpoint, the creation of these objects differs. We'll discuss each of the objects in the next section.

Input JSON address object

A `Locator` service can accept either a `Point` (for reverse geocoding) or a `JSON` object that represents an address. The JSON object defines an address that is formatted in the form of an object, as seen in the following code example. The address is defined as a series of name/value pairs defined within brackets, which are defined within your JavaScript code. Individual name/value pairs are defined for the street, city, state, and zip code in this case, but the name/value pairs will vary depending upon the type of geocoding service you've defined in your locator.

```
var address = {
    street: "380 New York",
    city: "Redlands",
    state: "CA",
    zip: "92373"
}
```

Input Point object

For reverse geocoding, the input to a `Locator` service takes the form of a `esri/geometry/Point` object, which is often defined through a user click on the map or perhaps through application logic. The `Point` object is returned through a `Map.click` event, which can be retrieved and used as the input object to the `Locator` service.

The Locator object

The `Locator` class contains methods and events that can be used to execute a geocode or reverse geocode operation using the input `Point` or `Address` object. `Locator` needs a URL pointer to your geocoding service, as defined within ArcGIS Server. A code example showing how to create a new instance of a `Locator` object is presented as follows:

```
var locator = new Locator
  ("http://sampleserver1.arcgisonline.com/ArcGIS/rest/
   services/Locators/ESRI_Geocode_USA/GeocodeServer")
```

Once a new instance of a `Locator` class has been created, you can call the `addressToLocations()` method to geocode an address or the `locationToAddress()` method to perform a reverse geocode. These methods result in an event that is fired at the completion of the operation. In the case of an address geocode, the `address-to-locations-complete()` event fires, and the `on-location-to-address-complete()` event fires on the completion of a reverse geocode operation. In either case, an `AddressCandidate` object is then returned to the event.

The AddressCandidate object

An `AddressCandidate` object is returned as a result of a `Locator` operation. Various properties are stored in this object, including the address, attributes, location, and score. The attributes property contains name/value pairs of field names and values. The location is, as the name would suggest, the x and y coordinate of the candidate address. The score property is a numeric value between 0 and 100 that indicates the quality of the address returned with a higher score, representing a better match. Multiple addresses can be stored in this object as an array of candidates.

Now, we're going to take a closer look at the Locator methods used to submit addresses and points. The `Locator.addressToLocations()` method sends a request to geocode a single address. An input address object is created and used as a parameter in the `addressToLocations()` method found on a `Locator` object. The results of the geocoding operation are returned in an `AddressCandidate` object. The address can then be plotted on the map as a graphic.

Reverse geocoding can also be performed by a `Locator` object through the `locationToAddress()` method. A `Point` object, created either by an end user click on the map or through application logic, is created and passed as a parameter into the `locationToAddress()` method. A second parameter is also passed into the method, indicating a distance in meters from the point where a matching address should be found. As with the `addressToLocations()` method, an `AddressCandidate` object is returned from the locator and contains an address, if one was found.

The geocoding process

We can summarize the geocoding process with the ArcGIS API for JavaScript. A `Locator` object is created through a reference to a geocoding service on an ArcGIS Server instance. An input address in the form of a JSON object is then created and submitted to the `Locator` object using the `addressToLocations()` method. This returns one or more `AddressCandidate` objects, which can then be plotted on the map. Take a look at the following diagram:

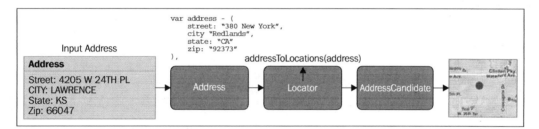

The reverse geocoding process

Let's review the reverse geocoding process as well. This process also uses a `Locator` object, which references a URL to a geocoding service. A `Point` geometry object is created as a result of either a location that has been clicked on the map or some other application-generated event. This `Point` object is then submitted to `Locator` through the `locationToAddress()` method, along with a distance value. The `distance` property, supplied in meters, determines the radius in which `Locator` will attempt to find an address.

If an address is found within the radius, an `AddressCandidate` object is created and can be decoded as an address. Take a look at the following diagram:

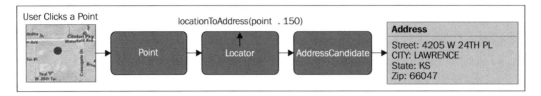

Time to practice with the Locator service

In this exercise, you will learn how to use the `Locator` class to geocode addresses and overlay the results on top of a basemap provided by ArcGIS Online. Open the JavaScript Sandbox at `http://developers.arcgis.com/en/javascript/sandbox/sandbox.html` and perform the following steps:

1. In your `ArcGISJavaScriptAPI` folder, open the file called `geocode_begin.html` in a text editor. I use Notepad++, but you can use whatever text editor you are most comfortable with. Some of the code for this exercise has already been written for you so that you can focus on the geocoding functionality.

2. Copy and paste the code in the file so that it completely replaces the code currently in Sandbox.

3. Add the following references for the objects that we'll use in this exercise:

```
var map, locator;
require([
        "esri/map", "esri/tasks/locator", "esri/graphic",
        "esri/InfoTemplate", "esri/symbols/SimpleMarkerSymbol",
        "esri/symbols/Font", "esri/symbols/TextSymbol",
        "dojo/_base/array", "dojo/_base/Color",
        "dojo/number", "dojo/parser", "dojo/dom", "dijit/
registry","dijit/form/Button", "dijit/form/Textarea",
        "dijit/layout/BorderContainer",
          "dijit/layout/ContentPane", "dojo/domReady!"
    ], function(
        Map, Locator, Graphic,
        InfoTemplate, SimpleMarkerSymbol,
        Font, TextSymbol,
        arrayUtils, Color,
        number, parser, dom, registry
    ) {
        parser.parse();
```

4. Now inside the `require()` function, we are going to initialize the `locator` variable and then register it to `Locator.address-to-locations-complete`. Add the following two lines of code just after the code block used to create the `Map` object:

```
locator = new
  Locator("http://geocode.arcgis.com/arcgis/rest/
  services/World/GeocodeServer");
locator.on("address-to-locations-complete", showResults);
```

The constructor for `Locator` must be a valid URL pointer to a locator service. In this case, we are using the World Geocoding Service. We've also registered the `Locator.address-to-locations-complete` event for the `Locator` object. This event fires when the geocoding has been completed and in this case, will call the `showResults()` function specified as a parameter to `on()`.

5. Let's also register the `click` event for the button that will trigger the geocoding by adding the following line of code just after the two lines that you just created. This will trigger the execution of a JavaScript function called `locate()`, which we'll create in the next step:

```
registry.byId("locate").on("click", locate);
```

6. In this step, you're going to create a `locate()` function, which will perform several tasks, including clearing any existing graphics, creating an `Address` JSON object from the input textbox on the web page, defining several options, and calling the `Locator.addressToLocations()` method. Add the code block just after the last line of code you entered, shown as follows:

```
function locate() {
  map.graphics.clear();
  var address = {
    "SingleLine": dom.byId("address").value
  };
locator.outSpatialReference = map.spatialReference;
var options = {
  address: address,
  outFields: ["Loc_name"]
}
locator.addressToLocations(options);
}
```

The first line of code in this function clears any existing graphics for the map. This is needed when the user is entering more than one address in a session. Next, we will create a variable called `address`, which is a JSON object that contains the address entered by the user. We then set the output spatial reference and create an `options` variable that contains the address and output fields as a JSON object. Finally, we call the `Locator.addressToLocations()` method and pass in the `options` variable.

7. The `showResults()` function will take the results returned by the `Locator` service and plot them on the map. In this case, we're going to display only an address with a score of greater than 80 on a scale of 0 to 100. Part of the `showResults()` function has already been written for you. Create a new variable to hold the `AddressCandidate` object by adding the highlighted line of code as follows:

```
function showResults(evt) {
  var candidate;
  var symbol = new SimpleMarkerSymbol();
  var infoTemplate = new InfoTemplate(
    "Location",
    "Address: ${address}<br />Score: ${score}<br />Source
      locator: ${locatorName}"
  );
  symbol.setStyle(SimpleMarkerSymbol.STYLE_SQUARE);
  symbol.setColor(new Color([153,0,51,0.75]));
```

8. Just after the line of code that creates the `geom` variable, start a loop that will loop through each of the addresses that are returned from `Locator`:

```
arrayUtils.every(evt.addresses, function(candidate) {

});
```

9. Start an `if` statement that checks the `AddressCandidate.score` property for a value greater than 80. We only want to display addresses with a high match value:

```
arrayUtils.every(evt.addresses, function(candidate) {
    if (candidate.score > 80) {

    }
});
```

10. Inside the `if` block, create a JSON variable with new attributes, which contain the address, score, and field values from the `AddressCandidate` object. In addition to this, the `location` property will be saved to the `geom` variable:

```
arrayUtils.every(evt.addresses, function(candidate) {
    if (candidate.score > 80) {
        var attributes = {
          address: candidate.address,
          score: candidate.score,
          locatorName: candidate.attributes.Loc_name
        };
        geom = candidate.location;


    }
});
```

11. Create a new `Graphic` object using the `geometry`, `symbol`, `attributes`, and `infoTemplate` variables that you either created earlier or were created for you and add them to the `GraphicsLayer`:

```
arrayUtils.every(evt.addresses, function(candidate) {
    if (candidate.score > 80) {
        var attributes = {
          address: candidate.address,
          score: candidate.score,
          locatorName: candidate.attributes.Loc_name
        };
        geom = candidate.location;
        var graphic = new Graphic(geom, symbol, attributes,
infoTemplate);
        //add a graphic to the map at the geocoded location
        map.graphics.add(graphic);


    }
});
```

12. Add a text symbol for the location(s):

```
arrayUtils.every(evt.addresses, function(candidate) {
    if (candidate.score > 80) {
        var attributes = {
          address: candidate.address,
          score: candidate.score,
          locatorName: candidate.attributes.Loc_name
        };
        geom = candidate.location;
var graphic = new Graphic(geom, symbol, attributes, infoTemplate);
```

```
        //add a graphic to the map at the geocoded location
        map.graphics.add(graphic);
//add a text symbol to the map listing the location of the matched
  address.
        var displayText = candidate.address;
        var font = new Font(
          "16pt",
          Font.STYLE_NORMAL,
          Font.VARIANT_NORMAL,
          Font.WEIGHT_BOLD,
          "Helvetica"
        );

          var textSymbol = new TextSymbol(
            displayText,
            font,
            new Color("#666633")
          );
          textSymbol.setOffset(0,8);
          map.graphics.add(new Graphic(geom, textSymbol));


      }
    });
```

13. Break out of the loop after one address with a score of greater than 80 has been found. Many addresses will have more than one match, which can be confusing. Take a look at the following code snippet:

```
arrayUtils.every(evt.addresses, function(candidate) {
    if (candidate.score > 80) {
      var attributes = {
        address: candidate.address,
        score: candidate.score,
        locatorName: candidate.attributes.Loc_name
      };
      geom = candidate.location;
var graphic = new Graphic(geom, symbol, attributes,
  infoTemplate);
      //add a graphic to the map at the geocoded location
      map.graphics.add(graphic);
//add a text symbol to the map listing the location of the
  matched address.
      var displayText = candidate.address;
      var font = new Font(
        "16pt",
```

```
        Font.STYLE_NORMAL,
        Font.VARIANT_NORMAL,
        Font.WEIGHT_BOLD,
        "Helvetica"
    );

    var textSymbol = new TextSymbol(
      displayText,
      font,
      new Color("#666633")
    );
    textSymbol.setOffset(0,8);
    map.graphics.add(new Graphic(geom, textSymbol));
    return false; //break out of loop after one candidate
with score greater  than 80 is found.
    }
  });
```

14. You may want to double check your code by examining the solution file `geocode_end.html` located in your `ArcGISJavaScriptAPI/solution` folder.

15. When you click on the **Run** button, you should see the following map. If not, you may need to recheck your code for accuracy.

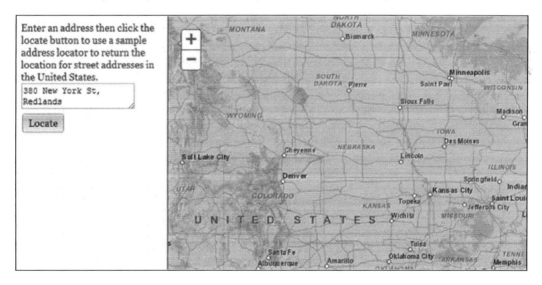

16. Enter an address or accept the default and click on **Locate**, as shown in the following screenshot:

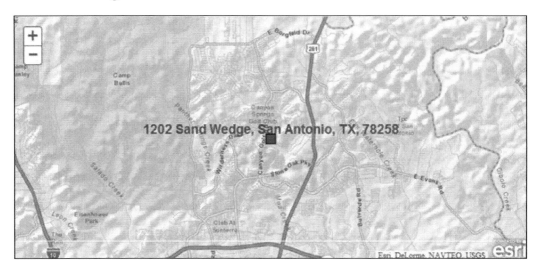

Summary

An ArcGIS Server Locator service can perform geocoding and reverse geocoding. Using the ArcGIS API for JavaScript, you can submit an address to the Locator service and retrieve geographic coordinates for the address, which can then be plotted on a map. An address, defined by a JSON object in JavaScript, is an input to a Locator object, which geocodes the address and returns the results in an AddressCandidate object that can then be displayed as a point on your map. This pattern is the same as the other tasks we've seen in previous chapters, where an input object (the Address object) provides input parameters to the task (Locator), which submits the job to ArcGIS Server. A result object (AddressCandidate) is then returned to a callback function, which processes the returned data. In the next chapter, you will learn how to use various Network Analyst tasks.

9
Network Analyst Tasks

Network analysis services allow you to perform analyses on street networks such as finding the best route from one address to another, finding the closest school, identifying a service area around a location, or responding to a set of orders with a fleet of service vehicles. The services can be accessed using their REST endpoints. There are three types of analysis that can perform the services: routing, closest facility, and service area. We'll examine each of the service types in this chapter. All network analysis services require you to have the network analyst plugin for ArcGIS Server.

In this chapter, we will cover the following topics:

- RouteTask
- Time to practice routing
- The ClosestFacility task
- The ServiceArea task

RouteTask

Routing in the API for JavaScript allows you to use a `RouteTask` object to find routes between two or more locations and optionally get driving directions. The `RouteTask` object uses network analysis services to calculate the routes and can include both simple and complex routes such as multiple stops, barriers, and time windows.

The `RouteTask` object uses a least-cost path between multiple locations in a network. Impedance on the network can include time and distance variables. The following screenshot shows the output of a `RouteTask` implementation:

As with the other tasks we have examined in this class, routing is accomplished through a series of objects including `RouteParameters`, `RouteTask`, and `RouteResult`. The following diagram illustrates the three route objects:

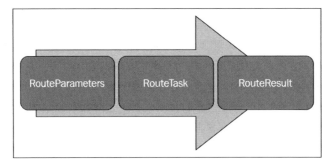

The `RouteParameters` object provides the input parameters to `RouteTask`, which submits a routing request to ArcGIS Server using the input parameters. Results are returned from ArcGIS Server in the form of a `RouteResult` object.

The `RouteParameters` object serves as an input to the `RouteTask` object and can include stop and barrier locations, impedance, whether or not to return driving directions and routes, and many others. You can obtain a full list of all the parameters at `https://developers.arcgis.com/en/javascript/jsapi/` `routeparameters-amd.html` for the JavaScript API. A brief code example is also provided showing how to create an instance of `RouteParameters`, add stops, and define the output spatial reference:

```
routeParams = new RouteParameters();
routeParams.stops = new FeatureSet();
routeParams.outSpatialReference = {wkid:4326};
routeParams.stops.features.push(stop1);
routeParams.stops.features.push(stop2);
```

The `RouteTask` object executes a routing operation using the input parameters supplied by `RouteParameters`. The constructor for `RouteTask` takes a pointer to a URL that identifies the network service to use for the analysis. Calling the `solve()` method on `RouteTask` executes a routing task against the network analysis service using the input parameters supplied:

```
routeParams = new RouteParameters();
routeParams.stops = new FeatureSet();
routeParams.outSpatialReference = {wkid:4326};
routeParams.stops.features.push(stop1);
routeParams.stops.features.push(stop2);
routeTask.solve(routeParams);
```

A `RouteResult` object is returned from the network analysis service to a callback function provided by `RouteTask`. The callback function then handles the data by displaying it to the user. The data returned is largely dependent upon the input supplied to the `RouteParameters` object. One of the most important properties on `RouteParameters` is the `stops` property. These are the points to be included in the analysis of the best route between points. Stops is defined as either an instance of `DataLayer` or `FeatureSet` and is a set of stops are to be included in the analysis.

The concept of barriers is also important in routing operations. Barriers restrict movement when planning a route. Barriers can include a car accident, construction work on a street segment, or other delays such as railroad crossings. Barriers are defined as either `FeatureSet` or `DataLayer` and specified through the `RouteParameters.barriers` property. The following code shows an example of how barriers are created in your code:

```
var routeParameters = new RouteParameters();
//Add barriers as a FeatureSet
routeParameters.barriers = new FeatureSet();
routeParameters.barriers.features.push(map.graphics.add(new
    Graphic(evt.mapPoint, barrierSymbol)));
```

Directions are returned only if `RouteParameters.returnDirections` is set to `true`. When you elect to have directions returned, you can also use various properties to control the returned directions. You have control over the language for the directions (`RouteParameters.directionsLanguage`), length units (`RouteParameters.directionsLengthUnits`), output type (`RouteParameters.directionsOutputType`), style name (`RouteParameters.StyleName`), and time attribute (`RouteParameters.directionsTimeAttribute`). The data returned in addition to directions can include the route between points, the route name, and an array of stops.

It is also possible to specify that the task should fail if one of the stops is unreachable. This is accomplished through `RouteParameters.ignoreInvalidLocations` property. This property can be set to `true` or `false`. You can also introduce time into the analysis through properties such as `RouteParameters.startTime`, which specifies the time the route begins, and `RouteParameters.useTimeWindows`, which defines that a time range should be used in the analysis.

Time to practice routing

In this exercise, you will learn how to implement routing in your applications. You'll create an instance of `RouteParameters`, add stops by allowing the user to click points on a map, and solve the route. The returned route will be displayed as a line symbol on the map. Follow the following directions to create an application that includes routing:

1. Open the JavaScript Sandbox at `http://developers.arcgis.com/en/javascript/sandbox/sandbox.html`.

2. Remove the JavaScript content from the `<script>` tag that I have highlighted in the following code snippet:

```
<script>
  dojo.require("esri.map");

  function init(){
   var map = new esri.Map("mapDiv", {
      center: [-56.049, 38.485],
      zoom: 3,
      basemap: "streets"
    });
  }
  dojo.ready(init);
</script>
```

3. Add the following references for the objects that we'll use in this exercise:

```
<script>
  require([
      "esri/map",
      "esri/tasks/RouteParameters",
      "esri/tasks/RouteTask",

      "esri/tasks/FeatureSet",
      "esri/symbols/SimpleMarkerSymbol",
      "esri/symbols/SimpleLineSymbol",
      "esri/graphic",
      "dojo/_base/Color"
    ],
    function(Map, RouteParameters, RouteTask,
      FeatureSet, SimpleMarkerSymbol, SimpleLineSymbol,
      Graphic, Color ){

  });
</script>
```

4. Inside the `require()` function, create the `Map` object as seen in the following code snippet and define variables to hold the route objects and symbols for display purposes:

```
<script>
  require([
      "esri/map",
      "esri/tasks/RouteParameters",
      "esri/tasks/RouteTask",
      "esri/tasks/RouteResult",
      "esri/tasks/FeatureSet",
      "esri/symbols/SimpleMarkerSymbol",
      "esri/symbols/SimpleLineSymbol",
      "esri/graphic",
      "dojo/_base/Color"
    ],
    function(Map, RouteParameters, RouteTask, RouteResult,
      FeatureSet, SimpleMarkerSymbol, SimpleLineSymbol,
      Graphic, Color ){
        var map, routeTask, routeParams;
        var stopSymbol, routeSymbol, lastStop;

        map = new Map("mapDiv", {
          basemap: "streets",
          center:[-123.379, 48.418], //long, lat
```

```
        zoom: 14
    });
  });
</script>
```

5. Just below the code block that created the `Map` object, add an event handler for the `Map.click()` event. This action should trigger the `addStop()` function:

```
map = new Map("mapDiv", {
    basemap: "streets",
    center:[-123.379, 48.418], //long, lat
    zoom: 14
});
map.on("click", addStop);
```

6. Create the `RouteTask` and `RouteParameters` objects. Set the `RouteParameters.stops` property equal to a new `FeatureSet` object. Also, set the `RouteParameters.outSpatialReference` property:

```
map = new Map("mapDiv", {
    basemap: "streets",
    center:[-123.379, 48.418], //long, lat
    zoom: 14
});
map.on("click", addStop);
routeTask = new RouteTask
  ("http://tasks.arcgisonline.com/ArcGIS/rest/services/
NetworkAnalysis/ESRI_Route_NA/NAServer/Route");
routeParams = new RouteParameters();
routeParams.stops = new FeatureSet();
routeParams.outSpatialReference = {"wkid":4326};
```

The following is a screenshot of the services directory that contains this network analysis service:

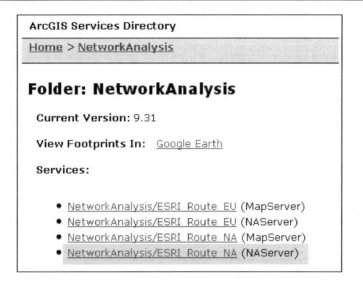

7. Add event handlers for the completion of the `RouteTask.solve-complete()` event and the `RouteTask.error()` event. The successful completion of a routing task should trigger the execution of a function called `showRoute()`. Any errors should trigger the execution of a function called `errorHandler()`:

```
routeParams = new RouteParameters();
routeParams.stops = new FeatureSet();
routeParams.outSpatialReference = {"wkid":4326};

routeTask.on("solve-complete", showRoute);
routeTask.on("error", errorHandler);
```

8. Create symbol objects for the beginning and ending points of the route as well as the line that defines the route between those points. The following lines of code should be added just below the two lines of code you added in the previous step:

```
stopSymbol = new
  SimpleMarkerSymbol().setStyle
    (SimpleMarkerSymbol.STYLE_CROSS).setSize(15);
stopSymbol.outline.setWidth(4);
routeSymbol = new SimpleLineSymbol().setColor(new
  Color([0,0,255,0.5])).setWidth(5);
```

9. Create the `addStop()` function that will be triggered when the user clicks on the map. This function will accept an `Event` object as its only parameter. The point clicked on the map can be extracted from this object. This function will add a point graphic to the map and add the graphic to the `RouteParameters.stops` property; on the second map click, it will call the `RouteTask.solve()` method, passing in an instance of `RouteParameters`:

```
function addStop(evt) {
    var stop = map.graphics.add(new Graphic(evt.mapPoint,
        stopSymbol));
    routeParams.stops.features.push(stop);

    if (routeParams.stops.features.length >= 2) {
        routeTask.solve(routeParams);
        lastStop = routeParams.stops.features.splice(0,
            1)[0];
    }
}
```

10. Create the `showRoute()` function, which accepts an instance of `RouteResult`. The only thing you need to do in this function is add the route as a line to `GraphicsLayer`:

```
function showRoute(solveResult) {
  map.graphics.add(solveResult.result.routeResults[0]
    .route.setSymbol(routeSymbol));
    }
```

11. Finally, add the error callback function in case there is a problem with the routing. This function should display an error message to the user and remove any leftover graphics:

```
function errorHandler(err) {
  alert("An error occurred\n" + err.message + "\n" +
    err.details.join("\n"));

  routeParams.stops.features.splice(0, 0, lastStop);
  map.graphics.remove
    (routeParams.stops.features.splice(1,    1)[0]);
}
```

12. You may want to review the solution file (`routing.html`) in your `ArcGISJavaScriptAPI` folder to verify that your code has been written correctly.

13. Click on the **Run** button. You should see the map as in the following screenshot. If not, you may need to recheck your code for accuracy.

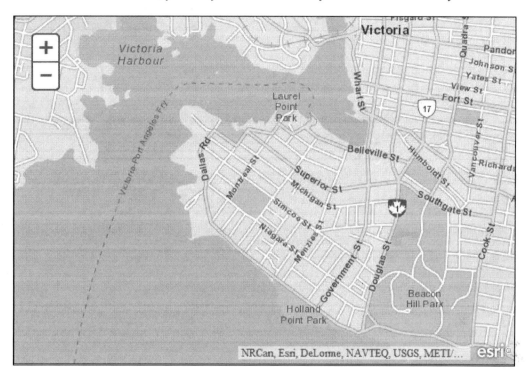

14. Click somewhere on the map. You should see a point marker as shown in the following screenshot:

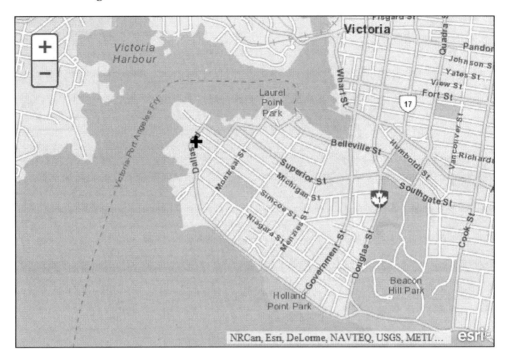

15. Click on another point somewhere on the map. This should display a second marker along with the best route between the two points, as seen in the following screenshot:

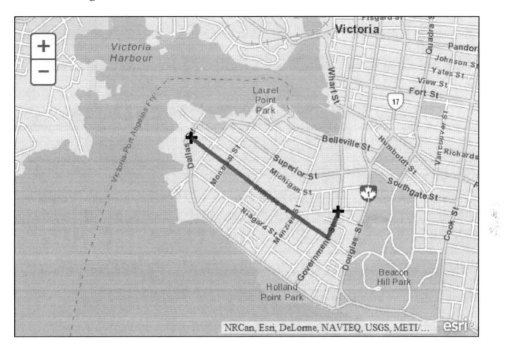

The ClosestFacility task

The ClosestFacility task measures the cost of traveling between incidents and facilities and determines which are nearest to one other. When looking for the closest facilities, you can specify how many to find and whether the direction of travel is towards or away from them. The closest facility solver displays the best routes between incidents and facilities, reports their travel costs, and returns driving directions.

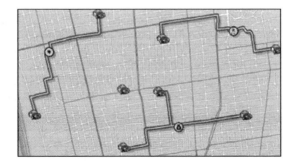

The classes involved in solving closest facility operations include
ClosestFacilityParameters, ClosestFacilityTask, and
ClosestFacilitySolveResults, shown as follows:

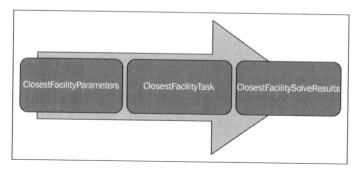

The ClosestFacilityParameters class includes input parameters such as the
default cutoff, whether or not to return incidents, routes, and directions, and more.
These parameters are used as inputs to the ClosestFacilityTask class, which
contains a solve() method. Finally, results are passed from ArcGIS Server back to
the client in the form of a ClosestFacilitySolveResults object.

The ClosestFacilityParameters object is used as an input to
ClosestFacilityTask. Some of the more commonly used properties on this object
will now be discussed. The incidents and facilities properties are used to set the
locations for the analysis. The data returned by the task can be controlled through
the returnIncidents, returnRoutes, and returnDirections properties, which are
simply true or false values indicating whether the information should be returned
in the results. The travelDirection parameter specifies whether travel should be to
or from the facility and defaultCutoff is the cutoff value beyond which the analysis
will stop traversing. The following code example shows how to create an instance of
ClosestFacilityParameters and apply the various properties:

```
params = new ClosestFacilityParameters();
params.defaultCutoff = 3.0;
params.returnIncidents = false;
params.returnRoutes = true;
params.returnDirections = true;
```

When you create a new instance of ClosestFacilityTask, you will need to point to a REST resource representing a network analysis service. Once created, the ClosestFacilityTask class accepts the input parameters provided by ClosestFacilityParameters and submits them to a network analysis service using the solve() method.

This is illustrated by the following code example. The solve() method also accepts callback and error callback functions:

```
cfTask = new
  ClosestFacilityTask("http://<domain>/arcgis/rest/services/network/
ClosestFacility");
params = new ClosestFacilityParameters();
params.defaultCutoff = 3.0;
params.returnIncidents = false;
params.returnRoutes = true;
params.returnDirections = true;
cfTask.solve(params, processResults);
```

The result returned from a ClosestFacilityTask operation is a ClosestFacilitySolveResult object. This object can contain various properties including a DirectionsFeatureSet object, which is an array of directions. This DirectionsFeatureSet object contains the turn-by-turn directions text and geometry of the route. The attributes for each feature provide the information associated with the corresponding route segment. The returned attributes include the direction text, the length of the route segment, the time to travel along the route segment, and the estimated time of arrival at the route segment. Other properties contained within ClosestFacilitySolveResults include an array containing the facilities and incidents, an array of polylines representing the routes returned, any messages returned, and arrays containing barriers.

The ServiceArea task

The new `ServiceArea` task, illustrated in the following screenshot, calculates the service area around an input location. This service area is defined in minutes and is a region that encompasses all the accessible streets within that time range.

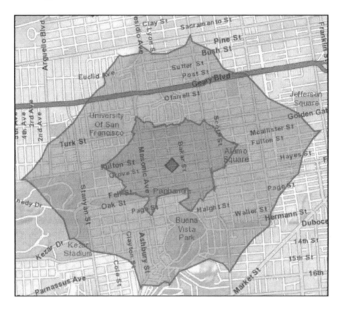

The classes involved in service area operations include `ServiceAreaParameters`, `ServiceAreaTask`, and `ServiceAreaSolveResults`. These objects are illustrated in the following diagram:

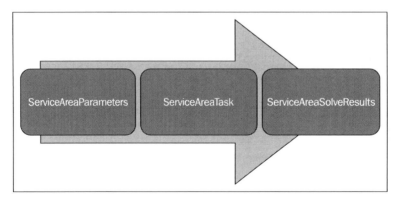

The `ServiceAreaParameters` class includes input parameters such as the default break, facilities involved, barriers and restrictions, travel direction, and more. These parameters are used as inputs to the `ServiceAreaTask` class, which calls `solve()`. Parameters defined in `ServiceAreaParameters` are passed in to `ServiceAreaTask`. Finally, results are passed from ArcGIS Server back to the client in the form of a `ServiceAreaSolveResults` object. The `ServiceAreaParameters` object is used as an input to `ServiceAreaTask`. Some of the more commonly used properties on this object are discussed in this section of the chapter. The `defaultBreaks` property is an array of numbers defining the service area. For instance, in the following code example, a single value of 2 is provided to indicate that we'd like to return a 2-minute service area around the facility. The `returnFacilities` property, when set to `true`, indicates that the facilities should be returned with the results. Various point, polyline, and polygon barriers can be set as well through the barriers property. Travel direction for the analysis can be to or from the facility and is set with the `travelDirection` property. There are many other properties that can be set on `ServiceAreaParameters`. A code example is provided as follows:

```
params = new ServiceAreaParameters();
params.defaultBreaks = [2];
params.outSpatialReference = map.spatialReference;
params.returnFacilities = false;
```

The `ServiceAreaTask` class finds service areas around a location using a street network. The constructor for `ServiceAreaTask` should point to a REST resource representing a network analysis service. To submit a request to solve a service area task, you will need to call the `solve()` method on `ServiceAreaTask`.

The result returned from a `ServiceAreaTask` operation is a `ServiceAreaSolveResult` object. This object can contain various properties including a `ServiceAreaPolygons` property, which is an array of service area polygons returned from the analysis. In addition, other properties include facilities, messages, and barriers.

Summary

Routing enables you to add the functionality that finds routes between two or more locations to your application. In addition, you can generate driving directions between the locations. This is accomplished through a `RouteTask` object that performs network analysis. This functionality, along with the other network analysis services, requires the use of the network analysis plugin for ArcGIS Server. Other network analyst tasks include the closest facility task, which allows you to measure the cost of traveling between incidents and facilities and determines which are nearest to one other, and the service area task, which calculates the service area around an input location. In the next chapter, you will learn how to execute geoprocessing tasks from your applications.

10
Geoprocessing Tasks

Geoprocessing refers to the automation and chaining of GIS operations in a logical fashion to accomplish some sort of GIS task. For example, you may want to buffer a stream layer and then clip a vegetation layer to this newly created buffer. A model can be built in ArcGIS for Desktop and run in an automated fashion from either a desktop environment or via a centralized server accessed through a web application. Any tool found in ArcToolbox, whether a built-in tool for your ArcGIS license level or a custom tool that you've built, can be used in a model and chained together with other tools. This chapter examines how you can access these geoprocessing tasks through the ArcGIS API for JavaScript.

In this chapter, we will cover the following topics:

- Models in ArcGIS Server
- Using Geoprocessor – what you need to know
- Understanding the service page for a geoprocessing task
- The Geoprocessor task
- Running the task
- Time to practice with the geoprocessing tasks

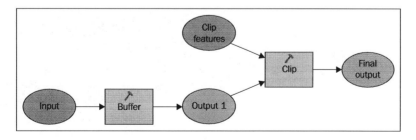

The preceding diagram shows us the components of a model that is built using ModelBuilder. These models can be published to ArcGIS Server as geoprocessing tasks and then accessed through your applications.

Models in ArcGIS Server

Models are built in ArcGIS for Desktop using ModelBuilder. Once built, these models can be published to ArcGIS Server as geoprocessing tasks. Web applications then use the `Geoprocessor` object found in the ArcGIS API for JavaScript to access these tasks and retrieve information. These models and tools are run on ArcGIS Server due to their computationally intensive nature and the need for ArcGIS software. Jobs are submitted to the server through your application and the results are picked up after the service is complete. Submitting jobs and retrieving the results can be accomplished through the `Geoprocessor` object. This process is illustrated in the following diagram:

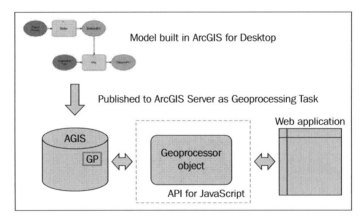

Using Geoprocessor – what you need to know

There are three things that you need to know when using a geoprocessing service:

- First, you need to know the URL where the model or tool is located. An example URL is `http://sampleserver1.arcgisonline.com/ArcGIS/ rest/services/Demographics/ESRI_Population_World/GPServer/ PopulationSummary`.

- When you go to this link, you can also find information about the input and output parameters, whether the task is asynchronous or synchronous, and much more. Speaking of input and output parameters, you need to know the data types associated with these parameters and whether or not each of these parameters is required.

- Finally, you need to know whether the task is asynchronous or synchronous and how your code should be configured based on that knowledge. All of this information can be found on the service page for the geoprocessing task.

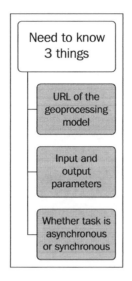

Understanding the service page for a geoprocessing task

The service page for a geoprocessing service includes metadata information about the service. This includes the execution type that can be either synchronous or asynchronous. In the case of the service seen in the following screenshot, the **PopulationSummary** service is a synchronous task, which indicates that the application will wait for the results to be returned. This type of execution is typically used with tasks that execute quickly. Asynchronous tasks are submitted as a job and then the application can continue to function while the geoprocessing service is doing its work. When the task is complete, it notifies your application that the processing is complete and the results are ready.

Other information includes the parameter names, parameter data type, whether the parameter is an input or output type, whether the parameter is required or optional, the geometry type, spatial reference, and fields.

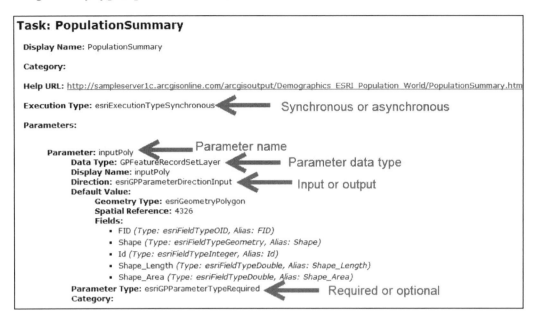

Input parameters

There are a number of details you must remember regarding input parameters that are submitted to the geoprocessing task. Almost all geoprocessing tasks will require one or more parameters. These parameters can be either required or optional and are created as JSON objects. In this section, you'll see a code example showing you how to create these JSON objects. When creating parameters as JSON objects, you must remember to create them in the exact order that they appear on the service page. The parameter names must also be named exactly as they are named on the service page. Please see the following screenshot for an example of how to read the input parameters of a service:

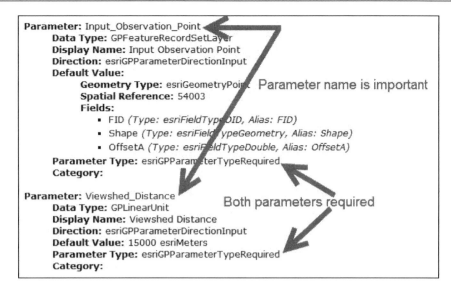

The following code example is correct because the parameter names are spelled exactly as seen in the service page (also notice that the casing is the same) and are provided in the correct order:

```
var params = {
    Input_Observation_Point: featureSetPoints,
    Viewshed_Distance: 250
};
```

In comparison, the following code example would be incorrect since the parameters are provided in reverse order:

```
var params = {
    Viewshed_Distance: 250,
    Input_Observation_Point: featureSetPoints
};
```

The previous screenshot shows the input parameters supplied to a geoprocessing task. When coding your JSON input parameters object, it is critical that you provide the exact parameter name as given on the service page and that you provide the parameters in the order they appear on the page. Notice in our code example that we are providing two parameters: `Input_Observation_Point` and `Viewshed_Distance`. Both parameters are required and we have named them exactly as they appear on the service page and they are in the correct order.

The Geoprocessor task

The Geoprocessor class in the ArcGIS API for JavaScript represents a GP task resource, which is a single task in a geoprocessing service. Input parameters are passed into the Geoprocessor class through a call to either Geoprocessor.execute() or Geoprocessor.submitJob(). We'll discuss the difference between these two calls later. After executing the geoprocessing task, the results are returned to the Geoprocessor object, where they are processed by a callback function. Creating an instance of the Geoprocessor class simply requires you to pass in the URL that points to the geoprocessing service exposed by ArcGIS Server. It does require you to import esri/tasks/gp. The following code example shows you how to create an instance of the Geoprocessor object:

```
gp = new Geoprocessor(url);
```

Running the task

Once you have an understanding of the geoprocessing models and tools available to you for an ArcGIS Server instance as well as the input and output parameters, you can begin writing the code that will execute the task. Geoprocessing jobs are submitted to ArcGIS Server for either synchronous or asynchronous execution. A synchronous execution implies that the client calls for execution of the task and then waits for the result before continuing with the application code. In an asynchronous execution, the client submits a job, continues to run other functions, and checks back later for completion of the job. By default, the client checks back for completion every second until the job is finished. The service page tells you how to submit your job for each geoprocessing task. Simply look for the execution type on the service page. The execution type is set when the model is published as a service. As a developer, you don't have any control over the type after it has been published.

Synchronous tasks

Synchronous tasks require your application code to submit a job and wait for a response before continuing. Because your end users must wait for the results to be returned before continuing to interact with your application, this type of task should only be used with tasks that return data very quickly. If a task takes more than just a few seconds, it should be defined as asynchronous instead of synchronous. Users quickly become frustrated with applications when data is returned within a very short period of time.

You will need to use the Geoprocessor.execute() method with the property input parameters and supplied callback function. The callback function is executed when the geoprocessing task returns the results of the job that was submitted. These results are stored in an array of ParameterValue.

Asynchronous tasks

Asynchronous tasks require you to submit a job, continue working on other functions while waiting for the process to finish, and then check back in with ArcGIS Server on a periodic basis to retrieve the results after completion. The advantage of an asynchronous task is that it doesn't force your end users to wait for the results. Instead, the task is submitted and your end users continue to interact with the application until the task has finished processing. When processing is complete, a callback function is triggered in your application and you can handle the results that are returned.

The Geoprocessor.submitJob() method is used to submit a job to the geoprocessing task. You will need to supply input parameters, a callback function, and a status callback function. The status callback function executes each time your application checks back for the results. By default, the status is checked once per second. However, this interval can be changed using the Geoprocessor.setUpdateDelay() method. Each time the status is checked, a JobInfo object is returned and contains information indicating the status of the job. When JobInfo.jobStatus is set to STATUS_SUCCEEDED, the complete callback function is called.

A visual diagram of the process flow that occurs on asynchronous tasks is provided in the following figure and might help reinforce how these types of tasks operate. Input parameters are created and input to the Geoprocessor object, which uses these parameters to submit a geoprocessing job to ArcGIS Server. The Geoprocessor object then executes the statusCallback() function at regular intervals. This function checks with the geoprocessing service to see if the job is finished. A JobInfo object is returned and contains a status indicator, indicating its completion status. This process continues until the job is completed, at which time a complete callback function is called and which passes the results of the job.

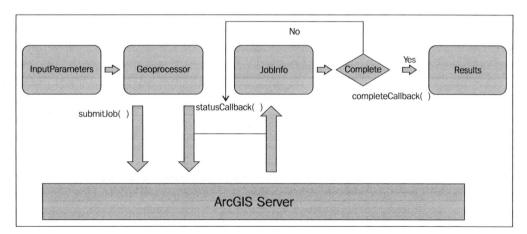

Time to practice with geoprocessing tasks

In this exercise, you will code a simple application that displays drive time polygons on a map by accessing the **CreateDriveTimePolygons** model provided by Esri. The application will create 1-, 2-, and 3-minute drive time polygons around a point clicked on the map.

1. Open the JavaScript Sandbox at `http://developers.arcgis.com/en/javascript/sandbox/sandbox.html`.

2. Remove the JavaScript content from the `<script>` tag that I have highlighted in the following code snippet:

    ```
    <script>
    dojo.require("esri.map");

    function init(){
    var map = new esri.Map("mapDiv", {
    center: [-56.049, 38.485],
    zoom: 3,
    basemap: "streets"
            });
        }
    dojo.ready(init);
    </script>
    ```

3. Add the following references for the objects that we'll use in this exercise:

    ```
    <script>
    require([
            "esri/map",
            "esri/graphic",
            "esri/graphicsUtils",
            "esri/tasks/Geoprocessor",
            "esri/tasks/FeatureSet",
            "esri/symbols/SimpleMarkerSymbol",
            "esri/symbols/SimpleLineSymbol",
            "esri/symbols/SimpleFillSymbol",
    "dojo/_base/Color"],
    function(Map, Graphic, graphicsUtils, Geoprocessor, FeatureSet,
      SimpleMarkerSymbol, SimpleLineSymbol, SimpleFillSymbol,
      Color){

        });
    </script>
    ```

4. Create the Map object as seen in the following code snippet and define variables to hold the Geoprocessor object and drive times:

```
<script>
require([

        "esri/map",
        "esri/graphic",
        "esri/graphicsUtils",
        "esri/tasks/Geoprocessor",
        "esri/tasks/FeatureSet",
        "esri/symbols/SimpleMarkerSymbol",
        "esri/symbols/SimpleLineSymbol",
        "esri/symbols/SimpleFillSymbol",
"dojo/_base/Color"],
function(Map, Graphic, graphicsUtils, Geoprocessor,
  FeatureSet, SimpleMarkerSymbol, SimpleLineSymbol,
  SimpleFillSymbol, Color){
var map, gp;
var driveTimes = "1 2 3";

// Initialize map, GP and image params
map = new Map("mapDiv", {
  basemap: "streets",
  center:[-117.148, 32.706], //long, lat
  zoom: 12
});    });
</script>
```

5. Inside the `require()` function, create the new Geoprocessor object and set the output spatial reference:

```
// Initialize map, GP and image params
map = new Map("mapDiv", {
  basemap: "streets",
  center:[-117.148, 32.706], //long, lat
  zoom: 12
});

gp = new
  Geoprocessor("http://sampleserver1.arcgisonline.com/
ArcGIS/rest/services/Network/ESRI_DriveTime_US/GPServer/
CreateDriveTimePolygons");
gp.setOutputSpatialReference({wkid:102100});
```

6. Set up an event listener for the `Map.click()` event. Each time the user clicks on the map, it will trigger the execution of the geoprocessing task that calculates drive times:

```
gp = new Geoprocessor("http://sampleserver1.arcgisonline.
com/ArcGIS/rest/services/Network/ESRI_DriveTime_US/GPServer/
CreateDriveTimePolygons");
gp.setOutputSpatialReference({wkid:102100});
map.on("click", computeServiceArea);
```

7. Now you'll create the `computeServiceArea()` function that serves as the handler for the `Map.click()` event. This function will clear any existing graphics, create a new point graphic that represents the point where the user clicked on the map, and execute the geoprocessing task. First, create the stub for the `computeServiceArea()` function just below the line of code that defined the handler:

```
gp = new Geoprocessor("http://sampleserver1.arcgisonline.
com/ArcGIS/rest/services/Network/ESRI_DriveTime_US/GPServer/
CreateDriveTimePolygons");
gp.setOutputSpatialReference({wkid:102100});
map.on("click", computeServiceArea);

function computeServiceArea(evt) {

}
```

8. Clear any existing graphics and create the new `SimpleMarkerSymbol` that will represent the point that is clicked on the map:

```
function computeServiceArea(evt) {
  map.graphics.clear();
  var pointSymbol = new SimpleMarkerSymbol();
  pointSymbol.setOutline = new
    SimpleLineSymbol(SimpleLineSymbol.STYLE_SOLID, new
    Color([255, 0, 0]), 1);
  pointSymbol.setSize(14);
  pointSymbol.setColor(new Color([0, 255, 0, 0.25]));
}
```

9. When the `Map.click()` event is triggered, an `Event` object is created and passed to the `computeServiceArea()` function. This object is represented in our code by the `evt` variable. In this step, you're going to create a new `Graphic` object by passing in the `Event.mapPoint` property, which contains the `Point` geometry returned from the map click as well as the instance of `SimpleMarkerSymbol` that you created in the last step. You'll then add this new graphic to `GraphicsLayer` so that it can be displayed on the map:

```
function computeServiceArea(evt) {
  map.graphics.clear();
  varpointSymbol = new SimpleMarkerSymbol();
  pointSymbol.setOutline = new
    SimpleLineSymbol(SimpleLineSymbol.STYLE_SOLID, new
    Color([255, 0, 0]), 1);
  pointSymbol.setSize(14);
  pointSymbol.setColor(new Color([0, 255, 0, 0.25]));

  var graphic = new Graphic(evt.mapPoint,pointSymbol);
  map.graphics.add(graphic);
}
```

10. Now, create an array called `features` and place the `graphic` object into the array. This array of graphics will eventually be passed into a `FeatureSet` object that will be passed to the geoprocessing task:

```
functioncomputeServiceArea(evt) {
  map.graphics.clear();
  var pointSymbol = new SimpleMarkerSymbol();
  pointSymbol.setOutline = new
    SimpleLineSymbol(SimpleLineSymbol.STYLE_SOLID, new
    Color([255, 0, 0]), 1);
  pointSymbol.setSize(14);
  pointSymbol.setColor(new Color([0, 255, 0, 0.25]));

  var graphic = new Graphic(evt.mapPoint,pointSymbol);
  map.graphics.add(graphic);

  var features= [];
  features.push(graphic);
}
```

11. Create a new `FeatureSet` object and add the array of graphics to the `FeatureSet.features` property:

```
function computeServiceArea(evt) {
  map.graphics.clear();
  var pointSymbol = new SimpleMarkerSymbol();
  pointSymbol.setOutline = new
    SimpleLineSymbol(SimpleLineSymbol.STYLE_SOLID, new
    Color([255, 0, 0]), 1);
  pointSymbol.setSize(14);
  pointSymbol.setColor(new Color([0, 255, 0, 0.25]));

  var graphic = new Graphic(evt.mapPoint,pointSymbol);
  map.graphics.add(graphic);
```

```
    var features= [];
    features.push(graphic);
    var featureSet = new FeatureSet();
    featureSet.features = features;
}
```

12. Create a JSON object that will hold the input parameters to be passed to the geoprocessing task and call the `Geoprocessor.execute()` method. The input parameters include `Input_Location` and `Drive_Times`. Remember that each input parameter must be spelled exactly as it is seen in the service page, including casing. The order of the parameters is also very important and is also defined on the service page. We define the `Input_Location` parameter to be a `FeatureSet` object. The `FeatureSet` object contains an array of graphics which in this case is only a single graphic point. The `Drive_Times` object has been hard coded with values of 1, 2, and 3 and set in the `driveTimes` variable we created earlier. Finally, we called the `Geoprocessor.execute()` method, passing in the input parameters as well as a callback function that will process the results. We'll create this callback function next:

```
function computeServiceArea(evt) {
map.graphics.clear();
varpointSymbol = new SimpleMarkerSymbol();
pointSymbol.setOutline = new
   SimpleLineSymbol(SimpleLineSymbol.STYLE_SOLID, new
   Color([255, 0, 0]), 1);
pointSymbol.setSize(14);
pointSymbol.setColor(new Color([0, 255, 0, 0.25]));

var graphic = new Graphic(evt.mapPoint,pointSymbol);
map.graphics.add(graphic);

var features= [];
features.push(graphic);
varfeatureSet = new FeatureSet();
featureSet.features = features;
var params = { "Input_Location":featureSet,
   "Drive_Times":driveTimes };
gp.execute(params, getDriveTimePolys);
}
```

13. In the last step, we defined a callback function called `getDriveTimePolys()`, which will be triggered when the geoprocessing task has finished with the analysis of drive times. Let's create this `getDriveTimePolys()` function. Just below the closing brace of the `computeServiceArea()` function, start the stub for `getDriveTimePolys()`:

```
function getDriveTimePolys(results, messages) {

}
```

14. The `getDriveTimePolys()` function accepts two parameters including the result object and any messages that are returned. Define a new `features` variable that holds the `FeatureSet` object returned by the geoprocessing task:

```
function getDriveTimePolys(results, messages) {
  var features = results[0].value.features;
}
```

15. The geoprocessing task will return three `Polygon` graphics. Each `Polygon` graphic represents a drive time that we hardcoded as an input parameter (1, 2, and 3 minutes). Create a `for` loop to process each of the polygons:

```
function getDriveTimePolys(results, messages) {
  var features = results[0].value.features;

  for (var f=0, fl=features.length; f<fl; f++) {

  }
}
```

16. Inside the `for` loop, symbolize each of the polygons with a different color. The first graphic will be red, the second green, and the third blue. There will be three polygons in the `FeatureSet` object. Define a different polygon symbol for each using the following code block and add the graphic to the `GraphicsLayer`:

```
function getDriveTimePolys(results, messages) {
var features = results[0].value.features;

for (var f=0, fl=features.length; f<fl; f++) {
  var feature = features[f];
  if(f == 0) {
    var polySymbolRed = new SimpleFillSymbol();
    polySymbolRed.setOutline(new
      SimpleLineSymbol(SimpleLineSymbol.STYLE_SOLID, new
      Color([0,0,0,0.5]), 1));
    polySymbolRed.setColor(new Color([255,0,0,0.7]));
    feature.setSymbol(polySymbolRed);
```

```
    }
    else if(f == 1) {
      var polySymbolGreen = new SimpleFillSymbol();
      polySymbolGreen.setOutline(new
        SimpleLineSymbol(SimpleLineSymbol.STYLE_SOLID, new
        Color([0,0,0,0.5]), 1));
      polySymbolGreen.setColor(new Color([0,255,0,0.7]));
      feature.setSymbol(polySymbolGreen);
    }
    else if(f == 2) {
      var polySymbolBlue = new SimpleFillSymbol();
      polySymbolBlue.setOutline(new
        SimpleLineSymbol(SimpleLineSymbol.STYLE_SOLID, new
        Color([0,0,0,0.5]), 1));
      polySymbolBlue.setColor(new Color([0,0,255,0.7]));
      feature.setSymbol(polySymbolBlue);
    }
    map.graphics.add(feature);
  }
```

17. Set the map extent to be the extent of `GraphicsLayer`, which now contains the three polygons you just created:

```
function getDriveTimePolys(results, messages) {
  var features = results[0].value.features;

  for (var f=0, fl=features.length; f<fl; f++) {
    var feature = features[f];
    if(f === 0) {
      var polySymbolRed = new SimpleFillSymbol();
      polySymbolRed.setOutline(new
        SimpleLineSymbol(SimpleLineSymbol.STYLE_SOLID, new
        Color([0,0,0,0.5]), 1));
      polySymbolRed.setColor(new Color([255,0,0,0.7]));
      feature.setSymbol(polySymbolRed);
    }
    else if(f == 1) {
      var polySymbolGreen = new SimpleFillSymbol();
      polySymbolGreen.setOutline(new
        SimpleLineSymbol(SimpleLineSymbol.STYLE_SOLID, new
        Color([0,0,0,0.5]), 1));
      polySymbolGreen.setColor(new Color([0,255,0,0.7]));
      feature.setSymbol(polySymbolGreen);
    }
    else if(f == 2) {
      var polySymbolBlue = new SimpleFillSymbol();
```

```
        polySymbolBlue.setOutline(new
            SimpleLineSymbol(SimpleLineSymbol.STYLE_SOLID, new
            Color([0,0,0,0.5]), 1));
        polySymbolBlue.setColor(new Color([0,0,255,0.7]));
        feature.setSymbol(polySymbolBlue);
    }
    map.graphics.add(feature);
  }
  map.setExtent(graphicsUtils.graphicsExtent
      (map.graphics.graphics), true);
}
```

18. Add a `<div>` tag that will hold the instructions for the application:

```
<body>
<div id="mapDiv"></div>
<div id="info" class="esriSimpleSlider">
    Click on the map to use a Geoprocessing(GP) task to
        generate and zoom to drive time polygons. The drive time
        polygons are 1, 2, and 3 minutes.
</div>
</body>
```

19. Alter the `<style>` tag at the top of the code, as seen in the highlighted part of the following code:

```
<style>
html, body, #mapDiv {
height: 100%;
margin: 0;
padding: 0;
width: 100%;
        }
        #info {
bottom: 20px;
color: #444;
height: auto;
font-family: arial;
left: 20px;
margin: 5px;
padding: 10px;
position: absolute;
text-align: left;
width: 200px;
z-index: 40;
        }
</style>
```

20. You may want to review the solution file (`drivetimes.html`) in your `ArcGISJavaScriptAPI` folder to verify that your code has been written correctly.

21. Click on the **Run** button. You should see the map in the following screenshot. If not, you may need to recheck your code for accuracy.

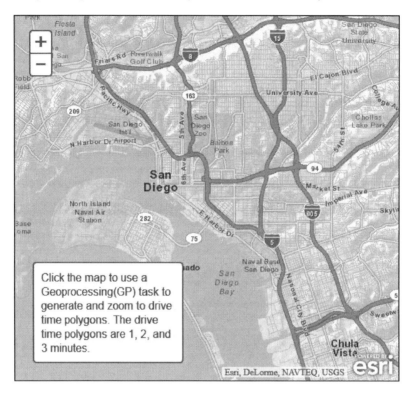

22. Click somewhere on the map. In just a few moments, you should see the drive time polygons displayed. Be patient. Sometimes this can take a little while.

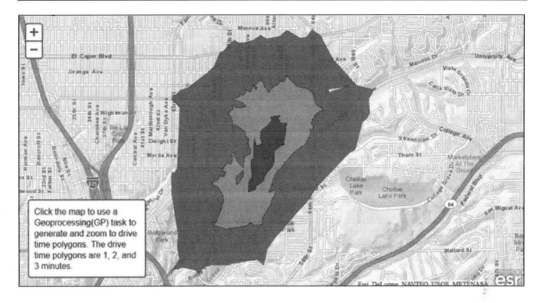

Summary

ArcGIS Server can expose geoprocessing services such as models and tools, which your application can access. These tools are run on ArcGIS Server due to their computationally intensive nature and need for ArcGIS software. Jobs are submitted to the server through your application and the results are returned after the task is complete. Geoprocessing tasks can be synchronous or asynchronous and are configured to run as one of these types by an ArcGIS Server administrator. As an application programmer, it is important for you to understand what type of geoprocessing service you are accessing as the method call that you make to the service depends upon this information. In addition, to know whether a task is synchronous or asynchronous, you also need to know the URL of the geoprocessing model or tool as well as the input and output parameters. In the next chapter, you will learn how to add data and maps from ArcGIS Online to your application.

11
Integration with ArcGIS Online

ArcGIS Online is a website designed for working with maps and other types of geographic information. On this site, you will find applications for building and sharing maps. You will also find useful basemaps, data, applications, and tools that you can view and use, plus the communities that you can join. For application developers, the really exciting news is that you can integrate ArcGIS Online content into your custom developed applications using the ArcGIS Server API for JavaScript. In this chapter, you'll explore how ArcGIS Online maps can be added to your applications.

In this chapter, we will cover the following topics:

- Adding ArcGIS Online maps to your applications with the webmap ID
- Adding ArcGIS Online maps to your applications with JSON
- Time to practice with ArcGIS Online

Adding ArcGIS Online maps to your applications with the webmap ID

The ArcGIS Server API for JavaScript includes two utility methods for working with maps from ArcGIS Online. Both methods are found on the `esri/arcgis/utils` resource. The `createMap()` method is used to create a map from an ArcGIS Online item.

Each map in the ArcGIS Online gallery has a unique ID. This unique ID, called webmap, will be important when you begin creating custom applications that integrate maps from ArcGIS Online. To get the webmap ID for a map that you'd like to add to your JavaScript API application, simply click on a map shared in ArcGIS Online that you've found. The address bar will contain the webmap ID for the map. You'll want to make note of this ID. The following screenshot shows how you can obtain the webmap ID from the address bar of a browser for a particular map:

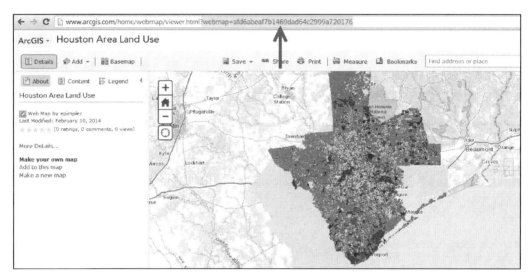

Once you have obtained the webmap ID for the ArcGIS Online map that you'd like to integrate into your custom JavaScript API application, you'll need to call the getItem() method, passing in the webmap ID. The getItem() method returns a dojo/Deferred object. The Deferred object is built specifically for tasks that may not complete immediately. It allows you to define success and failure callback functions that will be executed when the task is completed. In this case, a successful completion will pass in an itemInfo object to the success function.

This itemInfo object will be used to create the map from ArcGIS Online inside your custom application. You'll see a code example illustrating some of these topics as follows:

```
var agoId = "fc160a96a98d4052ae191cc486961b61";
var itemDeferred = arcgisUtils.getItem(agoId);

itemDeferred.addCallback(function(itemInfo) {
var mapDeferred = arcgisUtils.createMap(itemInfo, "map", {
mapOptions: {
  slider: true
```

```
    },
    geometryServiceURL: "http://sampleserver3.arcgisonline.com/ArcGIS/
rest/
    services/Geometry/GeometryServer"
    });
mapDeferred.addCallback(function(response) {
map = response.map;
    map.on("resize", resizeMap);
    });
mapDeferred.addErrback(function(error) {
console.log("Map creation failed: " , json.stringify(error));
    });
itemDeferred.addErrback(function(error) {
console.log("getItem failed: ", json.stringify(error));
    });
}
```

We'll cover this entire function in two separate examples. For now we'll examine the use of the `getItem()` method along with setting up callback functions for success or failure. These lines of code are highlighted in the preceding code example. In the first line of code, we create a variable called `agoId` and assign it the webmap ID that we'd like to use. Next we call `getItem()`, passing in the `agoId` variable containing our webmap ID. This creates a new `dojo/Deferred` object, which we assign to a variable called `itemDeferred`. Using this object, we can then create `success` and `error` callback functions. The `success` function, called `addCallback` is passed an `itemInfo` object that we'll use to create our map. We'll cover the actual creation of the map in the next section. In the event of some type of error condition, the `addErrback` function would be called. Now let's see how the map is created. The highlighted lines of the following code snippet illustrate the creation of the map:

```
    var agoId = "fc160a96a98d4052ae191cc486961b61";
    var itemDeferred = arcgisUtils.getItem(agoId);

    itemDeferred.addCallback(function(itemInfo) {
    varmapDeferred = arcgisUtils.createMap(itemInfo, "map", {
    mapOptions: {
      slider: true
      },
      geometryServiceURL: "http://sampleserver3.arcgisonline.com/ArcGIS/
rest/services/
      Geometry/GeometryServer"
      });
    mapDeferred.addCallback(function(response) {
    map = response.map;
      map.on("resize", resizeMap);
```

```
    });
  mapDeferred.addErrback(function(error) {
  console.log("Map creation failed: " , json.stringify(error));
    });
  itemDeferred.addErrback(function(error) {
  console.log("getItem failed: ", json.stringify(error));
    });
  }
```

The `createMap()` method is used to actually create the map from ArcGIS Online. This method takes an instance of `itemInfo`, which is returned from a successful call to `getItem()`; or, you can simply provide the webmap ID. As with any map that you create with the ArcGIS Server API for JavaScript, you also need to provide a reference to a `<div>` container that will hold the map and any optional map options that you'd like to provide. Just as with the `getItem()` method we examined earlier, `createMap()` also returns a `dojo/Deferred` object that you can use to assign success and error callback functions. The success function accepts a `response` object, which contains the `map` property that we use to retrieve the actual map. The error function runs when an error that would prevent the creation of the map occurs.

Adding ArcGIS Online maps to your applications with JSON

An alternative to creating a map using the webmap ID is to create a map using a JSON object that is a representation of the web map. This can be useful in situations where the application will not have access to ArcGIS Online. Take a look at the following code snippet:

```
var webmap = {};
webmap.item = {
  "title":"Census Map of USA",
  "snippet": "Detailed description of data",
  "extent": [[-139.4916, 10.7191],[-52.392, 59.5199]]
};
```

Next, specify the layers that make up the map. In the preceding snippet, the World Terrain basemap from ArcGIS Online is added along with an overlay layer that adds additional information to the map such as boundaries, cities, water features and landmarks, and roads. An operational layer is added that displays U.S. census data:

```
webmap.itemData = {
"operationalLayers": [{
  "url": " http://sampleserver1.arcgisonline.com/ArcGIS/rest/
  services/Demographics/ESRI_Census_USA/MapServer",
  "visibility": true,
  "opacity": 0.75,
  "title": "US Census Map",
  "itemId": "204d94c9b1374de9a21574c9efa31164"
}],
"baseMap": {
  "baseMapLayers": [{
  "opacity": 1,
  "visibility": true,
  "url": "http://services.arcgisonline.com/ArcGIS/rest/services/
  World_Terrain_Base/MapServer"
  },{
  "isReference": true,
  "opacity": 1,
  "visibility": true,
  "url": "http://services.arcgisonline.com/ArcGIS/rest/services/
  Reference/World_Reference_Overlay/MapServer"
  }],
  "title": "World_Terrain_Base"
},
"version": "1.1"
};
```

Once `webmap` is defined, use `createMap()` to build a map from the definition:

```
var mapDeferred = arcgisUtils.createMap(webmap, "map", {
mapOptions: {
slider: true
  }
});
```

Time to practice with ArcGIS Online

In this exercise, you will learn how to integrate ArcGIS Online maps into your applications. This simple application will display a public map of supermarket access in the U.S., pulled from ArcGIS Online. This map shows data for the entire U.S. The following screenshot illustrates this map. The supermarkets included in the analysis have annual sales of $1 million or more. The population in poverty is represented by taking the block group poverty rate (for example, 10 percent) from the census and symbolizing each block in that block group based on that percentage. Take a look at the following screenshot:

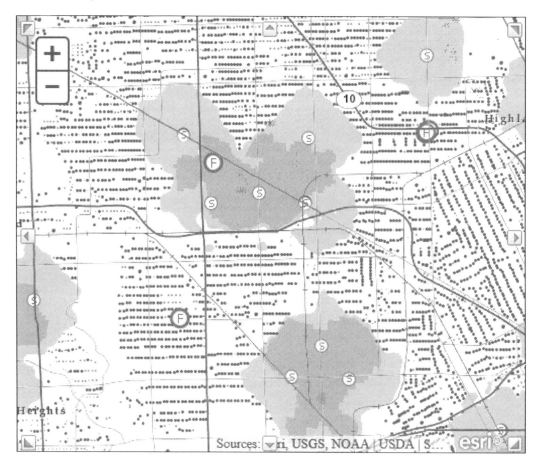

The green dots represent populations in poverty who live within one mile of a supermarket. The red dots represent the population in poverty that live beyond a one mile walk to a supermarket, but may live within a 10 minute drive, assuming they have access to a car. The grey dots represent the total population in a given area. Perform the following steps:

1. Before you begin coding the application, let's explore ArcGIS Online and see how you can find maps and retrieve their unique identifiers. Open a web browser and go to http://arcgis.com.

2. In the search box, type Supermarket as shown in the following screenshot:

3. This will return a list of results. We're going to add the **Supermarket Access Map** result to our application:

Search Results

Show

All Results
Maps
Layers
Apps
Tools
Files

☐ Show ArcGIS Desktop Content

Related Searches

Find items published by Esri related to "Supermarket"

Find groups related to "Supermarket"

385 results

Relevance   Title   Owner   Rating   Views   Date

Supermarket Access Map

Supermarkets are one way people have access to healthy food. This map shows where the supermarkets are. Areas that are within a 10 minute drive are depicted, as are areas within a 1 mile walk. At certain scales, populations living in poverty are represented.

Web Map by jimhe
Last Modified: October 29, 2013
★★★★☆ (15 ratings, 18 comments, 92,414 views)

Supermarket Access Map Service

Supermarkets are one way people have access to healthy food. This map shows where the supermarkets are. Areas that are within a 10 minute drive are depicted, as are areas within a 1 mile walk.

Map Images by jimhe
Last Modified: December 1, 2010
☆☆☆☆☆ (0 ratings, 2 comments, 23,996 views)

More Information

What types of items can I find here?

Advanced search options

Finding layer packages and other ArcGIS desktop content.

4. Click on the **Open** link under the thumbnail image of the map.

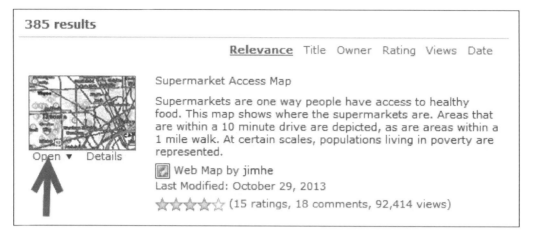

5. This will open the map in the ArcGIS Online viewer. You'll want to copy the web map number as shown in the following screenshot. I would suggest either writing the number down somewhere or copying and pasting to the Notepad. This is a unique ID for the map:

6. Open the JavaScript Sandbox at `http://developers.arcgis.com/en/ javascript/sandbox/sandbox.html`.

7. Remove the JavaScript content from the `<script>` tag that I have highlighted as follows:

```
<script>
dojo.require("esri.map");

function init(){
var map = new esri.Map("mapDiv", {
center: [-56.049, 38.485],
zoom: 3,
basemap: "streets"
    });
  }
dojo.ready(init);
</script>
```

8. Add the following references for the objects that we'll use in this exercise:

```
<script>
require([
        "dojo/parser",
        "dojo/ready",
        "dojo/dom",
        "esri/map",
        "esri/arcgis/utils",
        "esri/dijit/Scalebar",
        "dojo/domReady!"
    ], function(
parser,ready,dom,Map,arcgisUtils,Scalebar) {
    });
</script>
```

9. In this simple example, we're going to hardcode the webmap ID into the application. Inside the `require()` function, create a new variable called `agoId` and assign it the webmap ID you obtained as follows:

```
<script>
require([
        "dojo/parser",
        "dojo/ready",
        "dojo/dom",
        "esri/map",
        "esri/arcgis/utils",
        "esri/dijit/Scalebar",
        "dojo/domReady!"
    ], function(
parser,ready,dom,Map,arcgisUtils,Scalebar) {
```

```
      var agoId = "153c17de00914039bb28f6f6efe6d322";

    });

</script>
```

10. In the last two steps in this exercise, we will deal with the `arcgisUtils.`
    `getItem()` and `arcgisUtils.createMap()` methods. Both these methods
    return what is known as a `Dojo/Deferred` object. You need to have a
    basic understanding of `Deferred` objects, or the code won't make a lot of
    sense. The `dojo/Deferred` object is built specifically for tasks that may not
    complete immediately. It allows you to define success and failure callback
    functions that will execute when the task does complete. A success callback
    function will be called by `Deferred.addCallback()`, while a failure function
    will take the form `Deferred.errCallback()`. In the case of `getItem()`, a
    successful completion will pass in an `itemInfo` object to the success function.
    This `itemInfo` object will be used to create the map from ArcGIS Online
    inside your custom application. A failure to complete due to some reason
    will result in the generation of an error being passed to the `Deferred.`
    `addErrback()` function. Add the following code block to your application
    and then we'll discuss its details further:

```
<script>
require([
        "dojo/parser",
        "dojo/ready",
        "dojo/dom",
        "esri/map",
        "esri/arcgis/utils",
        "esri/dijit/Scalebar",
        "dojo/domReady!"
    ], function(
parser,ready,dom,Map,arcgisUtils,Scalebar) {

    var agoId = "153c17de00914039bb28f6f6efe6d322";
    var itemDeferred = arcgisUtils.getItem(agoId);

    itemDeferred.addCallback(function(itemInfo) {
    var mapDeferred = arcgisUtils.createMap(itemInfo,
  "mapDiv", {
    mapOptions: {
    slider: true,
    nav:true
    }
```

```
        });

        });
        itemDeferred.addErrback(function(error) {
        console.log("getItem failed: ",
    json.stringify(error));
        });

    });
```

```
</script>
```

In the first line of code, we call the getItem() function, passing in the agoId variable, which references the **Supermarket Access Map** from ArcGIS Online. This method returns a Dojo/Deferred object, which is stored in a variable called itemDeferred.

The getItem() function gets details about the ArcGIS Online item (webmap). The object passed back to the callback is a generic object with the following specification:

```
{
item: <Object>,
itemData: <Object>
}
```

Assuming that the call to getItem() was successful, this generic item object is then passed into the addCallback() function. Inside the callback function, we then make a call to the getMap() method, passing in the itemInfo object, a reference to the map container, and any optional parameters that define the map functionality. The map parameters in this case include the presence of a navigation slider and navigation buttons. The getMap() method then returns another Dojo/Deferred object, which is stored in the mapDeferred variable. In the next step, you'll define the code blocks that handle the Deferred object that will be passed back.

11. The object returned to the mapDeferred.addCallback() function will take the following form:

```
{
  Map: <esri/Map>,
itemInfo: {
item: <Object>,
itemData: <Object>
  }
}
```

12. Add the following code to handle the information returned:

```
<script>
require([
        "dojo/parser",
        "dojo/ready",
        "dojo/dom",
        "esri/map",
        "esri/arcgis/utils",
        "esri/dijit/Scalebar",
        "dojo/domReady!"
    ], function(
parser,ready,dom,Map,arcgisUtils,Scalebar) {

    var agoId = "153c17de00914039bb28f6f6efe6d322";
    var itemDeferred = arcgisUtils.getItem(agoId);

    itemDeferred.addCallback(function(itemInfo) {
    var mapDeferred = arcgisUtils.createMap(itemInfo,
  "mapDiv", {
       mapOptions: {
       slider: true,
       nav:true
       }
    });
        mapDeferred.addCallback(function(response) {
    map = response.map;
    });
    mapDeferred.addErrback(function(error) {
        console.log("Map creation failed: ", json.
          stringify(error));
    });

    });
    itemDeferred.addErrback(function(error) {
        console.log("getItem failed: ",
    json.stringify(error));
    });

    });

</script>
```

The success function (`mapDeferred.addCallback`) pulls the map from the response and assigns it to the map container.

13. You may want to review the solution file (`arcgisdotcom.html`) in your `ArcGISJavaScriptAPI` folder to verify that your code has been written correctly.

14. After clicking on the **Run** button, you should see the following map. If not, you may need to recheck your code for accuracy:

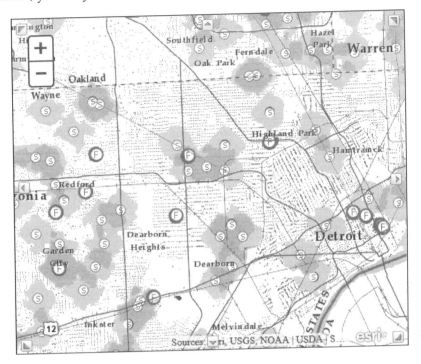

Summary

ArcGIS Online is becoming increasingly important as a platform for creating and sharing maps and other resources. As a developer, you can integrate these maps into your custom applications. Each map has a unique identifier that you can use to pull the map into your custom application developed with ArcGIS Server and the JavaScript API. Because it can take some time to return these maps from ArcGIS Online, the `getItem()` and `createMap()` methods return `Dojo/Deferred` objects, which provide callback functions for both success and failure. Once the maps have been successfully obtained from ArcGIS Online, they can then be presented in your application just like any other map service. In the next chapter, you will learn how to use the ArcGIS API in JavaScript for mobile applications.

12
Creating Mobile Applications

The ArcGIS Server API for JavaScript provides support for mobile platforms. Support is currently provided for iOS, Android, and BlackBerry operating systems. The API is integrated with `dojox/mobile`. In this chapter, you'll learn about the compact build of the API that makes web mapping applications possible through WebKit browsers as well as the built-in gesture support. Keep in mind that this is not the same as the ArcGIS API for iOS or Android, which is what you'd use to build native applications that can be made available through an app store. JavaScript API applications are rendered through the WebKit browser that is part of the mobile device.

We'll also cover the Geolocation API and how it can be integrated into your ArcGIS Server applications. The Geolocation API is a part of HTML5 and is used to get the location of a mobile device. Most mobile browsers support the Geolocation API specification that provides scripted access to geographical location information associated with a hosting device.

In this chapter, we will cover the following topics:

- ArcGIS API for JavaScript – a compact build
- Setting the viewport scale
- Time to practice with the compact build
- Integrating the Geolocation API
- Time to practice with the Geolocation API

ArcGIS API for JavaScript – a compact build

The ArcGIS API for JavaScript has a compact build that can be used to limit the footprint of the API, resulting in quicker downloads for mobile devices. This smaller footprint is a great choice for mobile applications, including the iPhone and iPad. There are two primary differences between the standard and compact builds of the API:

- The first difference is that the compact build only loads objects that are needed for your application. For example, if you don't need a `Calendar` widget, then it's not loaded.

- The second difference is that the compact build only loads 32 code modules instead of the 80 modules loaded with the standard build. If you need to use a code module that is not downloaded as part of the compact build, then you can use the `require()` function to load the specific module that you use.

Referencing the compact build is as simple as adding the word `compact` to the end of your reference to the API. You will see an example later. Using the API in a mobile application isn't any different from the techniques you've learned for creating web applications. However, you will need to learn some new techniques for creating the user interface for mobile applications. There are a number of good JavaScript mobile frameworks available for accomplishing this task, including Dojox Mobile and jQuery Mobile. The mobile frameworks style the web content to make it look like a mobile application. Safari browsers look like an iPhone application and Android browsers look like an Android application. Creating mobile user interfaces is beyond the scope of this text but there are many good resources available in print and online. In the following code example, you will see how to add a reference to the compact build of the ArcGIS API for JavaScript. Note the inclusion of the compact keyword at the end of the API.

```
<script src="http://js.arcgis.com/3.7compact/"></script>
```

Setting the viewport scale

You will want to use the `viewport` `<meta>` tag to set some initial display characteristics for your application. The `<meta>` tag should be included in the `<head>` section of your web page. A value of `1.0` for the initial scale is recommended and will fill the entire viewport of the screen. Values can be set between `0` and `1.0`. If you don't set a width, your mobile browser will use `device-width` when in portrait mode. If you don't set a height, the browser will use `device-height` when in landscape mode:

```
<meta name="viewport" content="width=device-width, initial-
   scale=1" maximum-scale=1.0 user-scalable=0>
```

Time to practice with the compact build

In this exercise, you will build the most basic mobile mapping application possible. We're simply going to use the compact build of the ArcGIS Server API for JavaScript to create a mapping application centered on the town of Banff, Alberta, Canada. The application won't be able to do anything other than zoom and pan. There won't be any sort of user interface beyond just the map. The goal is just to illustrate the basic structure of a mobile application built with the API for JavaScript.

This exercise will be a little different from the exercises you've worked on in previous chapters. You won't use the ArcGIS API for JavaScript Sandbox. Instead, you'll write your code in a text editor (I recommend Notepad++) and test using a mobile emulator.

1. Before starting this exercise, you'll want to make sure you have access to a web server. If you don't have access to a web server or one that isn't already installed on your computer, you can download and install the open source web server, Apache (`http://httpd.apache.org/download.cgi`). Microsoft IIS is another commonly used web server and there are many others that you can use as well. For the purposes of this exercise, I will assume that you are using the Apache web server.

2. A web server installed on your local computer will be referred to through the URL `http://localhost`, which is used to access the web server. This points to the `htdocs` folder under `C:\Program Files\Apache Software Foundation\Apache2.2` if you've installed Apache on a Windows platform.

3. In your `ArcGISJavaScriptAPI` folder, you'll find a file called `mobile_map.html`. I have prewritten some of the code that you will use in this step, so that you can focus on adding referencing to the compact build as well as some other items related to mobile development. Use this file as your starting point and copy it to the root directory of your web server (`C:\Program Files\Apache Software Foundation\Apache2.2\htdocs` if you're using Apache on Windows).

4. Open `mobile_map.html` in your favorite text editor. I recommend Notepad++, but you can use any text editor.

5. Add a reference to the compact version of the API as well as the Esri stylesheet. Add the following highlighted lines of code to your application:

    ```
    <head>

      <meta http-equiv="Content-Type" content="text/html;
        charset-utf-8">
    ```

```
<meta http-equiv="X-UA-Compatible" content="IE=7,IE=9,
   IE=10" />
<title>Simple Map</title>
<link rel="stylesheet"
   href="http://js.arcgis.com/3.7/js/esri/css/esri.css">
<link rel="stylesheet"
   href="http://code.jquery.com/mobile/1.1.0-
   rc.1/jquery.mobile-1.1.0-rc.1.min.css" />
<script src="http://code.jquery.com/jquery-
   1.7.1.min.js"></script>
<script src="http://code.jquery.com/mobile/1.1.0-
   rc.1/jquery.mobile-1.1.0-rc.1.min.js"></script>
<script src="http://js.arcgis.com/3.7compact/"></script>
```

6. You will want to use the `viewport` `<meta>` tag attribute to set some initial display characteristics for your application. A value of `1.0` for the initial scale is recommended and will fill the entire viewport of the screen. Values can be set between `0` and `1.0`. If you don't set a width, mobile browsers will use `device-width` when in portrait mode, and if you don't set a height, they will use `device-height` when in landscape mode. Add the following line of code under the `<head>` tag at the start of the code:

```
<meta name="viewport" content="width=device-width, initial-
   scale=1">
```

7. In the `<script>` tag, add the `require()` function seen highlighted in the following code snippet as well as the references that we'll use in this exercise:

```
<script>
   require([
        "esri/map",
        "dojo/domReady!"
     ], function(Map) {
   });
</script>
```

8. As is the case with a traditional web mapping application built with the API for JavaScript, you will create a `<div>` tag to hold the map for your mobile application. With a mobile application, you will want to style the map so that it takes up the entire viewport of the mobile application. This is accomplished by setting the width and height to `100%`, respectively. Add the `<div>` map container to your application. Make sure that you set the style of the width and height to `100%`:

```
<div data-role="page">
  <div data-role="header">
    <h1>Simple Map</h1>
  </div><!-- /header -->
```

```
<div data-role="content">
    <div id="mapDiv" style="width:100%;
      height:100%;"></div>
</div><!-- /content -->

<div data-role="footer">
  <h4>Page Footer</h4>
</div><!-- /footer -->
</div><!-- /page -->
```

9. Mobile devices can display their viewport in the standard or landscape mode simply by rotating the device. Your application will need to deal with these events as and when they occur. Add the onorientationchange() event to the <body> tag. The onorientationchange() event references a JavaScript function called orientationChanged(), which we have not yet defined. We'll do that in the next step:

```
<body onorientationchange="orientationChanged();">
```

10. Create a new Map object, set the basemap, and center the map as well as the zoom scale level:

```
<script type="text/javascript">
  require([
      "esri/map",
      "dojo/domReady!"
    ], function(Map) {
      map = new Map("mapDiv", {
          basemap: "streets",
          center:[-115.570, 51.178], //long, lat
          zoom: 12
      });
});
</script>
```

11. Create the orientationChanged() JavaScript function, as seen in the following code. This function can be added anywhere inside the <script> tag:

```
<script type="text/javascript">
    require([
      "esri/map",
      "dojo/domReady!"
    ], function(Map) {

      map = new Map("mapDiv", {
        basemap: "streets",
        center:[-115.570, 51.178], //long, lat
        zoom: 12
      });

    function orientationChanged() {
```

```
    if(map) {
        map.reposition();
        map.resize();
    }
  }
  });
</script>
```

12. Save the file.

13. Open a web browser and load an emulator. I recommend `iphone4simulator.com` but there are many others that you can use. These sites emulate how a website or application will look and behave.

 You are also welcome to upload these exercise files to a web server that is outside the firewall if you'd prefer to view them on an actual mobile device rather than an emulator.

14. If you are using Apache, then you've most likely saved the file to the root location of the web server, which is `C:\Program Files\Apache Software Foundation\Apache2.2\htdocs`. The file can then be accessed through a web browser using the URL `http://localhost/mobile_map.html`. Type `http://localhost/mobile_map.html` in the emulator address bar, as seen in the following screenshot. You should see a map appear.

The compact version of the API for JavaScript creates a *minified* version of the zoom scale slider. This is about as simple as a mapping application can get but hopefully it illustrates the basic characteristics of building a mobile mapping application.

15. You can use the zoom slider to zoom in and out and keep in mind that the ArcGIS Server API for JavaScript also supports gestures, so you can use a pinch gesture to zoom in and out as well. However, keep in mind that this will not work in the emulator. Use the zoom in and zoom out buttons on the interface for the application to zoom in and out as seen in the following screenshot:

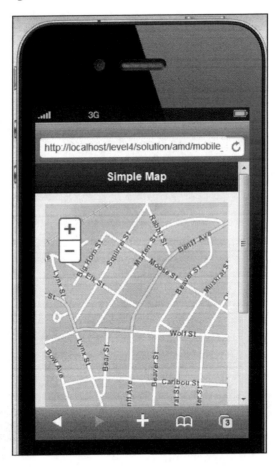

16. You may want to review the solution file (`mobile_map_solution.html`) in your `ArcGISJavaScriptAPI` folder to verify that your code has been written correctly.

Integrating the Geolocation API

The Geolocation API can be integrated with your ArcGIS Server applications to get the location of a mobile device. It can also be used to get the location from a web-based application, but this isn't nearly as accurate as it uses the IP address rather than a GPS or cell tower triangulation.

This API has built-in security that requires explicit permission from the end user before this functionality can be used in an application. Mobile and web applications will both display a prompt that requests permission to obtain the current location of a device. This prompt will appear similar to what is shown in the following screenshot:

Most browsers support the Geolocation API specification, which provides scripted access to geographical location information associated with a hosting device. The primary purpose of the Geolocation API is to identify the location of a mobile device. There are various ways in which a mobile device can be located, including cell tower triangulation, IP address, and GPS location. The `Geolocation.getCurrentPosition()` method returns the current location of the mobile device. You could easily use this API to place a point on the mapping application that corresponds to the current user location. The `Geolocation.watchPosition()` method can be used to track a location as it changes with a callback method being fired each time the position changes. So, if your application needs to be able to track the location of a device over time, then you'll want to use `watchPosition()` instead of `getCurrentPosition()`, which simply gets the location at a single point in time.

The following code snippet contains a simple example detailing the basic use of a Geolocation API. The first thing we do is check whether the browser supports the Geolocation API. This is done with the `navigator.geolocation` property, which returns a value of `true` or `false`. Generally, this will prompt the user to allow the application to collect the current location and also make sure that the browser supports Geolocation.

 To see if your browser supports Geolocation or any other HTML5 feature, go to `http://caniuse.com/`.

If the browser supports the Geolocation API and the end user gives it permission to collect the location, then we call the `geolocation.getCurrentPosition()` method. The first parameter passed to this method indicates a success callback function, which will be executed if the device is located successfully. Similarly, an error callback function can also be provided (`locationError`). A `Position` object is passed to the success callback function. This `Position` object can then be examined to obtain the latitude/longitude coordinates of the location. That's what we've done in the `zoomToLocation()` function which accepts a `Position` object as the only parameter. This function then obtains the latitude/longitude coordinates and plots the point on the map:

```
if (navigator.geolocation){
   navigator.geolocation.getCurrentPosition(zoomToLocation,
locationError);
}

function zoomToLocation(location) {
  var symbol = new SimpleMarkerSymbol();

  symbol.setStyle(SimpleMarkerSymbol.STYLE_SQUARE);
  symbol.setColor(new Color([153,0,51,0.75]));

  var pt = esri.geometry.geographicToWebMercator(new
    Point(location.coords.longitude, location.coords.latitude));
  var graphic = new Graphic(pt, symbol);
  map.graphics.add(graphic);
  map.centerAndZoom(pt, 16);
}

function locationError(error) {
  switch (error.code) {
    case error.PERMISSION_DENIED:
      alert("Location not provided");
```

```
      break;
   case error.POSITION_UNAVAILABLE:
     alert("Current location not available");
     break;
   case error.TIMEOUT:
     alert("Timeout");
     break;
   default:
     alert("unknown error");
     break;
   }
 }
```

Time to practice with the Geolocation API

In this exercise, you will learn how to integrate the Geolocation API into an ArcGIS
Server API for JavaScript application.

1. Open the JavaScript Sandbox at `http://developers.ArcGIS.com/en/
    javascript/sandbox/sandbox.html`.

2. Remove the JavaScript content from the `<script>` tag that I have highlighted
    in the following code snippet:

    ```
    <script>
      dojo.require("esri.map");

      function init(){
        var map = new esri.Map("mapDiv", {
           center: [-56.049, 38.485],
           zoom: 3,
           basemap: "streets"
         });
      }
      dojo.ready(init);
    </script>
    ```

3. Add the following references for the objects that we'll use in this exercise:

    ```
    <script>
      require([
          "dojo/dom",
          "esri/map",
          "esri/geometry/Point",
          "esri/symbols/SimpleMarkerSymbol",
          "esri/graphic",
    ```

```
    "esri/geometry/webMercatorUtils",
    "dojo/_base/Color",
    "dojo/domReady!"
    ], function(dom, Map, Point, SimpleMarkerSymbol, Graphic,
      webMercatorUtils, Color) {
  });
</script>
```

4. Create a new Map object centered on San Diego, CA, with a basemap layer of the streets. This will serve as the default map and zoom extent if the browser you are using doesn't support the Geolocation API or if permission to access the current device location is not provided:

```
<script>
  require([
      "dojo/dom",
      "esri/map",
      "esri/geometry/Point",
      "esri/symbols/SimpleMarkerSymbol",
      "esri/graphic",
      "esri/geometry/webMercatorUtils",
      "dojo/_base/Color",
      "dojo/domReady!"
    ], function(dom, Map, Point, SimpleMarkerSymbol,
      Graphic, webMercatorUtils, Color) {

    map = new Map("mapDiv", {
        basemap: "streets",
        center:[-117.148, 32.706], //long, lat
        zoom: 12
    });
  });
</script>
```

5. Create an `if` statement that checks for browser support of the Geolocation API and gains permission to access the current device location. The `Navigator.geolocation` property will return a `true` or `false` value. If the browser supports the Geolocation API and permission is given by the end user, then this property will contain a `true` value:

```
map = new Map("mapDiv", {
  basemap: "streets",
  center:[-117.148, 32.706], //long, lat
  zoom: 12
});
if (navigator.geolocation){
```

```
navigator.geolocation.getCurrentPosition(zoomToLocation,
locationError);
}
```

6. As you can see from the code you've added in the previous step, the `Geolocation.getCurrentPosition()` function defines two callback functions—one for success (`zoomToLocation`) and one for failure (`locationError`). In this step, you'll create the success callback function by adding the following code block. The success callback function, called `zoomToLocation`, will zoom to the location of the mobile device:

```
if (navigator.geolocation){
  navigator.geolocation.getCurrentPosition(zoomToLocation,
    locationError);
        }

  function zoomToLocation(location) {
    var symbol = new SimpleMarkerSymbol();

    symbol.setStyle(SimpleMarkerSymbol.STYLE_SQUARE);
    symbol.setColor(new dojo.Color([153,0,51,0.75]));

    var pt = webMercatorUtils.geographicToWebMercator(new
      Point(location.coords.longitude,
      location.coords.latitude));
    var graphic = new Graphic(pt, symbol);
    map.graphics.add(graphic);
    map.centerAndZoom(pt, 16);
  }
```

7. Now, let's add the error callback function called `locationError()`. This function will test for various types of errors related to not being able to find the current location of the device. Add the following function just below the success callback function that you created in the previous step:

```
function locationError(error) {
  switch (error.code) {
    case error.PERMISSION_DENIED:
      alert("Location not provided");
      break;
    case error.POSITION_UNAVAILABLE:
      alert("Current location not available");
      break;
```

```
case error.TIMEOUT:
  alert("Timeout");
  break;
default:
  alert("unknown error");
  break;
}
}
```

8. You may want to review the solution file (`geolocation.html`) in your `ArcGISJavaScriptAPI` folder to verify that your code has been written correctly.

9. Click on the **Run** button. Initially, you should see a message similar to that displayed in the following screenshot:

10. Click on **Share Location** and if the browser you are using supports the Geolocation API, then a new map should be displayed with your current location, represented by a symbol. Your location will obviously differ from mine.

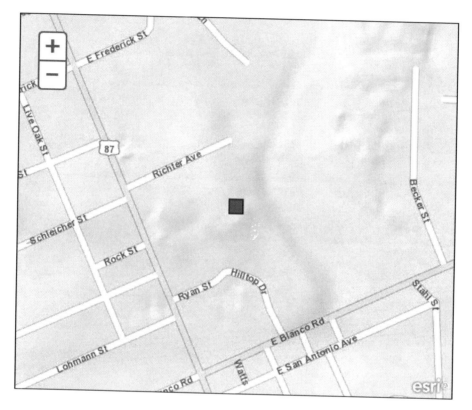

Summary

Mobile GIS applications are becoming very popular and the ArcGIS Server API for JavaScript can be used to quickly develop applications that are supported in both web and mobile applications. The API comes with built-in gesture support and supports iOS, Android, and BlackBerry platforms. The compact version of the API provides a smaller footprint that downloads quickly on mobile platforms. In addition, you can combine the Geolocation API into your applications, in order to locate the device and update the map to show the current location. In the next chapter, you will learn basic techniques used for designing and creating the layout of your application.

Application Design with ArcGIS Templates and Dojo

One of the most difficult tasks for many web developers when building GIS applications is designing and creating the user interface. The ArcGIS API for JavaScript and Dojo greatly simplifies this task. Dojo's layout dijits provide a simple, efficient way to create application layouts, and Esri provides a number of sample application layouts and templates that you can use to get up and running quickly. In this appendix, the reader will learn techniques to quickly design the layout of an application.

The Dojo BorderContainer dijit

Since the AGIS API for JavaScript is built directly on top of the Dojo JavaScript framework, you automatically have access to the user interface Dojo libraries, including layout dijits such as BorderContainer. The layout dijits are a set of user interface elements you can add to an application that give you control over the layout of the application. The BorderContainer dijit serves primarily as a container for other child containers and can be one of these two design types: headline or sidebar. You define the design type using the design attribute. The design type can be either headline or sidebar and both can be split into as many as 5 different regions: top, bottom, right, left, and center. Each region is normally filled by a Dojo layout element. It is also possible to nest regions for greater control over the layout of an application. For example, you might include a second BorderContainer within the center region of a master BorderContainer. Using this second BorderContainer, you could then further divide the center region.

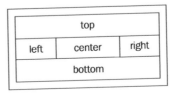

In the following code example, we are defining `design` to be of type `headline`. This results in the general configuration that you see in the code, with the `top` and `bottom` regions stretching across the entire width of the screen space. In this case, you only need to set the `height` property for the `top` and `bottom` regions:

```
<div id="main-pane" dojoType="dijit.layout.BorderContainer"
    design="headline">
```

In the following code example, we define `design` as `sidebar`. With the `sidebar` design, the `left` and `right` regions expand to take up `100%` of the height of the window, sacrificing the area available to the `top` and `bottom` regions. In this case, you need to define only the `width` style property as the height will always be `100%`.

```
<div id="main-pane" dojoType="dijit.layout.BorderContainer"
    design="sidebar">
```

In either case, the center region will conform to fit the amount of space available, based on the sizing of the other regions. The following screenshots that you will see depict both of the design types available for `BorderContainer`. The first shows a `headline` style while the second shows a `sidebar` style.

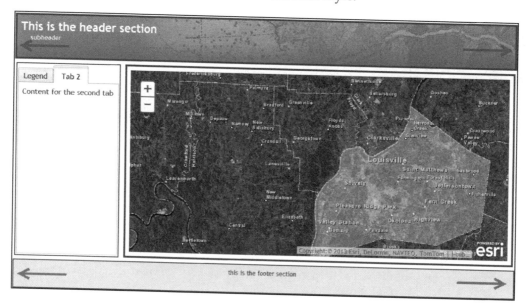

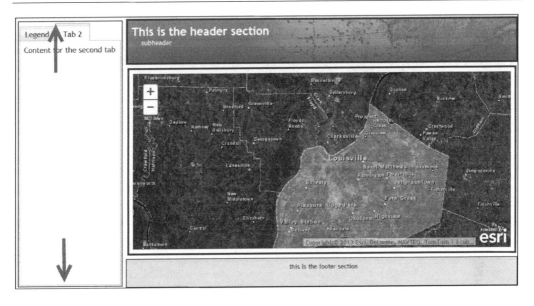

Additional Dojo layout elements

Each region of BorderContainer (top, bottom, left, right, and center) can be filled by a Dojo layout element. These elements are AccordionContainer, SplitContainer, StackContainer, and TabContainer. You can also create a nested set of BorderContainer objects to further divide the available layout space.

Child elements are placed inside a region through the use of the region attribute, as seen in the following code example. Notice that in the highlighted section, the region attribute is set to left. This will create ContentPane in the left region. ContentPane is a very basic layout element and is used as a container for other widgets. In this case, it is going to hold TabContainer (highlighted), which contains additional ContentPane objects.

```
<div dojotype="dijit.layout.ContentPane" id="leftPane"
  region="left">
  <div dojotype = "dijit.layout.TabContainer">
    <div dojotype="dijit.layout.ContentPane" title = "Tab 1"
      selected="true">
      Content for the first tab
    </div>
    <div dojotype="dijit.layout.ContentPane" title = "Tab 2" >
      Content for the second tab
    </div>
  </div>
</div>
```

The following screenshot illustrates the location and content that was generated using `ContentPane` and `TabContainer`:

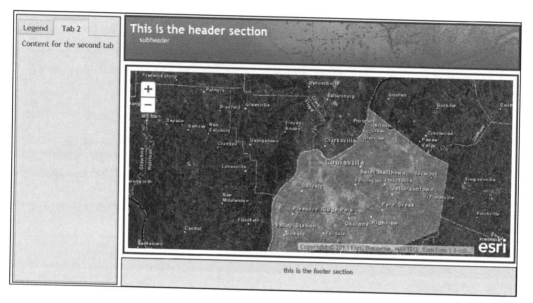

`AccordionContainer` holds a set of panes whose titles are visible, but only one pane's content is visible at a time. As the user clicks on a title, the pane contents become visible. These are excellent user interface containers that can hold a lot of information in a small area.

Esri has provided a number of sample layouts that you can use to get started with the layout of your application. The help page for the ArcGIS API for JavaScript includes a **Samples** tab containing dozens of sample scripts you can use in your application including various layout samples. In the next section, you'll learn how to integrate one of these sample layouts into your application.

Time to practice with sample layouts

In this exercise, you will download a sample layout provided by Esri. You'll then examine the layout to get a feel of the basic layout elements provided by Dojo. Finally, you'll make some changes to the layout.

1. Before starting this exercise, you'll want to make sure that you have access to a web server. If you don't have access to a web server or if a web server isn't already installed on your computer, you can download and install the open source web server Apache (http://httpd.apache.org/download. cgi). Microsoft IIS is another commonly used web server and there are many

others that you can use as well. For the purpose of this exercise, I will assume that you are using the Apache web server.

2. A web server installed on your local computer will be referred to through URL as `http://localhost`. This points to the `htdocs` folder under `C:\Program Files\Apache Software Foundation\Apache2.2\` if you've installed Apache on a Windows platform.

3. On the **Samples** tab of the ArcGIS API for JavaScript site (`https://developers.arcgis.com/en/javascript/jssamples/`), search for `Layouts` in the search box to generate a list of available layout samples.

4. Scroll down the list of search results until you see the **Layout with left pane** sample seen in the following screenshot. Click on this item:

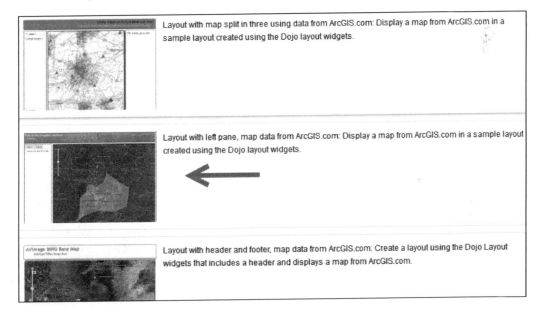

Layout with map split in three using data from ArcGIS.com: Display a map from ArcGIS.com in a sample layout created using the Dojo layout widgets.

Layout with left pane, map data from ArcGIS.com: Display a map from ArcGIS.com in a sample layout created using the Dojo layout widgets.

Layout with header and footer, map data from ArcGIS.com: Create a layout using the Dojo Layout widgets that includes a header and displays a map from ArcGIS.com.

5. Click on the **Download as a zip file** link to download the sample.

6. Create a new folder in your `htdocs` folder under `C:\Program Files\Apache Software Foundation\Apache2.2\` and name it `layout`. Unzip the file that you downloaded into this folder. This will create a file called `index.html`, along with the `css` and `images` folders.

7. Open a web browser and go to the URL `http://localhost/layout/index.html` so you can see the current layout. You should see something similar to the following screenshot:

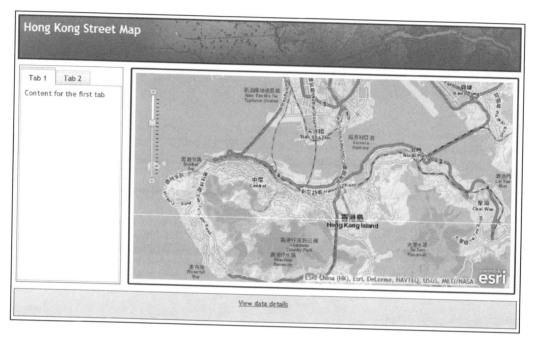

8. Open `index.html` in your favorite text or web editor.

9. Scroll to the bottom of the file until you see the `<body>` tag.

10. The highest level layout container is `BorderContainer`. A `<div>` tag will contain `BorderContainer` and all other child layout elements need to be located inside this `<div>` tag. Examine the following code. The highlighted section is the code used to define our top level `BorderContainer`. Notice that the design has been set to `headline`, which means that the top and bottom regions will be scrolled across the entire width of the screen:

```
<body class="claro">
  <div id="mainWindow"
    data-dojo-type="dijit.layout.BorderContainer"
    data-dojo-props="design:'headline'"
  style="width:100%; height:100%;">

    <div id="header"
      data-dojo-type="dijit.layout.ContentPane"
      data-dojo-props="region:'top'">
        <div id="title">
        </div>
```

```
    </div>

    <div data-dojo-type="dijit.layout.ContentPane"
      id="leftPane" data-dojo-props="region:'left'">
      <div data-dojo-type="dijit.layout.TabContainer">
        <div data-dojo-type="dijit.layout.ContentPane"
          data-dojo-props="title:'Tab 1', selected:'true'">
          Content for the first tab
        </div>
        <div data-dojo-type="dijit.layout.ContentPane"
          data-dojo-props="title:'Tab 2'">
          Content for the second tab
        </div>
      </div>
    </div>

    <div id="map" data-dojo-type="dijit.layout.ContentPane"
      data-dojo-props="region:'center'"></div>

    <div id="footer"
      data-dojo-type="dijit.layout.ContentPane"
      data-dojo-props="region:'bottom'">
      <span id="dataSource">
      </span>
    </div>

  </div>
</body>
```

11. Inside `BorderContainer`, you will find several child layout elements defined with the `ContentPane` dijit. `ContentPane` is a very generic layout element that simply holds either text or additional layout elements, such as `TabContainer` or `AccordionContainer`.

```
<body class="claro">
  <div id="mainWindow"
    data-dojo-type="dijit.layout.BorderContainer"
    data-dojo-props="design:'headline'"
    style="width:100%; height:100%;">

    <div id="header" data-dojo-type="dijit.layout.ContentPane"
      data-dojo-props="region:'top'">
      <div id="title">
      </div>
    </div>
```

```
<div data-dojo-type="dijit.layout.ContentPane"
  id="leftPane" data-dojo-props="region:'left'">
  <div data-dojo-type="dijit.layout.TabContainer">
    <div data-dojo-type="dijit.layout.ContentPane"
      data-dojo-props="title:'Tab 1', selected:'true'">
      Content for the first tab
    </div>
    <div data-dojo-type="dijit.layout.ContentPane"
      data-dojo-props="title:'Tab 2'">
      Content for the second tab
    </div>
  </div>
</div>

<div id="map" data-dojo-type="dijit.layout.ContentPane"
  data-dojo-props="region:'center'"></div>

<div id="footer" data-dojo-type="dijit.layout.ContentPane"
  data-dojo-props="region:'bottom'">
  <span id="dataSource">
  </span>
</div>

  </div>
</body>
```

Notice that in the previous code example, each ContentPane layout element has a region that has been designed for each layout element. In this case, we have defined all of the available regions, with the exception of the right region. This is illustrated in the following screenshot:

top		
left	center	right
bottom		

12. Next, examine the following highlighted code. The highlighted code defines the content for the left region. A simple ContentPane layout element is defined, which as I mentioned previously is a very simple container for other layout elements or text. Inside this ContentPane, we have created a TabContainer layout element and assigned two tabs. Each tab is created as ContentPane.

```
<body class="claro">
  <div id="mainWindow"
    data-dojo-type="dijit.layout.BorderContainer"
    data-dojo-props="design:'headline'"
    style="width:100%; height:100%;">

    <div id="header"
      data-dojo-type="dijit.layout.ContentPane"
      data-dojo-props="region:'top'">
      <div id="title">
      </div>
    </div>

    <div data-dojo-type="dijit.layout.ContentPane"
      id="leftPane" data-dojo-props="region:'left'">
      <div data-dojo-type="dijit.layout.TabContainer">
        <div data-dojo-type="dijit.layout.ContentPane"
          data-dojo-props="title:'Tab 1', selected:'true'">
          Content for the first tab
        </div>
        <div data-dojo-type="dijit.layout.ContentPane"
          data-dojo-props="title:'Tab 2'">
          Content for the second tab
        </div>
      </div>
    </div>

    <div id="map"
      data-dojo-type="dijit.layout.ContentPane"
      data-dojo-props="region:'center'"></div>

    <div id="footer"
      data-dojo-type="dijit.layout.ContentPane"
      data-dojo-props="region:'bottom'">
    <span id="dataSource">
    </span>
    </div>

  </div>
</body>
```

13. A common scenario would be to create a tab container that holds a legend for the map, as seen in the following screenshot:

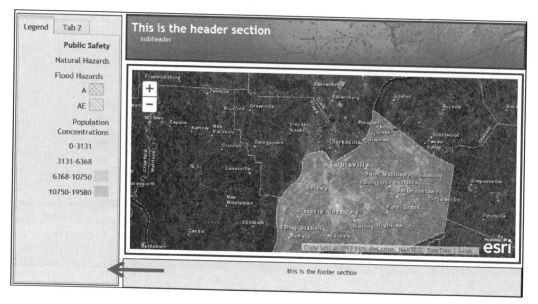

14. Now that you understand the basic concepts of creating layout elements, you can add content for the `right` region. Add the following highlighted code:

```
<body class="claro">
  <div id="mainWindow"
    data-dojo-type="dijit.layout.BorderContainer"
    data-dojo-props="design:'headline'"
    style="width:100%; height:100%;">

    <div id="header"
      data-dojo-type="dijit.layout.ContentPane"
      data-dojo-props="region:'top'">
      <div id="title">
      </div>
    </div>

    <div data-dojo-type="dijit.layout.ContentPane"
      id="leftPane" data-dojo-props="region:'left'">
      <div data-dojo-type="dijit.layout.TabContainer">
        <div data-dojo-type="dijit.layout.ContentPane"
          data-dojo-props="title:'Tab 1', selected:'true'">
          Content for the first tab
        </div>
        <div data-dojo-type="dijit.layout.ContentPane"
```

```
          data-dojo-props="title:'Tab 2'">
          Content for the second tab
      </div>
    </div>
  </div>

  <div data-dojo-type="dijit.layout.ContentPane"
    id="rightPane" data-dojo-props="region:'right'">
    Content for right pane
  </div>


  <div id="map" data-dojo-type="dijit.layout.ContentPane"
    data-dojo-props="region:'center'"></div>

  <div id="footer"
    data-dojo-type="dijit.layout.ContentPane"
    data-dojo-props="region:'bottom'">
    <span id="dataSource">
    </span>
  </div>

  </div>
</body>
```

15. In the `css` folder that you extracted earlier in the exercise, there is a file called `layout.css`. This contains the styling information for our application. Open this file in your text editor.

16. Find the text `#rightPane` as seen in the following code example. Properties are defined for the background color, foreground color, border styling, and width of the region:

```
#rightPane {
  background-color:#FFF;
  color:#3f3f3f;
  border:solid 2px #224a54;
  width:20%;
}
```

17. Recall that in the previous code block that you added, we gave `id` of `rightPane` to the `right` region. The CSS section will style our pane by giving it a background color (white), foreground color, width, and border.

18. Save the file.

19. If necessary, open your web browser and reload `http://localhost/ layout/index.html`, or simply refresh the page if you already have it opened. Now you should see new content for the `right` region of the application. Currently, it only holds some text as the content, but you could easily add additional content, including user interface widgets (dijits). We'll do that in the next step when we add `AccordionContainer`.

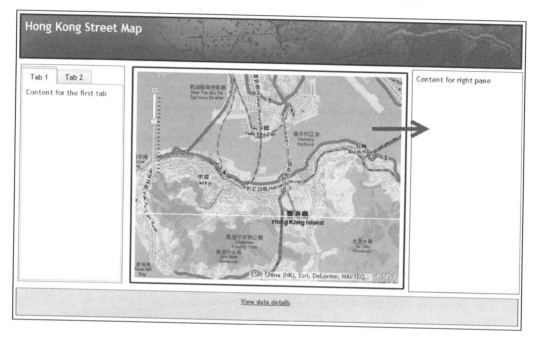

20. Next, we'll add `AccordionContainer` to the `right` region.

21. First, add a reference to the `AccordionContainer` resource, as seen in the following highlighted code:

```
dojo.require("dijit.layout.BorderContainer");
dojo.require("dijit.layout.ContentPane");
dojo.require("dijit.layout.TabContainer");
dojo.require("esri.map");
dojo.require("esri.arcgis.utils");
dojo.require("esri.IdentityManager");
dojo.require("dijit.layout.AccordionContainer");
```

22. Now, add `AccordionContainer` inside `ContentPane` for the `right` region as well as the content for each of the panes. The highlighted code below should be added to the `ContentPane` you created in step 14:

```
<div data-dojo-type="dijit.layout.ContentPane"
  id="rightPane" data-dojo-props="region:'right'">
  <div data-dojo-type="dijit.layout.AccordionContainer" >
    <div data-dojo-type="dijit.layout.ContentPane"
      title="Pane 1">
    Content for Pane 1
    </div>
    <div data-dojo-type="dijit.layout.ContentPane" title="Pane
      2">
      Content for Pane 2
    </div>
    <div data-dojo-type="dijit.layout.ContentPane" title="Pane
      3">
    Content for Pane 3
    </div>
  </div>
</div>
```

23. Save the file.

24. Refresh your browser to see the new `AccordionContainer` layout element as seen in the following screenshot. In this exercise, you learned how to quickly create an application layout using Esri sample layouts.

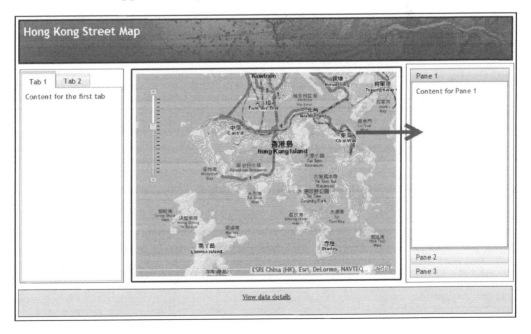

Summary

Designing and implementing the appearance of a GIS web mapping application is often a difficult task for developers. Design and development are two very different skill sets. Most people aren't good at both. However, Dojo's layout widgets and Esri sample templates make it much easier to build complex designs with very little coding. In this appendix, you learned how to use an Esri sample to quickly define and build the layout of an application.

Index

E

editing widgets
    about 121
    AttachmentEditor 125, 127
    AttributeInspector 124, 125
    Editor 121, 122
    Edit toolbar 127
    TemplatePicker 122, 123
Editor widget 121, 122
Edit toolbar 127
errorCallback() function 135
errorHandler() function 179
Event.mapPoint property 155, 198
Event object 55
executeIdentifyTask() function 154
execute method 68
execute() method 135
external stylesheet
    used, for inserting CSS in application 25

F

facilities property 184
feature editing
    about 119
    feature service 120
feature layer
    about 75
    definition expression, setting 80
    display mode, defining 78
    feature, selecting 80, 81
    rendering 82-86
    snapshot mode 79, 80
featureLayer.getDefinitionExpression()
        method 80
FeatureLayer object
    about 75
    creating 76, 77
    optional constructor parameters 77, 78
    using 87-92
feature service 120
FeatureSet.features property 199
FeatureSet object 58, 130, 178, 199
FindParameters object 147
FindTask
    about 158
    FindParameters object 157, 158

FindResult 158
    used, for feature attributes getting 156-158
FindTask.execute() method 158
FindTask object 147
fullExtent() method 53
function keyword 18
functions 18

G

Gauge widget 107, 108
Geocoder widget
    about 102
    adding, to application 102-107
geocoding
    about 162
    example 162
    Locator Service used 162-166
Geolocation API
    integrating 228-234
    practicing with 230-234
geolocation.getCurrentPosition() method
        229, 232
Geolocation.getCurrentPosition() method
        228
Geolocation.watchPosition() method 228
geometry
    creating, for graphics 60
geometry property 130
geom variable 168
geoprocessing task
    about 194
    asynchronous tasks 195
    input parameters 192, 193
    running 194
    synchronous tasks 194
    working with 196-204
geoprocessor
    service page, understanding 191
    using 190
Geoprocessor class 194
Geoprocessor.execute() method 194, 200
Geoprocessor.setUpdateDelay() method 195
Geoprocessor.submitJob() method 195
getDriveTimePolys() function 201
getItem() method 208, 209
getMap() method 217

graphic
  adding, to graphics layer 64
  attributes, assigning to 62
  composition 59
  creating 59, 64
  creating, on map 65-73
  displaying, on map 65-73
  geometry, creating for 60
  symbolizing 60-62
graphic attributes
  displaying, in info template 63
Graphic.setInfoTemplate() method 72
graphics layer
  graphics, adding to 64
  multiple graphics layers 65
GraphicsLayer object 91

H

handler function 54
HistogramTimeSlider dijit 114
HomeButton widget 115
HTML
  seperating, from CSS and JavaScript 26, 28
HTML code
  creating, for web page 32, 33
  validating, W3C HTML validator used
    10-12
HTML DOCTYPE declaration
  about 9
  HTML 4.01 Strict 9
  XHTML 1.0 Strict 9
HTML page concepts
  about 7, 8
  DOCTYPE declaration 9
  HTML code, validating 10-12
  primary tags 9

I

identify functionality
  implementing 151-156
IdentifyParameters class 148
IdentifyParameters.layerIds property 149
IdentifyParameters object
  about 147, 148
  using 149

IdentifyTask
  about 148
  IdentifyParameters object 148, 149
  IdentifyTask attribute 149, 150
  used, for feature attributes getting 148
IdentifyTask attribute
  about 149, 150
  IdentifyResult 150, 151
IdentifyTask.execute() method 150, 155
incidents property 184
info template
  graphic attributes, displaying in 63
InfoTemplate object 72, 91
inline styling
  used, for inserting CSS in application 25
input parameter objects
  about 163
  Input JSON address object 163
  Input Point object 164
input parameters
  about 192
  Input_Observation_Point 193
  Viewshed_Distance 193
instance
  creating, of Navigation toolbar 96
internal stylesheet
  used, for inserting CSS in application 25
itemDeferred variable 209
itemInfo object 208

J

JavaScript
  case sensitivity 15
  code, commenting in 13
  constructors 20
  decision-supporting statements 17
  events 20
  functions 18
  fundamentals 13
  looping statements 17
  methods 19, 20
  objects 19
  properties 20
  seperating, from HTML and CSS 26, 27
  variable datatypes 15, 16
  variables 14

JobInfo object 195
JSON
  used, for ArcGIS Online maps adding to
    applications 210, 211

L

layer classes
  using 43
layerIds property 157
LayerSwipe widget 118
left-to-right (LTR) orientation 109
Legend widget 110, 111
LocateButton widget 116, 117
locationError() function 232
locationToAddress() method 164, 165
Locator.addressToLocations() method 164,
    167
Locator class 161, 164
Locator object
  about 164
  AddressCandidate object 164, 165
Locator Service
  practicing with 166-172
  used, for geocoding in ArcGIS API for
    JavaScript 162
Locator Service, used for geocoding
  geocoding process 165
  input parameter objects 163, 164
  Locator object 164, 165
  reverse geocoding process 165
locator variable 167
looping statements 17

M

map
  about 40
  creating 36, 37
  events 53-55
  layers, adding to 47
  service layers 41-53
Map.addLayer() method 44
map.centerAt(pt) method 20
Map.click event 154, 164, 178
mapDeferred.addCallback() function 217
mapDeferred variable 217
Map.disableScrollWheelZoom() method 52

map events
  about 53, 55
  types 55
map extent
  getting 52, 53
  setting 52, 53
Map.extent property 53
Map.fullExtent method 53
map navigation
  about 49
  controlling, keyboard used 52
  controlling, mouse used 52
  toolbars 49, 51
  widgets 49, 50
Map object 34, 37
mapPoint property 141
map service layers
  definition expression, setting 48
  dynamic map service layers 45-47
  individual layers, visibility setting 47, 48
  layer classes, using 43
  layers, adding to map 47
  map extent, setting 52, 53
  map navigation 49-52
  tiled map service layers 44
  working with 41, 42
Map.setExtent() method 53
Map.setExtent property 53
Measurement widget 108
modules
  loading 34, 35

N

Navigation toolbar
  instance, creating of 96
Navigator.geolocation property 231

O

objects
  about 19
  actions 19, 20
onExtentChange event 53
on() method 54
onorientationchange() event 225
options parameter 36
options variable 168

[PACKT]
PUBLISHING

Thank you for buying
Building Web and Mobile ArcGIS Server Applications with JavaScript

About Packt Publishing

Packt, pronounced 'packed', published its first book "*Mastering phpMyAdmin for Effective MySQL Management*" in April 2004 and subsequently continued to specialize in publishing highly focused books on specific technologies and solutions.

Our books and publications share the experiences of your fellow IT professionals in adapting and customizing today's systems, applications, and frameworks. Our solution based books give you the knowledge and power to customize the software and technologies you're using to get the job done. Packt books are more specific and less general than the IT books you have seen in the past. Our unique business model allows us to bring you more focused information, giving you more of what you need to know, and less of what you don't.

Packt is a modern, yet unique publishing company, which focuses on producing quality, cutting-edge books for communities of developers, administrators, and newbies alike. For more information, please visit our website: www.packtpub.com.

Writing for Packt

We welcome all inquiries from people who are interested in authoring. Book proposals should be sent to author@packtpub.com. If your book idea is still at an early stage and you would like to discuss it first before writing a formal book proposal, contact us; one of our commissioning editors will get in touch with you.

We're not just looking for published authors; if you have strong technical skills but no writing experience, our experienced editors can help you develop a writing career, or simply get some additional reward for your expertise.

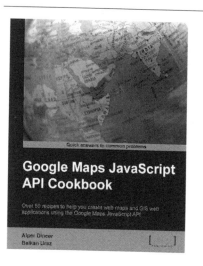

Object-Oriented JavaScript
Second Edition

ISBN: 978-1-84969-312-7   Paperback: 382 pages

Learn everything you need to know about OOJS in this comprehensive guide

1. Think in JavaScript

2. Make object-oriented programming accessible and understandable to web developers

3. Apply design patterns to solve JavaScript coding problems

4. Learn coding patterns that unleash the unique power of the language

Jasmine JavaScript Testing

ISBN: 978-1-78216-720-4   Paperback: 146 pages

Leverage the power of unit testing to create bigger and better JavaScript applications

1. Learn the power of test-driven development while creating a fully-featured web application

2. Understand the best practices for modularization and code organization while putting your application to scale

3. Leverage the power of frameworks such as BackboneJS and jQuery while maintaining the code quality

Please check **www.PacktPub.com** for information on our titles

Made in the USA
Lexington, KY
16 July 2015